New Ways in Teaching Visual Literacy

Lisa Horvath and Susan Iannuzzi, Editors

This book has a companion website.
Go to **tesol.org/teachingvisualliteracy**
for additional resources.

bookstore.tesol.org

TESOL International Association
1925 Ballenger Avenue, Ste. 550
Alexandria, VA 22314 USA
tesol.org

Associate Director of Publications: Tomiko Breland
Copy Editor: Suzy Richardt
Reviewers: Moisés Alcántara Ayre, Elsa Anderson, Jason May
Cover: Citrine Sky Design
Interior Design: Kathleen Dyson
Head of Education and Events: Sarah Sahr

Recommended citation:
Horvath, L., & Iannuzzi, S. (2026). *New ways in teaching visual literacy*. TESOL Press.

ISBN 978-1-953745-24-8
ISBN (ebook) 978-1-953745-25-5
Library of Congress Control Number 2026933310

This book is dedicated to Ana Preto-Bay, whose advice in 1996—to join TESOL if I was serious about teaching English—deeply impacted the course of my career. Thank you, Ana.

—*LH*

For my teachers, who taught me how to notice: Harvey Cornell, Phillip Bianco, and Val Emslie

—*SI*

Contents

Part II. Videos

Part III. Social Media

Part IV. Student-Generated Art

Part VI. Multimodalities

Part VII. Visualization

Introduction

In its most simple definition, visual literacy is the ability to understand (receive) and create (produce) visual media. As defined by the Visual Literacy Standards Task Force, visual literacy is:

> … a set of abilities that enables an individual to effectively find, interpret, evaluate, use, and create images and visual media. Visual literacy skills equip a learner to understand and analyze the contextual, cultural, ethical, aesthetic, intellectual, and technical components involved in the production and use of visual materials. A visually literate individual is both a critical consumer of visual media and a competent contributor to a body of shared knowledge and culture (2011, para. 2).

VISUAL LITERACY AND COMMUNICATIVE COMPETENCE

The goal of language learning is to develop communicative competence, and communication in today's world depends heavily on visual elements. Social media and electronic resources are commonplace in all corners of the globe, and students engage with these media regularly. Therefore, literacy is incomplete without visual literacy (Kress, 2003).

Despite the prevalence of images and media in nearly every activity in the language classroom, visual literacy is often inadequately addressed in teacher training programs (Donaghy & Xerri, 2017). This book aims to fill that gap and provide support materials to teachers who recognize the role of visual literacy in language learning. Supporting learners to become both linguistic and visual communicators prepares them to navigate the full multimodal spectrum of communication in the 21st century.

VISUAL LITERACY AND LIFE SKILLS

Besides being an essential element of communicative competence, visual literacy enhances the acquisition and development of vocabulary, grammar, listening, speaking, reading, and writing. In addition to developing traditional language skills and improving communicative competence, visual literacy activities can provide a platform for processing trauma, developing social and emotional competencies, and increasing critical and creative thinking skills.

Furthermore, visual media communicates strong messages, greatly impacts our world view, and heavily influences our perception of reality. By bringing visual literacy to the forefront of what we do in the classroom, whether in person or online, we support learners in developing essential life skills.

The activities within this volume aim to facilitate exploration of the range of possibilities that development of visual literacy skills can address. These include self-reflection and greater awareness of others' biases, beliefs, and experiences. The range of activities enables teachers to focus on interpretation or creation of visual media while emphasizing how students' English language skills can be improved.

RECEPTIVE AND PRODUCTIVE VISUAL LITERACY

As with language skills, visual literacies can be divided into both receptive and productive skills. Receptive visual skills include observing, understanding, evaluating, reflecting, interpreting, experiencing, judging, and valuing. Productive visual skills include describing, creating, drafting, empathizing, envisioning, experimenting, presenting, realizing, and using.

Receptive and productive visual literacy skills can further be divided into competencies, similarly to how language is divided into competencies in the Common European Framework of Reference for Languages (CEFR). The Common European Framework of Reference for Visual Literacy (CEFR-VL) articulates specific visual competencies. For example, the personal domain includes the competency of observing foreign customs and rituals and understanding their aesthetic forms. This is particularly crucial for language learners who are exposed to a different culture alongside language learning—thus the development of intercultural awareness, critical thinking, openness, curiosity, empathy, appreciation, and active dialogue with a world different from their own enhances their ability to communicate (Haanstra & Wagner, 2017).

THE NEED FOR VISUAL LITERACY INSTRUCTION IN ENGLISH LANGUAGE TEACHING

Today's English language learners need strong visual literacy skills. As Donaghy and Xerri emphasize:

> … there is an urgent need for ELT [English language teaching] to finally come to terms with both multiliteracies pedagogy and visual literacy if we are to meet the needs of our students to communicate effectively in a world where communication is increasingly multimodal in nature. To do this, we need to increase the presence of multimodal texts in the ELT curriculum, incorporate specific visual literacy and media production training into pre-service and in-service teacher training courses, and extend specific visual literacy and media production strategies aimed at students (2017, p. 8).

This volume addresses the need for visual literacy instruction by providing activities that will support English language learners' development into active, informed, and literate consumers of visual media. These activities play an essential role in developing effective linguistic and visual communicators. They equip English language learners with the life skills they need to effectively communicate in and navigate an increasingly visual world.

ABOUT THIS VOLUME

We are deeply grateful for the contributions of our many dedicated authors, without whom this book would not be possible. Based on the activities they provided, we've divided the contents of this book into seven sections:

Still images

Videos

Social media

Student-generated art

Semiotics

Multimodalities

Visualization

Within each section, some activities cover the same topics as others but address them from different angles or target different audiences. Although many activities are based on digital resources, whenever possible, we have endeavored to make this volume relevant to teaching environments without internet or digital access by including analog alternatives.

We are confident that this book will provide teachers with a rich resource from which they can draw to support learners in the development of essential visual literacy competencies, creating competent and responsible consumers of and contributors to our increasingly visually dependent global landscape.

COMPANION SITE

Many of the appendixes, worksheets, links, and images from this book are also available on the companion site (www.tesol.org/teachingvisualliteracy). Visit the site to download these resources to use with students or to adapt for your own contexts.

REFERENCES AND FURTHER READING

Donaghy, K., & Xerri, D. (Eds.). (2017). *The image in English language teaching*. ELT Council. https://www.danielxerri.com/uploads/4/5/3/0/4530212/the_image_in_english_language_teaching_introduction__2017_.pdf

Haanstra, F., & Wagner, E. (2017). *Common European Framework of reference for visual literacy (CEFR-VL)*. https://envil.eu/wp-content/uploads/2017/09/CEFR_VL-Introduction.pdf

Karastathi, S. (2016). *Visual literacy in the language curriculum*. Visual Arts Circle. https://visualartscircle.com/2016/12/04/visual-literacy-in-the-language-curriculum/

Kress, G. (2000). Multimodality: Challenges to thinking about language. *TESOL Quarterly, 34*(2), 337–340.

Kress, G. (2003). *Literacy in the new media age*. Routledge.

Lundy, A. D., & Stephens, A. E. (2015). Beyond the literal: Teaching visual literacy in the 21st century classroom. *Procedia Social and Behavioral Sciences, 174*, 1057–1060. https://doi.org/10.1016/j.sbspro.2015.01.794

Royce, T. (2002). Multimodality in the TESOL classroom: Exploring visual-verbal synergy. *TESOL Quarterly, 36*(2), 191–205.

Schönau, D., Kárpáti, A., Kirchner, C., & Letsiou, M. (2020). A new structural model of visual competencies in visual literacy. *The Literacy, Preliteracy and Education Journal, 4*(3), 57–71. https://pages.pedf.cuni.cz/gramotnost/files/2021/06/04_Schonau_Karpati_Kirchner_Letsiou-1.pdf

Visual Literacy Standards Task Force. *ACRL visual literacy competency standards for higher education*. (2011, October 27). Association of College & Research Libraries (ACRL). https://www.ala.org/acrl/standards/visualliteracy

Wagner, E., & Schönau, D. (Eds.). (2016). *Common European framework of reference for visual literacy–Prototype*. Waxmann. https://envil.eu/wp-content/uploads/2016/10/Abstracts_-framework_formatiert_11.pdf

Part I

Still Images

Introduction: The Power of Still Images in the English Language Classroom

This section of the book delves into the use of still images as an instructional tool in English language teaching contexts. Still images, including photographs, paintings, and illustrations, offer learners a concrete way to engage with the language, making abstract concepts more tangible. The activities that follow explore how educators can leverage still images to enhance comprehension, stimulate critical thinking, and encourage creative expression, all while fostering a deeper connection with the language.

Still images occupy a central place as pedagogical tools that facilitate both linguistic and visual literacy development. Unlike moving images, still images—whether photographs, illustrations, or infographics—encourage learners to pause, observe closely, and engage in deeper interpretive practices (Callow, 2013; Serafini, 2014).

For example, in the activity "Critically Reading a Photo Through Decolonial Lenses," learners examine an image of a group of boys in a favela in Rio de Janeiro and engage with the visual content from a decolonial and antiracist perspective. This encourages learners to not only analyze the photograph's aesthetic qualities but also reflect on the social and political implications embedded in the image, ultimately developing their literacy on how race affects understanding (Coachman & Fernandes, 2023).

In "Making Inferences From Photographs," learners analyze a photograph and make inferences about the actions, emotions, and contexts depicted. This activity promotes higher order thinking by encouraging learners to support their inferences with evidence drawn directly from the image, honing their observation and reasoning skills.

Through analysis of still images, learners can contextualize language within meaningful visual frameworks. When learners challenge themselves to use new vocabulary or grammatical structures to describe images, they are more likely to retain and understand the content (Paivio, 2006). This dual-coding process—where verbal and visual information are processed through separate cognitive channels—enhances memory and retrieval, especially for learners with limited English proficiency.

In the activity "Using Landscape Photos to Prepare for Description Writing," learners transition from narrative to descriptive writing by engaging with a series of landscape photographs. This exercise helps learners practice describing scenes using varied and effective language, reinforcing their ability to observe, articulate, and connect with unfamiliar places and concepts in English.

Thus, still images offer a versatile and enriching approach to language instruction. As visual and verbal modes of communication become increasingly intertwined, incorporating still images thoughtfully allows language educators to support learners in navigating and making meaning from the world around them.

REFERENCES AND FURTHER READING

Callow, J. (2013). *The shape of text to come: How image and text work*. Primary English Teaching Association.

Coachman, E. F., & Fernandes, I. S. (2023). Addressing race in English language teaching. *AILA Review, 36*(1), 64–90. https://doi.org/10.1075/aila.22016.coa

New London Group. (1996). A pedagogy of multiliteracies: Designing social futures. *Harvard Educational Review, 66*(1), 60–92.

Paivio, A. (2006). *Mind and its evolution: A dual coding theoretical approach.* Erlbaum.

Serafini, F. (2014). *Reading the visual: An introduction to teaching multimodal literacy.* Teachers College.

Alte Zachen: Old Things to Learn New Skills

Tatia Gruenbaum

Levels	Intermediate to advanced
Ages Suitable for Activity	Preservice teachers
Aims	Extract meaning from illustrations
	Situate illustrations in cultural, social, and historical contexts
	Discover how including visual children's literature and the Holocaust in English language teaching can support the mission of remembrance and global citizenship education
Class Time	90 minutes–2 hours
Preparation time	20 minutes
Resources	Copy of *Alte Zachen: Old Things* (Hanaor, 2022)
	OR
	Selected pages from the book (Appendix)

Serafini (2009) argues that teachers can only support children in creating meaning from images once they have learned how to do so themselves. This activity draws on the graphic novel *Alte Zachen: Old Things* (Hanaor, 2022) as a teaching tool to support preservice and in-service English language teachers to develop visual literacy skills for English language teaching purposes.

Alte Zachen: Old Things tells the story of a boy named Benji who goes grocery shopping with his grandmother. Together, they travel across Brooklyn and Manhattan to pick up the necessary ingredients for a Friday dinner. The grandmother is a Holocaust survivor. Teachers can draw on this activity plan when teaching upper primary and lower secondary school–aged learners about concepts from global citizenship education (e.g., unity, inclusion, empathy) and to mark the International Day of Commemoration each January in memory of the victims of the Holocaust.

PROCEDURE

1. Begin by asking teachers to notice the illustration on the front cover of the book. Discuss the following general questions:

    a. Describe the grandmother and her grandson.

    b. Describe the scene. What is happening?

    c. Describe the illustrator's style. What materials did the illustrator use (e.g., paint, pencil, ink, charcoal)? What techniques did the illustrator apply (e.g., shading, sketching, blending)?

2. Then, continue to discuss the following specific questions:

    a. Where are the grandmother and the grandson positioned on the page? What does this position represent?

b. What do you think the difference between the grandmother's patterned clothes and her grandson's plain clothes could represent? What meaning could the grandmother's multiple layers of clothes have? Think about her age, and the age of her grandson.

c. The grandmother and her grandson are walking to the right. Does the chosen direction express the beginning or the end of a journey?

d. Look at the buildings in the background and the countless windows. What similarities or differences can you spot? What meaning do you attach to these buildings?

e. In your view, what does the white horizon add to the cover?

f. What color are the spine and the title? Why do you think the illustrator made this choice?

g. Look at the hand lettering (i.e., the font) on the cover page. In your view, does hand lettering reflect more of a child's or adult's perspective? What could this mean for the story?

3. Ask teachers to read and explore the rest of the book, or share the provided images (see Appendix). Give the following verbal directions:

While reading, you will notice that the story in this graphic novel is mostly told in panels of various shapes and sizes. Each panel shows action through an image or an image and word(s). The panels are separated by a blank (white) space called the *gutter*. Text and thoughts are presented in balloons. In addition, there is a shift between color and monochrome. According to the illustrator,

> "All the present-day images are produced in monochrome and the flashback scenes are in colour. This is to represent that the grandmother's memories are somehow more vivid and powerful than the current day world that she finds herself in. Her experiences have shaped her into the woman she is today, and she now feels somewhat detached and can't relate to New York and its people." (B. Phillips, personal communication, September, 2023)

4. After teachers have completed reading and exploring the book, use some or all of the following prompts to lead a discussion:

a. Look carefully at the first set of two pages. Focus on the gutters and use your imagination. What do we not see in the blank space?

b. Read the pages you have available, in the book or online, and notice the color changes. Can you identify the various (historical) events that are represented in color? What can you say about the illustrator's color palette? Can you attach emotions or a mood to the various scenes?

c. Read the pages you have available, in the book or online. Look out for icons or symbols and establish their meaning.

d. Return to the front cover and recall your answer regarding the question on the color of the spine and the title. Reflect on the word *Alte* (see bottom right corner for translation) and the meaning behind the color and monochrome shift. Does this influence your initial answer?

CAVEATS AND OPTIONS

- When working with visual children's literature and the Holocaust, such as graphic novels and picture books, preparation is essential to ensure the safety of the younger learner. Some pages require mediation, sensitivity, and perhaps additional information. Advise (preservice) teachers to lean on the Safe In & Safe Out approach by Gruenbaum (2025) for English language teaching embedded in a children's rights perspective.

- The following suggestions connect visual literacy activities with developing English language skills. When exploring the covers and pages, lead students through some or all of the following supplemental activities:

- Create a vocabulary A–Z.

- Focus on language to express personal views, experiences, and emotions.

- Focus on language for making predictions.

- Focus on language for comparison and contrast (e.g., cultures, societies, present and past).

- Determine the opportunities that the use of English and Yiddish in this graphic novel can offer in the multilingual English language classroom (i.e., discuss translanguaging).

- Prepare discussion questions and preteach terminology on challenging topics, such as antisemitism, discrimination, inclusion, and migration.

- Use the following questions to encourage and guide (preservice) teachers' reflection:
  — How has this graphic novel supported the development of your own visual literacy skills?
  — How can you use this book to teach visual literacy skills to your learners?
  — What was your favorite or least favorite illustration (i.e., scene) in this book? Why?

REFERENCES AND FURTHER READING

Cicada Books. (2022). *Alte zachen: Old things.* https://www.cicadabooks.co.uk/books/p/alte-zachen-old-things

Gruenbaum, T. (2025). *Visual Holocaust children's literature in English language teaching: Teaching guide.* https://heyzine.com/flip-book/01af577e7c.html

Hanaor, Z. (2022). *Alte zachen: Old things* (B. Phillips, Illus.). Cicada Books.

Phillips, B. (n.d.). *Alte zachen.* https://benjaminphillips.co.uk/Alte-Zachen

Serafini, F. (2009). Understanding visual images in picturebooks. In J. Evans (Ed.), *Talking beyond the page: Reading and responding to contemporary picturebooks* (pp. 10–25). Routledge.

Thames & Hudson Sales. (2022, May 9). *Alte zachen* [Video]. YouTube. https://www.youtube.com/watch?v=FkO7hu2Mu0c

UNESCO. (n.d.). *Addressing antisemitism through education.* https://www.unesco.org/en/education-addressing-antisemitism

Note: Images reproduced from *Alte zachen: Old things* (Hanaor & Phillips, 2022). Used with permission.

Analyzing and Interpreting Photographs: Paying Attention to Detail

Gabriela Kleckova

Levels	Intermediate to advanced
Ages Suitable for Activity	Secondary to adult
Aims	Read a photograph for detail
	Draw conclusions based on observations
	Express opinions
	Ask questions
Class Time	40–50 minutes
Preparation Time	5 minutes
Resources	Photograph (Appendix A or teacher's own choice)
	Worksheet (Appendix B)

This activity teaches learners a step-by-step strategy to scrutinize photographs. They develop the skills to decode a photograph, pay attention to detail, and build meaning from their observations to draw conclusions about the photograph.

PROCEDURE

1. Hand out the worksheet to learners.
2. Show the photograph to learners (see Appendix A or use your own photograph). Tell them to study the photograph quietly for 2 minutes to form an overall impression. It is important that learners take 2 minutes to examine the photograph. It allows them to process the image more thoroughly.
3. Distribute the worksheet and tell learners they will work independently for 5 minutes with Part A of the worksheet. Tell them to analyze the photograph by applying the four-quadrant strategy:
   a. Divide the photograph into four visual quadrants.
   b. Then, study each quadrant and note down the people, objects, and activities they see in each quadrant.

   Stress that it is important that learners only record what can be visually observed.
4. Have learners form groups of three or four and share their observations about people, objects, and activities in the photograph. Tell them to add their peers' ideas to their own.
5. As a whole class, ask learners how much detail they noticed in the photograph after applying the four-quadrant strategy, compared to when they first observed the whole photograph at once during Step 2.

6. Tell learners they will form an opinion about the photograph based on their observations (e.g., it is a choir practice; people are standing in a choir formation and holding their music script). After some time for reflection, tell learners to independently complete Part B of the worksheet.

7. Have learners return to their small groups and share their opinions about the photograph. Remind them to use reasons to support their opinions.

8. As a whole class, elicit how their opinions about the photographs were similar to or different from their peers' opinions.

9. Ask learners to complete Part C of the worksheet independently.

10. Assign each corner of your classroom to one of the questions from Part C. Tell learners to go to the corner of the question they chose to answer. Then, based on the number of learners in each corner, tell them to form pairs or small groups and discuss their responses.

11. Encourage learners to share some of their answers with the whole class. During the following discussion, focus more on Questions 1 and 2, which are connected to developing thinking skills around photographs.

12. Refer students to Part D and give them a few minutes to write down as many questions as possible. Then, elicit the questions as a whole class activity. Learners listen to each other and share their questions. They are told that no question can be repeated. The goal is to see how many different questions the class can generate.

13. Close the activity by asking learners how they could find answers to some of the class-generated questions. Finally, you can share background information about the image.

CAVEATS AND OPTIONS

- Parts A and B of the worksheet are critical for building visual literacy (i.e., analyzing and interpreting images). Parts C and D develop learners' deeper thinking about images. It is possible to use only the first two parts of the worksheet if needed.

- You can apply this strategy to any image (e.g., photographs, illustrations) you choose. When selecting an image, consider the level of detail and information presented—the more, the better.

- The linguistic demands of the activity depend on the image's topic or theme and on the complexity of the worksheet questions, and both can be easily modified to fit the needs of a particular group of learners.

Note: This activity was adapted from educator resources at the U.S. National Archives (www.archives.gov/education/activities/worksheets/analyze-a-photograph-intermediate).

REFERENCES AND FURTHER READING

Baker, F. W. (2012). *Media literacy in the K–12 classroom.* International Society for Technology in Education.

APPENDIX A: *Photograph*

Image credit: Gabriela Kleckova. Used with permission.

This photograph was taken at a birthday party in the early evening in late April. The birthday man is standing on the stage and looking at the crowd. His friends are singing a song they wrote for him; one of them is playing the piano. It is a unique and fun moment, and two people are capturing the moment with their cameras. Before this moment, the man and his other friends had a little concert for everyone. The man carves wood and makes handmade wooden marionettes for a living, which explains all the wooden items in the picture. The author of the picture was up on a high deck when taking the picture.

APPENDIX B: *Worksheet*

Part A: What do I see?

Divide the photograph into four quadrants. Study each quadrant separately and pay attention to all the details. Note the people, objects, and activities you see:

People	Objects	Activities
What people do you see? What do they look like? What are they wearing? Where are they?	What objects do you see? What sizes and colors are they? Where are the objects in relation to the people? What are the objects for?	What are the people doing?

Part B: What do I think and why?

Based on what you have observed about the photograph, respond to the following questions:

Question 1	What is going on in the photograph?
My opinion	
My rationale	

Question 2	What sounds would the photograph make (if it could)?
My opinion	
My rationale	

Question 3	What does the space outside the photograph look like?
My opinion	
My rationale	

Question 4	What season of the year is it?
My opinion	
My rationale	

Question 5	What do you think happened before this photograph was taken?
My opinion	
My rationale	

Part C: What else do I think?

Choose one of the following questions and write your answer below it:

1. What title would you give the photograph? What made you decide on that title?

2. Why do you think this picture was taken? For whom? By whom?

3. Imagine you are inside the photograph. What does it feel like?

4. Does the photograph remind you of anything? How and why?

Part D: What questions do I have?

1. What questions does the photograph raise in your mind?

Caption the Photograph

Monika Bharti

Levels	All
Ages Suitable for Activity	Primary to secondary
Aims	Make sustained observations of visual images
	Interpret, analyze, and communicate the meanings of images and visual media
	Use images and visual media effectively
	Evaluate images and their sources
	Develop verbal knowledge in context with visual clues
	Develop observational, brainstorming, listening, and speaking skills
Class Time	45 minutes
Preparation Time	20 minutes
Resources	Photographs (Appendix, or teacher's choice)

Using pictures to support reading is one of the key early literacy concepts for new readers. After completing this activity, learners will understand how "reading" pictures for details and clues can help them predict what the picture is about. This activity aims to reveal that a single visual image can be open to several interpretations. Learners will further gain awareness of the power of a caption to frame an image's meaning, even if the caption is not accurate.

PROCEDURE

1. Divide the class into pairs.
2. *Warm-up:* Before handing out the photographs without captions in the Appendix, provide each pair of learners with another photograph with a caption.
   a. Have them discuss in pairs what they notice about the photograph and how the caption is related to it. This warm-up discussion will activate their knowledge about the concept of a caption.
   b. Conduct a whole-class discussion and ask learners what they think about the photograph and the caption.
   c. Elicit ideas about this image using questions like the following:
      i. What is happening in the photo?
      ii. Where do you think it is?
      iii. Describe the people, objects, and events shown.
      iv. Can you guess the story's topic (e.g., entertainment, sports, local news)?
      v. How is the caption related to the photo?
      vi. If we changed the caption, would it make you feel different about the photo?

3. *Writing a Caption:* Distribute the preselected photographs without captions (from the Appendix or your own choosing) to each pair of learners. Ask learners to closely examine the photograph and talk about it with each other in pairs, then write a caption to accompany the photograph.

   a. Make it clear that there are no correct answers; you simply want them to be creative.

   b. Visit each pair and monitor the conversations. If the learners are having a hard time brainstorming and producing a caption, ask guiding questions as in the previous warm-up stage:

      i. Are there any clues as to when it was taken?

      ii. What was happening in the picture?

      iii. Are there any clues as to where it was taken?

      iv. Are there any clues as to why it was taken or who took it?

      v. Is it a posed photograph? A natural scene? A selfie?

      vi. Invite a few pairs to discuss what they observed about their assigned photograph and why they chose a particular caption with the whole class.

4. *Class Discussion and Analysis:* Reveal the original captions (true nature) of the photographs discussed by the students' pairs and compare them with the captions given by the learners. Discuss the similarities and differences between the original captions and the captions assigned by the learners. Ask guiding questions like the following:

   a. What is the key information?

   b. What conclusions can you reach?

   c. How can you interpret the information?

   d. What is going on? What assumptions are you making?

   e. How does each caption change the perception of the photograph?

CAVEATS AND OPTIONS

- Adapt this activity to any age and level by changing the context and language level of the prompts.

- Use this activity alone or as a lead-in to a bigger topic. Choose photographs on themes relevant to your learning objectives or reading materials. This can make for a great introduction to draw out the learners' background knowledge and prepare them for a larger discussion or research project.

- This activity can also be easily adapted for a wide range of different types of images, including advertisements.

- Repeat the activity by giving the same photographs to different pairs or groups. Learners can compare and contrast the different captions they produced for the same photograph.

- You can use pictures that the students have already chosen, or they can bring pictures from outside of class. In this way, learners can select different themes to work with.

- You may want to preteach the vocabulary before doing the activity. One way to approach this is to ensure learners have multiple exposures to the target vocabulary words. For example, you can pronounce a new word, explain what it means, talk about the parts of the word, write the word on the board, use the word in a sentence or question, and show a video linked to that specific word or phrase. This approach can be adapted for any proficiency level.

REFERENCES AND FURTHER READING

Felten, P. (2008). Visual literacy. *Change: The Magazine of Higher Learning, 40*(6), 60–64.

National Institute for Literacy. (2007). *What content-area teachers should know about adolescent literacy.* National Institute of Child Health and Human Development, National Institute for Literacy. https://lincs.ed.gov/publications/pdf/adolescent_literacy07.pdf

APPENDIX: *Sample Photographs*

Critically Reading a Photo Through Decolonial Lenses

Izabelle da Silva Fernandes and Erika de Freitas Coachman

Level	High intermediate
Ages Suitable for Activity	Secondary to adult
Aims	Develop observation skills
	Practice responding verbally to visual stimuli
	Develop critical race literacy
	Promote critical thinking and social awareness
Class Time	30–45 minutes
Preparation Time	10 minutes
Resources	Image (Appendix)
	Laptop and projector

uring recent decades, decolonial and antiracist perspectives have brought forward novel proposals for the field of English language teaching (ELT). Ferreira's concept of critical race literacy (2014), for instance, has underscored the importance of submitting texts (whether visual, written or spoken) to a careful analysis to recognize how language actively shapes ideas on race and racism. This activity aims at decolonial and antiracist purposes by promoting a debate about a picture of a group of boys in Borel, a favela in the city of Rio de Janeiro, in Brazil.

PROCEDURE

1. Distribute copies of the image (see Appendix) or project the image digitally.
2. Ask students what elements draw their attention in the image and discuss why these particular features stand out.
3. Invite students to analyze the source from which the photograph was retrieved (www.favelagrafia.com.br) and discuss the kind of content that is available on this website.
4. Ask students to relate elements from the photo itself to the name of the website (www.favelagrafia.com.br).
5. Ask students where they assume the photograph was taken and whether they have lived in or near places like the favela from the picture.
6. Have students discuss the reason why the boys from the picture have their faces covered.
7. Draw students' attention to the boy whose face is covered by a yellow soccer jersey of the Brazilian team and invite them to discuss possible implications and interpretations they could associate with it.
8. Ask students to discuss whether the picture would convey the same meanings if it were black and white.

9. Organize learners into small groups and have them discuss the following questions:

   a. What is the role of music and art according to the image? Do you agree with this view on the social function of art? Why (not)?

   b. Have you ever seen any similar photos? If so, where were they published?

   c. This image has gone viral on different social media. Why do you think this happened?

   d. The title of the photo (originally in Portuguese) is *Alguns lutam com outras armas* [Some people fight with other weapons]. To what sort of "fight" does such a name probably refer to?

   e. From your experience or background knowledge, what are favelas usually associated with?

   f. To what extent do you think the image contradicts or reinforces those stereotypes? Why?

10. Ask each group to provide a brief overview on their internal debate. Did they all agree while answering the questions? Why (not)?

11. Elicit the meaning of *hashtag*. Ask students what hashtags are used for in social media.

12. Finally, ask each student to imagine they are going to share this photo online. Invite each of them to create an original hashtag to be posted with it.

CAVEATS AND OPTIONS

To extend this activity, have students exchange hashtags and comment on each other's ideas.

REFERENCES AND FURTHER READING

Ferreira, A. J. (2014). Teoria racial crítica e letramento racial crítico: Narrativas e contranarrativas de identidade racial de professores de línguas [Critical race theory and critical race literacy: Narratives and counternarratives of language teachers]. *Revista Da Associação Brasileira De Pesquisadores/As Negros/As (ABPN)*, 6(14), 236–263.

Mignolo, W. (2010). Delinking: The rhetoric of modernity, the logic of coloniality and the grammar of decoloniality. In W. Mignolo & A. Escobar (Eds.), *Globalization and the decolonial option* (pp. 303–368). Routledge.

APPENDIX: *Teenage Boys Carrying Musical Instruments in Borel, Rio de Janeiro*

The photograph examined in this activity went viral a few years ago. What is particularly striking about it is the fact that the boys are posing as some criminals stereotypically do (also covering their faces), but instead of carrying guns, they are holding musical instruments.

The photographer's name is Ton Valentim, and the boys are participants in a social project aimed at teaching jazz to children and teenagers from lower income communities.

The questions offered in this activity plan have been designed to invite students to talk about racism and racialized identities in their societies.

Image credit: Anderson Cunha Valentim. Used with permission.

Decoding World War I and World War II Propaganda Posters

Constance Leonard

Levels	High intermediate to advanced
Ages Suitable for Activity	Secondary to adult
Aims	Decode propaganda posters
	Practice presenting in class
	Develop critical consumption of media
Class Time	15–45 minutes
Preparation Time	10 minutes
Resources	Sample U.S. propaganda posters from the "Powers of Persuasion" online exhibit (www.archives.gov/exhibits/powers-of-persuasion), or Appendix
	Access to the internet on laptops or tablets
	Laptop and projector

Students are saturated with visual content in the 21st century. Multilingual learners of English need to know how to accurately decode what they are viewing in order to consume and use information in both academic and personal settings. According to the American Library Association, "visual literacy is a set of abilities that enables an individual to effectively find, interpret, evaluate, use, and create images and visual media" (Visual Literacy Standards Task Force, 2011). This activity examines World War I (WWI) and World War II (WWII) propaganda posters to develop critical visual literacy skills that learners can use, for example, to analyze disinformation surrounding current conflicts.

PROCEDURE

1. Before the activity, ask students to research whether their country was involved in either WWI or WWII and locate a propaganda poster in their home language. If their country was not involved in either of the two wars, students can select a country of their choice or a country where their home language is spoken.

2. Display a poster of your choice from either WWI or WWII from the "Powers of Persuasion" online exhibit at the U.S. National Archives (www.archives.gov/exhibits/powers-of-persuasion) or from another national archive. An example is provided in the Appendix.

3. Analyze the poster as a whole class, looking at the language, colors, images, placement and size of images, any cultural context, and the appeal to patriotism and civic duty. You may discuss all or some of the following points:

   a. For example, the language might appeal to patriotism (or it might demonize the "enemy") in an attempt to persuade citizens to join the cause by either enlisting in the military or serving in another capacity at home.

b. Also, these posters often use large bright images of flags and larger-than-life images of patriots working at home and abroad, eliciting emotion in the viewer.

c. The placement of imagery matters: Some items will be drawn large and in the foreground, drawing the eye to the main message, and other items will be dwarfed, denoting their insignificance.

d. Ask students to notice how people who are "others" or enemies in the conflict are often presented in cartoonish, demeaning, and racist ways, such as with exaggerated facial features.

4. Divide students into pairs or small groups, and ask each group to choose their own poster to analyze and present. Give students a time limit for discussing and decoding the visuals on their posters.

5. Circulate among the groups to help facilitate the decoding.

6. To close the activity, have each group display their poster and present their findings to the class. This is also an opportunity for the rest of the class to add their interpretations.

CAVEATS AND OPTIONS

- Extend the activity by asking students to search online and find propaganda posters in various languages and compare their images and rhetoric to English-language posters from the same conflict. You could facilitate an interesting cultural discussion with these images.

- Students could also compare and contrast WWI and WWII posters with recruitment posters in current conflicts.

- For sample posters in British English, the Imperial War Museums are a useful source of propaganda imagery. Both recruitment and civic duty posters are included, giving students a variety of options:

  — WWI poster archive (www.iwm.org.uk/learning/resources/first-world-war-recruitment-posters)

  — WWII poster archive (www.iwm.org.uk/learning/resources/second-world-war-posters)

  Calls for civic duty included saving gas by car sharing, victory gardens, and home recycling. Posters also exhorted civilians to save waste products like cooking fat, paper, aluminum foil and other materials and donate them to the military to be used in manufacturing. This call could be compared to recycling campaigns today.

- The U.S. National Archives and the Imperial War Museums websites listed earlier also include additional primary resources, such as audio recordings, photographs, film footage, and letters, which could lead to further activities on how to analyze such materials for academic research.

- The skills learned in this activity can easily be adapted to analyze news photographs, magazine covers, campaign posters, and advertisements.

REFERENCES AND FURTHER READING

Visual Literacy Standards Task Force. (2011, October 27). *ACRL visual literacy competency standards for higher education.* Association of College & Research Libraries (ACRL). www.ala.org/acrl/standards/visualliteracy

APPENDIX: *Sample WWII Civic Poster From the U.S. National Archives*

Image source: National Archives (https://www.archives.gov/exhibits/powers-of-persuasion)

In this poster, the viewer can note the bright red and blue colors and prominent position of the American flag at the top of the background, suggesting that all citizens are united under one flag. Below the flag and illustrated in grayscale, a white man and a Black man appear to be working together in either manufacturing or maintenance. Their expressions are serious and they are both focused on the task at hand. It is interesting to note the slogan, "United We Win," at the same time Black soldiers were fighting in separate units.

Note: The views expressed in this article are those of the author and not necessarily those of the U.S. Air Force Academy, the U.S. Air Force, the Department of Defense, or the U.S. Government. PA#: USAFA-DF-2023-372

Descriptive Taboo: Enhancing Visual Literacy Through Speaking

Linda Merzougui

Level	Intermediate to high intermediate
Ages Suitable for Activity	Adult
Aims	Develop visual literacy skills through interpreting and describing images
	Expand descriptive vocabulary by avoiding "taboo" words
	Enhance fluency and communication in English speaking
Class Time	45 minutes–1 hour
Preparation Time	15–20 minutes
Resources	Taboo word cards and sample images (Appendix)
	Timer or stopwatch

This activity helps learners improve their visual literacy by encouraging creative language use when describing images. By avoiding overused vocabulary, students engage more deeply with visual prompts and expand their descriptive abilities.

PROCEDURE

1. *Introduction (5–10 minutes):* Introduce visual literacy and explain that learners will describe images without using specific common words. Show an example of an image (e.g., a crowded market) and demonstrate how to describe it without using basic words like *shop, people,* or *buy.*

2. *Activity Setup (5 minutes):* Divide the class into small groups of three or four students. Each group receives an image and a card with a list of taboo words that they cannot use in their description (see Appendix). Explain that groups will take turns describing their image to the class while other groups guess what the image depicts. Encourage detailed descriptions of the images (focusing on colors, objects, people, and activities) and prompt students to use complete sentences rather than words.

3. *Activity Execution (25–30 minutes)*

   Step 1: The first group presents their description, avoiding the taboo words on their card.

   Step 2: The rest of the class guesses what the image is based on the description. If no correct guesses are made, the group can offer additional details. Finally, the group reveals their image card to the rest of the class.

   Step 3: Rotate through all the groups, providing feedback on creativity, language use, and clarity after each round.

4. *Discussion (5–10 minutes):* Facilitate a class discussion on how avoiding certain words pushed students to engage with the images differently. Discuss the

importance of visual literacy and how this activity connects to real-life communication, such as in IELTS speaking tasks.

CAVEATS AND OPTIONS

- For advanced learners, consider using more abstract images or asking follow-up questions that require deeper analysis (e.g., cultural significance, inferred emotions).
- For lower level learners, adapt the activity by using simpler and more concrete images and providing basic taboo cards with familiar vocabulary. This helps to make the activity more accessible and engaging.
- For online classes, use digital tools like Padlet (padlet.com) to share images and allow students to add notes before discussing.

APPENDIX: *Sample Images and Taboo Word Cards**

Taboo Words Card

future learning
holograms
technology
education
digital classroom
innovation

Taboo Words Card

cultural exchange
global connections
study abroad
international students
global citizenship

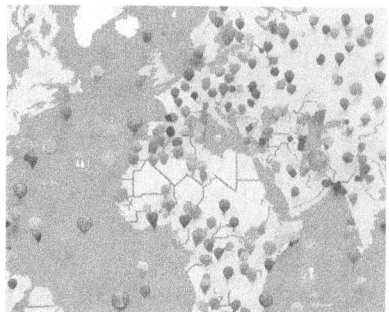

Taboo Words Card

teamwork
brainstorming
multicultural
collaboration
problem-solving
innovation hub

Taboo Words Card

identity

home

cultural pride

roots

personal story

Taboo Words Card

idiom

literal

figurative

weather

language play

humor

Taboo Words Card

software engineering
virtual
innovation
coding
digital
future
high-tech

Taboo Words Card

diversity

global learning

student community

knowledge exchange

inclusion

---

*All images in this appendix created by Linda Merzougi with Canva AI. Used with permission.

Eliciting Creative Responses to Still Images

Natalia Orlova

Levels	Advanced
Ages Suitable for Activity	Preservice and in-service teachers
Aims	Critically analyze and respond to still images
	Make inferences from an image
	Understand how to incorporate images as stimuli for skill integration
	Develop cross-cultural curiosity
Class Time	45 minutes–1 hour
Preparation Time	10 minutes
Resources	Images of Vermeer paintings (Appendixes A and B) or an image of another painting

Using visuals as prompts for developing productive and receptive skills is an important area in a teacher's competence. Analyzing still images stimulates (preservice) teachers' development of their own visual literacy—and further encourages them to integrate visuals in skill development activities in their own classrooms.

PROCEDURE

1. Ask the class if they like visiting museums or exhibitions. Elicit the names of some world-famous museums and check if the students know in which countries they are located. Ask a student to write responses on the board. Possible answers could include the following:
    a. Metropolitan Museum of Art (New York City, United States)
    b. Louvre (Paris, France)
    c. British Museum (London, United Kingdom)
    d. National Museum of India (New Delhi, India)
    e. Rijksmuseum (Amsterdam, Netherlands)
    f. Melbourne Museum (Melbourne, Australia)
    g. Marrakech Museum (Marrakech, Morocco)
    h. Gold Museum (Bogota, Colombia)
2. Elicit examples of artifacts one can see in history, art, and science museums. Further elicit what types of artifacts belong to fine art. Possible answers could include painting, sculpture, drawing, watercolor, graphics, and architecture.
3. Ask if students like paintings. Ask them to share names of their favorite artists (if they have any).

4. Tell them about your favorite visual artist, whose creative work you know or like. When the teacher is passionate about a topic, it can help learners engage and connect to the learning.

5. Give some background information about the artist of the paintings in Appendixes A and B (adapted from Mauritshuis, n.d.):

   For more than a century, Johannes Vermeer's name was missing from the history of art. His paintings depicted the life of the middle class and provided onlookers with a window into the lives of common people via scenes of the everyday life of the past. Currently, only 36 paintings are attributed to him. After his death, Vermeer's name was almost forgotten. Vermeer was rediscovered in the 19th century, and since that time he received a great deal of international attention, as he still does to this day.

6. Show the class two paintings by Vermeer: *The Love Letter* (see Appendix A) and *Mistress and Maid* (see Appendix B). Both paintings depict a lady, a maid, and a letter. Let students read the following text and guess which painting it describes:

   The picture "masterfully portrays the moment in which a maid delivers… a letter, presumably a love letter." In the picture, a young woman sits holding a lute by its neck in her left hand. In her right hand, there is a letter that she has seemingly been given by her maidservant. A viewer can also see a laundry basket, loafers, a broom, "and even a crumpled piece of sheet music strewn in apparent disorder" (Janson, n.d.).

7. Zoom in on the image of *The Love Letter*. Divide the class into pairs or small groups and ask them to discuss what they see in the picture. Use the following questions as verbal prompts:

   a. Who can you see in the picture?
   b. Where is the scene set?
   c. How would you entitle the picture?
   d. Does the depicted interior belong to a wealthy household? How do you know?
   e. What had the young woman been doing before the maidservant brought in the letter?

   Elicit answers from pairs or groups. Then, tell them the name of the painting.

8. With the whole class, continue eliciting answers to the following inferential questions:

   a. Who could have written the letter?
   b. Why is there a questioning expression in the lady's eyes?
   c. How can you describe the smile on the maid's face? Is it triumphant? wry? false? smug? amused?
   d. Does the maid know about the content of the letter? What makes you think so?

9. Divide learners into two groups. Tell one group to imagine the identity of the person who wrote the letter. Tell the other group to speculate on the lady's personal background and characteristics.

10. Tell each group to write a character profile for the person they've been discussing. After a few minutes, ask each group to present their profile to the class.

11. Then, give each group time to 1) write a letter to the lady and to the enigmatic person, 2) swap letters with a different group, and 3) write a reply.

12. If students have access to internet-enabled mobile devices, ask students to search online for other paintings by Vermeer which contain the motif of a letter. (Possible paintings include *Woman in Blue Reading a Letter*, *Girl Reading a Letter at an Open Window*, *Lady Writing a Letter with her Maid*, *A Lady Writing a Letter*, *Mistress and Maid*.)

13. Elicit opinions on why writing a letter was a popular motif in Vermeer's time.

14. Ask the class to compile a list of countries where pictures by Vermeer are on display. Which museum would they like to visit? Why?

CAVEATS AND OPTIONS

- Follow the same activity procedure with a painting of your choice.
- As an alternate opening to this activity, select photos of world-famous museums and ask students to match the names with the photos. Choosing world-famous museums with interesting and unconventional buildings may stimulate cross-cultural curiosity. For example, you might choose the Musée d'Orsay (Paris, France), Museo Soumaya (Mexico City, Mexico), the Modern Art Museum of Fort Worth (Texas, United States), or the Erawan Museum (Samut Prakan Province, Thailand).
- While showing the class both paintings, present the descriptions of *Love Letter* (Step 6) and *Mistress Maid*. Have students match the descriptions with the paintings.
  - *Mistress Maid*: The painting depicts the moment in which a maid delivers a letter to her lady. The lady is depicted with her head slightly turned from the viewers and her hand raised to the chin. Presumable, the lady has been writing a letter or was planning to do so.
- As a follow-up task, ask students to find their own images and design activities for peer teaching or, alternatively, design an activity they would teach their students.

REFERENCES AND FURTHER READING

Janson, J. (n.d.). The love letter by Johannes Vermeer. *Essential Vermeer 5.0: The complete interactive Vermeer catalogue*. https://www.essentialvermeer.com/catalogue/love_letter.html

Mauritshuis. (n.d.). Johannes Vermeer (1632–1675): "The sphinx of Delft." https://www.mauritshuis.nl/en/our-collection/our-masters/johannes-vermeer

APPENDIX A: *The Love Letter*

Image source: https://commons.wikimedia.org/wiki/File:Vermeer,_Johannes_-_The_Loveletter.jpg

APPENDIX B: *Mistress and Maid*

Image source: https://commons.wikimedia.org/wiki/File:Vermeer_Lady_Maidservant_Holding_Letter.jpg

Enhancing Writing With Visual Comparisons

Adelia Mazzella-Chace

Levels	Intermediate to advanced
Ages Suitable for Activity	Secondary to adult
Aims	Develop observational skills by analyzing visual images
	Respond to visual input both verbally and in writing
	Use appropriate academic vocabulary to describe similarities and differences
	Practice planning and organizing information in text form
Class Time	15 minutes–1 hour
Preparation Time	10–30 minutes
Resources	Visuals (Appendix A)
	Transitions signal chart (Appendix B)
	Writer's notebook or digital collaborative workspace

The ability to recognize and describe similarities and differences between concepts, ideas, or objects is a fundamental skill in the English language classroom, applicable at all levels from elementary school to higher education. When this skill is extended into writing, it can be very difficult for students to construct effective comparative text structures, so explicit instruction is recommended (Hammann & Stevens, 2003). In this activity, students first use visuals to practice verbally conceptualizing the similarities and differences between two subjects. Then, they will transfer their ideas into written form by creating sentences, using appropriate transition signals for comparison and contrast to effectively connect their ideas.

PROCEDURE

1. Ask the class to review the purpose of comparison and contrast in writing.
    a. Explain that we use comparison and contrast to explain and evaluate the similarities and differences between two subjects.
2. Put learners in pairs or small groups.
3. Give each group a set of printed visuals (Appendix A).
4. Ask the class to look at their visuals and answer the following questions with their partners:
    a. What two things are being compared?
    b. How are they similar?
    c. How are they different?
5. Ask the students to be as detailed as possible. Give groups time to think and respond.

6. Present each group with a chart of common transitions used in comparison/contrast writing (Appendix B). Review the phrases with the class, pointing out how the different types of transition signals can be used.

7. Ask students to look at their assigned visual again, write four to five sentences using at least one transition signal, and underline the transition in their writer's notebook.

   a. *Example sentence 1:* Both pictures have a tall building.

   b. *Example sentence 2:* Unlike the first picture, the second picture has white puffy clouds.

   c. *Example sentence 3:* One similarity between the pictures is that they both contain a body of water.

   d. *Example sentence 4:* Although the first picture was taken in the evening, the second picture was taken during the day.

8. Give students time to formulate their sentences. Walk around the room providing assistance and answering questions on correct vocabulary and grammar usage.

9. After students have completed their sentences, ask a few volunteers to share their examples with the rest of the class.

CAVEATS AND OPTIONS

- Adapt this activity for a lower level by changing the visual content and providing sentence frames like the following:
  - Both pictures have a _____ building.
  - Although the first picture was taken in the _____, the second picture was taken during the _____.
- Present the visuals digitally by placing them in a shared collaborative workspace such as Google Docs, Google Slides, or FigJam (www.figma.com/figjam). Students can then type their sentences directly on the shared document.
- Use this activity as a writing warm up or a review activity. Make it a full-length class session by having students describe several sets of pictures.
- Extend the learning or assign homework by having students focus on one set of pictures to write a well-developed paragraph or essay.

REFERENCES AND FURTHER READING

Hammann, L. A., & Stevens, R. J. (2003). Instructional approaches to improving students' writing of compare–contrast essays: An experimental study. *Journal of Literacy Research, 35*(2), 731–756. doi.org/10.1207/s15548430jlr3502_3

APPENDIX A: *Visuals*

Image credit: Nirmal Rajendharkumar on Unsplash.

Image credit: Alexander Shatov on Unsplash.

Image credit: Vitolda Klein on Unsplash. *Image credit:* Melinda Martin-Khan on Unsplash.

Image credit: dcbel on Unsplash.

Image credit: Peter Pryharski on Unsplash.

Image credit: Ryan Arnst on Unsplash.

Image credit: Liana Mikah on Unsplash.

APPENDIX B: *Comparison and Contrast Transition Signals*

Comparison	Contrast
Similarly	However
Both	Although
In the same way	In contrast
One similarity	Unlike
Another similarity	On the contrary
Like	On the other hand
Likewise	One difference

Expanding Vocabulary Through Photographs and Poetry

Ana Luisa Lado

Levels	Low beginner to low intermediate
Ages Suitable for Activity	Secondary to adult
Aims	Integrate graphic, oral, and written means of communication
	Describe people they love and with whom they identify
	Write a poem and illustrate it with their own photographs
Class Time	5 (20-minute) class periods
Preparation Time	10 minutes
Resources	Copy of *My People* (Hughes, 2009)
	Optional: A device for taking photographs (e.g., tablet or smartphone)

y People, by Langston Hughes (2009) with photography by Charles R. Smith Jr., is a Coretta Scott King Award–winning picture book that is an ideal springboard for students to create their own poetic and photographic works. The text has a Lexile level of 80L, making it accessible to early beginners, and the photographs are appropriate for older and adult students.

PROCEDURE

Activity 1: Vocabulary Comprehension

1. To prepare for this activity, select four nouns from the text (e.g., *faces, sun, eyes, night*) for which you will demonstrate meanings by referring to the photographs and/or making gestures.

    a. Make a word card for each noun and make a list of suggested substitutes. Use the photographs in the book as prompts.

    b. Plan an explanatory gesture for each of the following words: *faces, sun, eyes, souls*.

2. Read the poem while pausing at each selected noun to make the planned gesture and/or point to the photographs.

3. Reread the poem and pause on each page for students to chorally finish the phrase for you. They should speak out the key words (e.g., *faces, eyes, sun, souls*).

4. Give students your prepared word cards. Reread the text while pausing to ask "Who has this word?" Have the student with the card show it.

5. Have students trade their word cards with each other. Reread it again while pausing and have students raise their card in the air and say the word out loud.

6. If the technology is available, check comprehension by asking students to take photographs to represent the meanings of the words and having them identify each other's photographs.

Activity 2: Cloze Poem

1. Write the poem on the board, leaving four blanks for key nouns, such as *night, faces, people,* and *stars.* Have students come up to the board and put a word card into a blank.

2. Repeat with another set of four nouns, such as *eyes, people, sun,* and *souls.*

3. Develop fluency by helping students memorize the poem:

    a. Write the poem on the board and read it. Then erase one word per line. Read it again while having students orally fill in the erased word. Then erase one more word per line and reread it while students orally fill in all the erased words.

    b. Continue to erase one more word at a time until they can recite the poem with fluency.

4. Use the following steps to expand students' vocabulary knowledge:

    a. Teach the meaning of the word *people* through the photographs and with gestures.

    b. Then, provide similar words to use as substitutes for people, such as *class-mates, countrymen, family,* and *friends.* Allow students to make more suggestions for words that can be substituted, and write each of these words on a card.

    c. Assign each of the new words a distinct gesture. Use total physical response (TPR) to teach the subtle differences between their meanings. Say a word and elicit a gesture or movement from the students (Asher, 2009).

    d. Rewrite the complete poem on the board. Substituting one of the expanded vocabulary words for the word *people* in the poem, read the newly created phrases together.

5. Use the same method to expand the meaning of the word *beautiful*:

    a. Assign contrasting gestures for the word and its opposite, *not beautiful.*

    b. Then, expand students' vocabulary by selecting four other words to use as substitutes for *beautiful* that have a similar meaning and the same number of syllables, such as *wonderful, enchanting, delightful, attractive.* Write each of these words on a card. Allow students to make suggestions for words that can be substituted.

    c. Teach the subtle differences between the meanings of the new words by assigning each of them a distinct gesture.

    d. Have students select one of the cards and take turns substituting the words in the poem and reading the lines on the board.

Activity 3: Noticing Grammar

1. Write the first sentence of the poem on the board. As you read it, underline the words that will help students notice its grammatical structure. Have the students read it with you and notice the singular verb *is*:

    The night is beautiful, so are the faces of my people.

2. Show four possible singular nouns that can be substituted for *night* and correctly used with *is*, such as *sun, day, sunshine, garden,* or *meadow.*

3. Write the second sentence of the poem on the board and have students notice the plural verb *are*:

> The stars are beautiful, so are the eyes of my people.

Again, list four possible plural nouns that can be substituted for *stars* and *eyes*, such as *faces, souls, joys, arms, smiles, hugs,* or *laughs*.

4. Write the third and fourth patterned phrases on the board. Have students notice the new sentence patterns. Have them read the phrases out loud with you:

> Beautiful, also, <u>are</u> the souls
>
> Beautiful, also, *is* the sun

Activity 4: Application

Ask students to write their own poem using the patterns of *My People*, using their own choices of substituted nouns and adjectives drawn from Activity 2.

Activity 5: Sentence Scramble

1. Have two teams write the sentences from the poem on long pieces of paper, then cut each sentence to make word cards for each of the words in these sentences.
2. Scramble the words.
3. Have each team of students put the word cards into correct sentences together.
4. Teams get one point for each sentence that they correctly reconstruct.

CAVEATS AND OPTIONS

- After completing Activity 4, have students photograph and print scenes related to their poems and use these to make their own book.
- There are several ways to assess students depending on your learning objectives:
  — Write the pattern of the poem with blanks on a worksheet or on the board. Have students fill in the blanks.
  — Have students rehearse reciting this poem and assess their ability to do so with adequate pronunciation and fluency (i.e., accuracy, speed, and intonation).
  — Assess vocabulary comprehension and recall by creating a worksheet with photographs or illustrations of key vocabulary words and having students write the correct word under each image.
  — Use the students' own poems, with or without illustrations, for assessment.
- For students at more advanced levels, allow a wider variety of sentence structures.
- One way to adapt this activity for students at the earliest beginner levels of English proficiency is to limit the number of suggested vocabulary words in the word-substitution activities to one or two items.
- Another way to adapt the activity for low beginners is to lead them in the following speaking practice activity:
  — Begin by asking half the class to stand in a line facing the other half of the class.

— Students in one line ask the person facing them in the other half of the line a question, and that person answers, as in the following:

The night is beautiful.	
Is the night beautiful?	Yes, it is.
Is this photograph night?	Yes, it is.
Is this an eye?	Yes, it is.
Are the faces beautiful?	Yes, the faces are beautiful.
Is this a photograph of a face?	Yes, it is.
Are these more than one face?	Yes, they are.
Are these two eyes?	Yes, they are.
Beautiful are the eyes.	
Are the eyes beautiful?	Yes, they are.

— Once mastered, switch the roles or move random students into the opposite line.

REFERENCES AND FURTHER READING

Asher, J. (2009) *Learning another language through actions* (7th ed.). Sky Oaks Productions.

Hughes, L. (2009). *My People* (C. R. Smith, Jr., Illus.). Atheneum Books for Young Readers.

Lado, A. (2012) *Teaching beginner ELLs with picture books: Tellability*. Corwin/Sage.

Marymount University School of Education (n.d.). *Picture books for teaching English learners.* https://marymount.edu/academics/college-of-health-and-education/school-of-education/resources/esl/

Exploring Cultural Perspectives Through Visual Storytelling

Maki Hignett

Levels	Intermediate to advanced
Ages Suitable for Activity	University to adult
Aims	Improve understanding of visual literacy and storytelling
	Encourage critical thinking and cultural awareness
	Improve English communication skills, both written and oral
	Develop creative expression through visual storytelling
	Foster empathy and appreciation for diverse cultures
Class Time	2 (90-minute) class periods
Preparation Time	30–40 minutes
Resources	Laptop and projector
	Access to the internet on laptops or tablets
	Paper and drawing materials (e.g., pencils, markers)

In this activity, students engage in visual storytelling and examine how it reflects various cultural perspectives. This activity draws upon the foundational visual semiotics work of Kress and Van Leeuwen (2021), who assert that visual elements can be "read" much like text; it is also informed by Pauwels (2011), who underlines the importance of visual methodologies in examining societal and cultural dynamics.

Encouraging students to explore and appreciate cultural diversity by analyzing and creating visual stories is an effective method for improving their visual literacy and English communication skills. Care should also be taken to ensure that these discussions encourage openness and respect toward different cultures, especially when students are exploring cultures other than their own.

PROCEDURE

1. *(5 minutes)* Begin the activity by introducing the concept of visual literacy and its importance in communication. Explain that visual literacy involves the ability to interpret, understand, and create meaning from visual elements, such as images, illustrations, and videos.

2. *(5 minutes)* Introduce the term *visual storytelling* and discuss how it serves as a medium to communicate ideas, emotions, and narratives through visuals, rather than written or spoken words. Emphasize the importance of visual storytelling in today's media-rich world, where people often consume information through images and videos rather than traditional text.

3. *(10 minutes)* Project the Japanese Ukiyo-e print in Figure 1 as an example of visual storytelling. Explain how this visual story reflects the unique customs, values, and traditions of Japanese culture. Here are some ideas to get you started:

This iconic Ukiyo-e print depicts a large wave threatening boats off the coast of Kanagawa Prefecture. It serves as a powerful illustration of various aspects of Japanese culture—capturing the nation's complex relationship with nature, its spirituality, and its philosophical viewpoints. The wave is both a menacing force and a beautiful, natural form. This duality embodies the complexities often found in Japanese cultural narratives, making it a compelling example for discussion.

Figure 1. "The Great Wave off Kanagawa" by Hokusai (sourced from Ukiyo-e.org).

4. *(10 minutes)* Show students more examples of visual stories from diverse cultures (see Appendix A). Initiate a discussion on the messages, themes, and cultural elements found in each example, encouraging student input. These discussions should promote careful consideration of cultural differences and invite students to examine any stereotypes or preconceived notions that may emerge.

5. *(15 minutes)* Divide the class into small groups and assign each group a specific culture to research. Alternatively, groups may choose to explore images or visual stories from their own cultures to support a more informed discussion. Instruct them to find images or visual stories that represent their chosen culture to prepare a 3-minute presentation.

6. *(3 minutes per group)* Groups present their findings.

7. *(10 minutes)* Facilitate a class discussion to compare and contrast the presented visual stories, focusing on their reflection of diverse cultural perspectives.

8. *(10–15 minutes)* Instruct students to craft their own visual story, depicting an aspect of their assigned culture using either drawing materials or digital tools. Explain that they are preparing for an individual 3-minute presentation to be delivered in the subsequent class period. Provide time in class for students to begin their research and ask questions; the presentation should be completed as homework.

9. In the subsequent class, students present their visual stories, elaborating on the cultural elements and messages their work aims to convey. Peer feedback and discussion are encouraged.

CAVEATS AND OPTIONS

- For lower level students, provide a list of key vocabulary related to visual literacy and culture to support their understanding and communication (see Appendix B).
- For online instruction, use a digital platform for group work and presentations, and provide resources for digital image creation.
- To adapt to three or four 45-minute sessions:
  - — Session 1 covers the introduction and cultural examples (Steps 1-4).
  - — Session 2 focuses on group research and short presentations (Steps 5-7).
  - — Session 3 is for individual visual story presentations (Steps 8-9).
  - — A fourth session may be added for larger classes to accommodate additional individual presentations.

REFERENCES AND FURTHER READING

Kress, G. R., & Van Leeuwen, T. (2021). *Reading images: The grammar of visual design* (3rd ed.). Routledge.

Pauwels, L. (2011). An integrated conceptual framework for visual social research. In E. Margolis & L. Pauwels (Eds.), *The SAGE handbook of visual research methods* (pp. 3–23). SAGE.

APPENDIX A: *List of Sample Visual Stories or Images From Different Cultures*

Use the following ideas and keywords to conduct your research. Themes for each type of visual story are listed in parentheses.

- *Japan:* Ukiyo-e prints (historical scenes, folklore), manga (modern comics), anime (animated stories)
- *Brazil:* Cordel literature illustrations (folk tales, social commentary), street art (urban culture, activism)
- *India:* Mughal miniatures (historical events, myths), Bollywood movie posters (popular culture)
- *China:* Traditional ink paintings (nature, philosophy), contemporary Chinese art (modern
- life, political commentary), manhua (Chinese comics)
- *Mexico:* Murals (social and political messages), Day of the Dead imagery (cultural celebration of life and death)
- *Australia:* Indigenous rock art (traditional stories, spirituality), contemporary Indigenous paintings (modern interpretations of traditional themes)

To guide your research, use the following resource list for visual storytelling examples:

- Creative Commons Search (search.creativecommons.org/)
- Wikimedia Commons (commons.wikimedia.org/wiki/Main_Page)

- Open Educational Resources (OER) Repositories (oercommons.org/)

Note: The three image archives listed are licensed under Creative Commons, suitable for educational use.

APPENDIX B: *Key Vocabulary for Visual Literacy*

Provide the following key vocabulary terms to enhance lower level students' understanding of visual literacy and culture, and to support their communication during the activity.

- *Visual literacy:* The ability to interpret, understand, and create meaning from visual elements such as images, illustrations, and videos
- *Semiotics*: The study of signs and symbols and their use or interpretation
- *Visual storytelling*: Conveying narratives or ideas through visual elements such as images or illustrations
- *Culture*: The customs, arts, social institutions, and achievements of a particular nation, people, or social group
- *Perspective*: A point of view or way of thinking about something, often influenced by personal experiences or cultural background
- *Interpretation*: The act of explaining the meaning of something, such as an image or artwork
- *Symbolism*: The use of symbols to represent ideas or qualities
- *Context*: A framework of information that includes the cultural, historical, or social background
- *Aesthetic*: Relating to beauty or the appreciation of beauty, often in the context of art or design
- *Composition*: The arrangement of visual elements in a work of art or design

Exploring Images With the Question–Answer Relationship Strategy

Gabriela Kleckova

Level	Lower intermediate to advanced
Ages Suitable for Activity	Elementary to adult
Aims	Read a photograph for details
	Draw inferences about a photograph based on observed details
	Talk about books and reading experiences
Class Time	25–50 minutes
Preparation Time	5 minutes
Resources	Photograph (Appendix A)
	Worksheet (Appendix B, or one of your own choice)
	Paper and markers (optional)

This activity applies the question–answer relationship (QAR) strategy (Raphael, 1986) to teach comprehension of visual images. Traditionally, QAR is used to improve learners' reading comprehension by asking and answering questions about a text. The activity encourages understanding of images and their interpretation and analysis. It teaches learners to consider what they see in the image and draw inferences using their own background knowledge.

PROCEDURE

1. Introduce the activity by telling your learners they will study and discuss a photograph (Appendix A).

2. Share the worksheet (Appendix B) with the learners and explain the four levels of questions:

   a. **Right There**: The answer is clearly observable in the image.

   b. **Think and Search**: The answer requires learners to examine the image some more and make connections about what they see.

   c. **Author and You**: The answer involves a combination of information from what the author of the image presents and what the student knows.

   d. **On Your Own**: The answer comes from the student's background knowledge and experience, in interaction with the ideas in the image.

   These questions ask students to think about an image at four different levels, enhancing both comprehension and thinking skills.

3. Use think, pair, share for Parts A and B in the worksheet. First, have learners work independently, examining the photograph and noting their answers. Second, ask learners to pair up and share their responses with each other.

4. Wrap up this section by eliciting a few answers to questions in Parts A and B from your learners.

5. Leave students in pairs and tell them to address the questions in Part C by discussing their opinions and ideas and then noting them down.

6. Form groups of four. Tell pairs to share their responses and further discuss them. Ask them to identify anything they can all agree on in their groups.

7. Elicit responses (i.e., ideas they agree on in the groups). Ask for reasons to support their responses. Wrap up this discussion by explaining the background of the image.

8. Refer learners to Part D of the worksheet. Tell them to read the questions and choose one they would like to answer. Tell them to note down or think about their response.

9. Instruct learners to look for peers who have chosen the same question. Form groups based on their preferred question. (If the groups have more than five learners, divide into smaller groups.) In groups, students share their responses to Part D. To extend this step, they can also create a poster capturing their responses using visual maps or graphic organizers.

10. Conclude the activity by eliciting a sample response to each question in Part D, or conduct a gallery walk if posters were created, and have learners reflect on what they have learned.

CAVEATS AND OPTIONS

- Depending on the language level of your learners, consider scaffolding in the form of sentence starters.

- As a follow-up, you can ask learners to examine another image (i.e., one of their own choice) and write their own QAR questions. Have learners work in groups of three or four and present their questions to their peers.

- Apply the strategy to any image of your choice (e.g., photographs, illustrations). When selecting an image, consider the detail and information presented—the more, the better.
  — Plan the activity around your own image to activate learners' background on a topic (a relevant image is needed), practice topic-related lexis, and encourage speaking in the beyond stage of a reading/listening activity.

- Creating the four sets of questions for each category (as in Appendix B) can be challenging. Start with one or two questions per category. Think & Search questions can involve comparing and contrasting, describing cause and effect, listing, or giving examples.

- The language demands of the activity depend on the image's topic or theme as well as on the complexity of the questions. Both can be easily modified to fit a particular group of learners.

REFERENCES AND FURTHER READING

Cortese, E. E. (2003). The application of question–answer relationship strategies to pictures. *The Reading Teacher, 57*, 374–380.

Raphael, T. E. (1986). Teaching question-answer relationships. *The Reading Teacher, 39*, 516–520.

APPENDIX A: *Photograph*

The photograph was taken at Powell's City of Books in Portland, Oregon in March 2023. The bookstore sells new and used books and claims to be one of the largest bookstores of this kind in the world. It hosts kids' story time every Saturday morning.

Image credit: Gabriela Kleckova. Used with permission.

APPENDIX B: *Worksheet*

	Questions	Your Answers
In the Image		
A. Right There *Observe the image.*	Where are the people? What do you see on the round tables? What are the people doing?	
B. Think & Search *Observe the image and make connections.*	What is displayed around the room? What different age groups are the people? What is going on in the picture?	
In My Head		
C. Author & Me *Think about what you know and what is in the image.*	Who do you think the people are? Why do you think they are there? What questions could you ask the people?	
D. On My Own *Think about what you know.*	What books do you like to read? Why? How do you choose the books you read? If you could write a book, what would you write the book about? Why?	

Idioms Illustrated: A Visual Vocabulary Portfolio

Sheena Moleta

Levels	Intermediate to advanced
Ages Suitable for Activity	Secondary and university
Aims	Develop understanding of idioms
	Develop skills for collaboration
	Improve sentence-writing skills
Class Time	15–20 minutes per idiom
Preparation Time	10 minutes per idiom
Resources	Padlet (padlet.com; or any other digital platform for image sharing)
	Access to the internet on laptops or tablets
	Laptop and projector

Idioms can be challenging for language learners because the meaning of an idiom cannot always be understood literally. To help students develop a strong grasp of idiomatic expressions, in this activity, students create an ongoing visual vocabulary portfolio. This portfolio includes images that represent the figurative meanings of idioms along with sentences demonstrating their usage. Each time a new idiom is introduced, students add it to their portfolio, gradually building a visual reference collection. By associating idioms with images, students enhance their comprehension and retention of figurative language while also practicing their writing skills.

PROCEDURE

1. Explain that this will be an ongoing activity in which students will build and add to a visual idiom portfolio to help them understand and remember the meanings of idioms.

2. Share the definition of an idiom: a phrase where the meaning is different from the literal words.

3. Emphasize the importance of idioms in everyday language and how their meanings cannot always be understood literally.

4. Explain literal versus figurative meaning by showing two images—one illustrating the literal interpretation and the other illustrating the figurative meaning of a well-known idiom. Here is an example:

    a. *Idiom*: "It's raining cats and dogs."

    b. *Literal meaning*: Show an illustration of animals falling from the sky.

    c. *Figurative meaning*: Show an illustration or photo of rain falling heavily.

5. Introduce Padlet (padlet.com; or an alternative digital platform) where students will store their idioms.

6. Explain that for each idiom, students will work with a partner to:
    a. find or create an image that represents the figurative meaning,
    b. post the image on Padlet and write the idiom above it, and
    c. write a sentence using the idiom correctly to show understanding.
7. Show students an example (see Appendix A).
8. After introducing some new idioms and completing any related learning activities, have students work in pairs to find or create an image that represents the figurative meaning of their chosen idiom. (For instance, if they choose the idiom *hit the books*, they might post an image of a student studying intensely with a stack of textbooks.)
9. Have students post their selected image to their portfolio and write the idiom as a title above the image.
10. Below the image, ask students to write a sentence that uses the idioms correctly, showing their understanding (e.g., "After class, I will hit the books to study for my test."). Encourage students to make the sentence relevant to their personal experiences to help internalize the meaning.
11. After pairs have completed Steps 8–10, review a few images and sentences together as a whole class to check understanding. This reinforces the idioms and provides an opportunity for feedback.

Ongoing Process: Repeating the Activity as New Idioms Are Introduced

1. As you introduce each new idiom, explain its figurative and literal meanings. (See Appendix B for a list of suggested idioms to help you implement this activity more easily.)
2. Have students find or create an image that visually represents the figurative meaning and post it in their portfolio.
3. Have students write a sentence demonstrating correct usage.
4. Lead a whole-class review and discussion, where students share and explain their images and sentences.

CAVEATS AND OPTIONS

- Ensure that students choose appropriate images that reflect the figurative meaning, not the literal meaning, of the idioms.
- For lower level students, teachers may want to provide preselected images for students to match to idioms.
- If digital access is limited, students can create their portfolios in a physical notebook, where they draw, print, or cut out images and write their sentences by hand.
- Encourage creativity! Students who enjoy art can even sketch their own representations of idioms instead of using found images.

APPENDIX A: *Example Padlet Post With Image and Sentence*

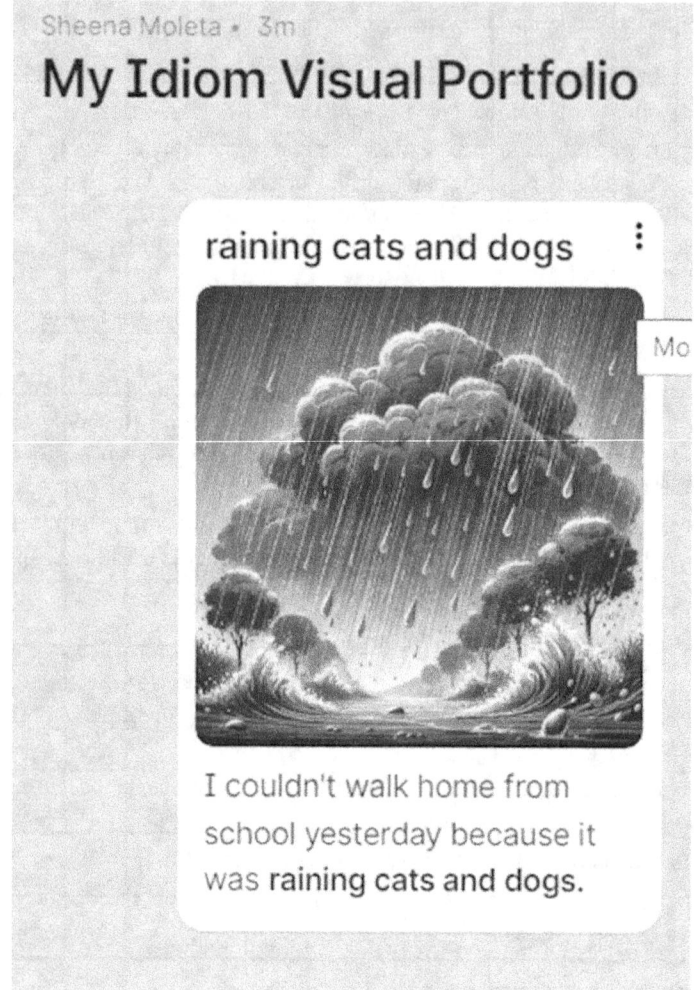

Image source: Created by Sheena Moleta with AI. Used with permission.

APPENDIX B: *Suggested Idioms*

Idiom	Figurative Meaning	Idiom	Figurative Meaning
Throw in the towel	Give up	Costs an arm and a leg	Very expensive
A blessing in disguise	A good thing that seemed bad at first	Once in a blue moon	Very rarely
Bittersweet	A mix of happy and sad feelings	Stay in touch	Keep in contact
Piece of cake	Something very easy	Take it easy	Relax
Call it a day	Finish work for the day	Over my head	Too complicated to understand
Caught red handed	Caught in the act of doing something wrong	Hang in there	Don't give up
Not my cup of tea	Not something you enjoy	Give me a hand	Help me
Idioms About Time			
Idiom	Figurative Meaning	Idiom	Figurative Meaning
Tied up	Very busy	It's about time	Finally happening after a delay
Only time will tell	The future will reveal the answer	Time to kill	Extra free time
Bide your time	Wait patiently	Time flies	Time goes by quickly
Idioms About Feelings			
Idioms for Feelings	Figurative Meaning	Idioms for Feelings	Figurative Meaning
Worn out	Exhausted	Blown away	Amazed or impressed
Fed up	No longer tolerant of a situation	No hard feelings	No resentment or bad feelings
I'm beat	Very tired	Butterflies in stomach	Feeling nervous
Under the weather	Sick or ill	Head over heels	Deep in love
Seeing red	Very angry	Beside yourself	Overwhelmed with strong emotions

Looking Into Photo Puzzle Pieces

Rosario Giraldez

Levels	Intermediate to advanced
Ages Suitable for Activity	Secondary to adults
Aims	Develop inference skills
	Describe places, people, actions, and feelings
	Foster creativity and critical thinking
Class Time	20–40 minutes
Preparation Time	5–15 minutes
Resources	Picture of someone looking at a smartphone (Appendix)
	Sample photographs cut in four pieces (Appendix)

aking inferences from photos involves studying visible details and then applying background knowledge to make assumptions about what an image is meant to convey. Photos can portray a myriad of different features and they can showcase features pertaining to different cultures. Students need to scrutinize an image in order to come to conclusions about what they see and then present their inferences to partners. In turn, partners can challenge others' inferences and present their arguments. This activity promotes the development of creativity by imagining what lies beyond images. In addition, it fosters the development of critical thinking by challenging inferences shared by others.

PROCEDURE

1. Show a picture of someone looking at their smartphone to the class and ask students to choose which of the following statements could describe the picture:

    a. The person is reading a post.

    b. The person is watching a video.

    c. The person is looking at something on their smartphone.

2. Since all the statements could potentially describe the picture, direct students' attention to what statement could be considered a fact (Option C). Explain that the other options are inferences, because they are conclusions or opinions formed by looking at facts. Ask students to think of times when they make inferences, and why inferences are important. If students cannot provide answers, give some examples. Write a few sample inferential questions on the board and leave them there as a reference to be used in Step 9:

    a. Why do you think…?

    b. What is most likely true about…?

    c. What can you conclude about…?

3. Divide the class into groups of four students. In each group, give every student one piece of a photo that you have previously cut into four equal pieces. (See Appendix for suggested photos).

4. Tell students to individually focus on their pieces. They should take a few minutes to look closely at all the details and then make inferences about the parts of the photo that they do not see. Highlight that they will be guessing (inferring) based on the details they can see.

5. Ask students to work individually and write a description of the whole photo based on viewing only their own pieces. Ask them to make inferences regarding the other three pieces they do not see. Allow 10–15 minutes to write these descriptions.

6. Within each group, have students read their descriptions of the whole image. After reading the descriptions, the four members of the group put their pieces together to reveal the image.

7. Have students vote on who wrote the most accurate description.

8. After having agreed on the most accurate description, have students make further inferences based on the entire photo.

9. As a class, have groups show their photos and share their descriptions. Encourage students to challenge the ideas presented by asking inferential questions, which are the ones usually answered by interpreting clues from parts of a scene or a text. Reinforce the use of inferences as explained in Step 2 and refer to the sample questions written on the board.

CAVEATS AND OPTIONS

- Add one further step before proceeding to Step 9: Have students reassemble to share their descriptions and inferences about the photo in a different group before presenting them to the whole class. After descriptions have been shared, ask students to go back to their initial groups and retell the descriptions they learned by changing groups.

- Instead of pictures cut in four, if students have smartphones, ask them to choose a (school-appropriate) photo from their camera roll and zoom in a portion of it for their partners to describe.

- Extend the activity by having groups write a story about the picture.

REFERENCES AND FURTHER READING

Albano, L. (2013, December 6). *How English language teachers can use pictures in class.* British Council. https://www.britishcouncil.org/voices-magazine/how-english-language-teachers-use-pictures-class

Dell'Angelo, T. (2014, December 1) *Literacy through photography for English language learners.* Edutopia. https://www.edutopia.org/blog/literacy-through-photography-for-ells-tabitha-dellangelo

APPENDIX: *Sample Photos*

Image credit: Kamal Uddin on Unsplash.

Image credit: Greg Rosenke on Unsplash.

Image credit: Cajeo Zhang on Unsplash.

Image credit: Constantin Panagopoulos on Unsplash.

Making Inferences From Photographs

Juli S. Sarris

Level	Any
Ages Suitable for Activity	Any
Aims	Analyze a photograph and describe people, animals, and actions depicted
	Infer reasons for the behaviors and actions depicted in a photograph
	Support reasons with evidence from a photograph
Class Time	50 minutes–1 hour
Preparation Time	10 minutes
Resources	Photographs (Appendix A)

hotographs provide rich visual imagery that can inspire imagination and creativity. They allow us to see the world from multiple perspectives and to build empathy and understanding of the world outside of our own personal experiences. In this activity, learners analyze a photograph, describe the people/animals and setting depicted, and infer behaviors and actions. Learners support their inferences with evidence from the photograph. This activity promotes higher order skills such as creative thinking, inferring, and evaluating as well as the 21st-century skills of analysis, collaboration, and communication.

PROCEDURE

1. Divide students into groups of three to four learners each.
2. Using the first sample photograph (see Appendix A), preteach the following sentence frames for making inferences:
   a. I think the _____ is/are _____ because _____.
      Example: *I think the children are carrying backpacks because they are going to school.*
   b. I think this because _____.
      Example: *I think this because I carry a backpack to school too.*
   c. The _____ might be _____.
      Example: *The children might be going home.*
   d. The _____ could be _____.
      Example: *The children could be singing a song together.*
   e. The _____ must be _____.
      Example: *The children must be very excited.*
   f. This reminds me of _____.
      Example: *This reminds me of my own school.*

g. This makes me think _____.

    Example: *This makes me think about my own school day.*

3. Display another photograph, either projected or printed. Photographs should depict an activity and/or action from which students can make inferences. Example photographs appear at the end of this activity in Appendix A. You can also search for photographs online at Unsplash (unsplash.com) and Pixabay (pixabay.com).

4. Ask students to discuss the following prompts in their groups:

Description

    a. Who is in this photograph?

    b. What do they look like?

    c. What else do you see in the photograph?

Making Inferences

    a. What do you think is happening in this photograph?

    b. What do you see in the photograph that makes you think this?

    c. What do you think the people/animals are thinking? What do you see in the photograph that makes you think this?

    d. Why do you think someone took this photograph? Why do you think that?

    e. What does this photograph make you wonder about?

5. Circulate and monitor the group discussions.

6. After 10 minutes, bring the class back together and ask groups to share some of their thoughts. Paraphrase student contributions to validate them.

7. Have students return to their groups and work together to write their description of the photograph in one paragraph and their inferences in a second paragraph. For classes with young children, the teacher may choose to group-write the description and inferences, with the children dictating their ideas and the teacher writing. In this case, steps 8 and 9 are not necessary.

8. Have groups swap their descriptions and inferences and add to the paragraphs, offering additional details and inferences.

9. Collect each group's writing for formative evaluation.

CAVEATS AND OPTIONS

- Extend the activity by asking student groups to perform their writing as a drama.

- Give each group different photographs to analyze.

- For advanced classes, in Step 8, have students add basic narrative structures for beginning, middle, and end, such as connectors/transitions and cohesive devices.

- Use this activity through Step 5 as a warm-up speaking activity.

- For a fiction-writing extension activity, see instructions in Appendix B.

REFERENCES AND FURTHER READING

Baker, L. (2015). How many words is a picture worth? *English Teaching Forum, 53*(4), 2–13. https://americanenglish.state.gov/resources/english-teaching-forum-2015-volume-53-number-4#child-2020

Hailey, D., Miller, A., & Yenawine, P. (2015). Understanding visual literacy: The visual thinking strategies approach. In D. Baylen & A. D'Alba (Eds.), *Essentials of teaching and integrating visual and media literacy* (pp. 49–73). Springer.

Visual Thinking Strategies. (n.d.). *Image of the week.* https://vtshome.org/weekly-image/

APPENDIX A: *Example Photographs*

Image source: Unsplash

APPENDIX B: *Extension Activity*

Procedure

1. In groups of three to four, have students collaborate to imagine and write a fictional narrative about the photograph. Allow for creativity. The following prompts can support the writing:

    a. What are the names of the people/animals in the photograph?

    b. What is the relationship between the people/animals in the photograph? Are the people related to each other in some way, or are they strangers? Who owns the animals, or are they wild animals?

    c. What are they saying to each other?

    d. Describe the setting in detail.

    e. Describe the people/animals in detail.

    f. How are the people/animals in the photograph feeling?

    g. What happened before, during, and after the actions shown in the photograph?

2. After 30 minutes, groups exchange their narratives and conduct a peer review to check for spelling, grammar, vocabulary, and accuracy. Writings are then returned to original groups.

3. After 10 minutes to review corrections, debrief as a whole class. Ask groups to summarize their narratives for the class.

4. Collect the narratives for formative assessment.

CAVEATS AND OPTIONS

Adapt prompts to fit the proficiency level of the class.

- For beginners, guide students to write their narratives in the simple present and present continuous, thereby describing just the events depicted in the photograph.

- For intermediate learners, have them write their narratives in past, present, and future.

- Challenge advanced classes to write a dialog and/or use reported speech.

- If you are teaching young children, have them draw their stories rather than write them.

Peer's Favorite Trip: Storytelling From an Image Collection

Abdulsamad Humaidan

Levels	Beginner to high intermediate
Ages Suitable for Activity	Adults
Aims	Practice critical thinking
	Create narrative stories from image collections with no text
	Practice oral storytelling and public speaking
	Build community with each other by learning more about their peers
Class Time	20–30 minutes
Preparation Time	5 minutes +
Resources	Student-provided photos

This activity gives learners the opportunity to construct oral stories about their peers' favorite trip from an image collection. Asking learners to practice storytelling with real photos selected by their classmates, rather than randomly selected photos, brings authenticity to the activity and empowers learners to think creatively and critically about photographs.

PROCEDURE

1. Before the activity, ask learners to think about a favorite trip they had in the past and collect five to eight photographs from the trip. Tell them to bring these photos to the next class (see Caveats and Options).

2. Pair learners and tell them to exchange photo collections. Ask learners to look at their peer's image collection creatively and critically and try to construct a story about their peer's favorite trip.

3. To help learners create a story about their peer's favorite trip, learners can think about the following:

    a. When was the trip (e.g., month, year)?

    b. Where did they go?

c. Who did they go with?

d. How did they get to their destination?

e. How long did they stay at the vacation site?

f. Describe each activity demonstrated in each picture.

4. Individually, allow time for brainstorming. Then, have learners write an imagined story based on the photographs.

5. Have learners share their imagined stories with their peers.

6. In pairs, learners compare the imagined story with the actual story.

CAVEATS AND OPTIONS

- For classrooms with limited technology, introduce this activity by having students simply exchange printed photographs or even drawings of a favorite trip.

- If technology allows, have learners insert their pictures into PowerPoint slides or a Microsoft Word document and then add a title for their trip.

- Ask learners to do the activity in small groups instead of pairs.

- For best results, lead this activity after a school break or vacation, such as spring break or summer vacation.

- Inform learners about the idea of the activity a few days or even 1 week in advance. This gives learners time to think about the topic and decide which pictures to include in their image collections.

- Some learners might not be willing to show their faces in pictures due to cultural practices or restrictions. In this case, ask these learners to share only the images of the places they visited while on trips.

Picture Stations for Active Speaking

Lynn W. Zimmerman

Level	High beginner to intermediate
Ages Suitable for Activity	Elementary to adult
Aims	Practice listening and speaking
	Respond verbally to visual input
	Develop observation skills
Class Time	≈ 45 minutes
Preparation Time	30 minutes
Resources	Several sets of age-appropriate pictures
	Question cards (Appendix A)

In this activity, students rotate through stations with different pictures to answer questions. The questions will represent various aspects of Bloom's Taxonomy, such as identification, description, and comparison/contrast. Students will practice their active speaking skills.

PROCEDURE

1. Begin with a warm-up by showing learners a picture that has people and objects that they can identify in English. Tell students they have 1 minute to write as many words as they can about the picture. Then, ask students to share some of their words by grammatical categories (e.g., nouns, adjectives, verbs). Point at the picture where the word they suggest is depicted.

2. Practice asking and answering questions to prepare students for the picture stations activity by eliciting answers for these questions:

    a. Who is in the picture?

    b. What is in the picture?

    c. Where was the picture taken? How do you know?

    d. When was the picture taken? How do you know?

    e. Why did the photographer/artist create this picture? How do you know?

    f. How does the picture make you feel? Why?

3. Form groups of four to five students by seating them together in a workspace. Put 8–10 pictures and a set of question cards in each group's workspace.

4. Have students spread their pictures out and place their question cards in a pile, face down, on the workspace.

5. When all groups are ready, have students look at the pictures, and ask each student to select one.

6. In their groups, have students take turns answering the general opening question: Why did you choose that picture?

7. Then, have students take turns selecting the top question card from the pile and reading it aloud. They then answer that question about their picture. Students continue in this way, asking and answering until all questions have been answered. If students answer all the questions before the teacher calls time, they can shuffle the cards, choose a new picture, and start again.

8. After around 5 minutes, call time. The students place their pictures back on their workspace and place the question cards in a pile. Then, each group moves to a different workspace where the pictures have a different theme.

9. Have students repeat Steps 4–8. If the students start to lose interest, end the activity or allow them to speak freely about aspects of the pictures that are most interesting to them. If they still seem engaged, ask them to move to a different workspace one more time.

10. To close the activity, ask some students to show a picture they chose and describe it to the class. Discuss their answers as a class.

CAVEATS AND OPTIONS

- This activity can be adapted for any age group and proficiency level, selecting appropriate pictures and providing level-appropriate question cards. Questions for lower level learners should focus more on describing, while questions for higher level learners could require them to make inferences about the picture.

- Decide if all students in a group should answer each question about a picture or if only the student who chose that picture should answer.

- Conduct informal or formative assessment of students' speaking by using a checklist or rubric with categories such as fluency, vocabulary (range and accuracy), grammar, and/or pronunciation.

- Project images for the entire class to see; in this case, in groups, students only select and answer the question cards.

APPENDIX A: *Question Cards*

What are three words that describe this picture?	What advice would you give to someone or something in the picture?	What is happening around this picture in the area you can't see?	If you were in the picture, what would you be doing?
What can't we see in this picture that is important?	What is something you would change in this picture?	Describe the mood in the picture.	What does this picture remind you of?
What is happening in the picture?	What happened before this picture?	What will happen after this picture?	How does this picture make you feel?
Where is this picture?	Who took the picture?	Why was this picture taken?	What is the artist trying to show?

Pursuing Dreams Amid Social Barriers

Maysaa Banat

Levels	Intermediate to high intermediate
Ages Suitable for Activity	Secondary
Aims	Analyze a visual narrative to understand societal and personal conflicts
	Discuss how societal expectations can influence personal choices
	Develop visual literacy by interpreting visual narratives
	Enhance students' ability to articulate their thoughts on cultural influences
	Foster empathy by connecting with characters' experiences
Class Time	50 minutes
Preparation Time	15 minutes
Resources	Visual narrative images (Appendixes A and B)
	Projector or printed copies of the visual narrative
	Whiteboard and markers
	Student notebooks

This activity uses visual narrative analysis to explore how societal expectations can influence personal aspirations. Throughout the activity, students develop skills in critical thinking and visual literacy. The provided visual narratives portray individuals facing conflicts between their personal dreams and societal expectations. As they analyze these narratives, students learn to interpret visual cues, symbols, and underlying messages, which are crucial for visual literacy. The activity also encourages meaningful discussions around how culture and community shape our choices, fostering empathy, self-awareness, and critical evaluation of the role community norms play in personal development.

PROCEDURE

1. *Introduction (5 minutes):* Begin by discussing students' dreams and aspirations. Ask students to think about their future goals and the factors that may affect these aspirations. Explain that today's activity will explore how societal expectations and limitations— including pressures from one's family, peers, and culture—can shape or limit personal choices.

2. *Visual Analysis (15 minutes):* Display the visual narrative for the class (Appendix A or Appendix B). Ask students to observe and note emotions, characters, and symbols present in each panel. Guide them to focus on visual elements like facial expressions, gestures, and settings that provide context about the characters' experiences. Use questions like "What emotions are conveyed?" or "What symbols can you identify?" Allow students to record their observations individually.

3. *Group Discussion (15 minutes):* Divide students into small groups to discuss the following questions:

    a. What dreams are depicted in the visual narrative?

    b. What obstacles do the characters face?

    c. How do these obstacles reflect real-world issues?

    Encourage students to consider both explicit and implicit messages. Encourage collaborative learning by allowing students to build on each other's ideas and gain different perspectives.

4. *Class Discussion (10 minutes):* Bring the class back together and invite representatives from each group to share their insights. Use this time to highlight common themes, surprising interpretations, or differing perspectives that emerged during group discussions. Use specific panels of the visual narrative to guide the discussion. Ask follow-up questions:

    a. What was the most powerful moment in the story, and why?

    b. How did societal expectations influence the characters' choices?

    c. Can you identify a turning point in the narrative?

    Encourage students to relate these moments to real-life examples, either from their own experiences or from stories they've heard. For instance, a student may mention a friend who chose a less conventional path, like taking a gap year to volunteer abroad despite family pressure to start university immediately. These connections help deepen understanding of how cultural norms shape individual decisions.

5. *Reflection Activity (5 minutes):* Ask each student to write a short reflection on an experience where they faced a societal pressure or limitation regarding their choices or aspirations. Instruct them to describe how they reacted or how they wish they had reacted.

    a. For students who haven't personally experienced such a situation, suggest they reflect on an observation of someone else facing a similar challenge. This could be a friend, a family member, or even a character in a book, movie, or news story. Encourage them to consider what they learned from this observation and how it relates to societal expectations and limitations.

    b. Students may share their written reflections with the class, if comfortable.

CAVEATS AND OPTIONS

- For lower proficiency students, provide key vocabulary related to the visual narrative. Simplify questions to focus on describing emotions and actions rather than analyzing abstract themes. Use sentence starters like "The character feels..." to help them articulate observations.

- For higher proficiency students, for Step 5, challenge them to relate the provided visual narrative to real-world examples and/or propose solutions for overcoming societal barriers. This will help them develop problem-solving skills and think critically about societal pressures.

- For younger students, focus more on describing what they see and identifying simple themes, such as happiness or challenges.

- For older students, focus on deeper discussions on societal pressure and explore broader cultural contexts.

APPENDIX A: *Visual Narrative Image 1*

Image credit: YamiSeif. Used with permission.

APPENDIX B: *Visual Narrative Image 2*

Image credit: YamiSeif. Used with permission.

Reading Images in the World Around Us

Amber Warren and Huili Hong

Levels	High beginner to advanced
Ages Suitable for Activity	Elementary to adult
Aims	Explore aspects of visual rhetoric and how they convey point of view
	Engage in authentic oral practice with associated grammar and target language
	Develop skills to interpret images for meaning
Class Time	30 minutes–1 hour
Preparation Time	≈ 20 minutes
Resources	Images or photographs, ideally taken in your local area and/or from local newspapers

Just like words and stories, the images around us convey meaning and contain information about the creator's point of view. Analyzing visual elements can support students' understanding of visual rhetoric and how the composition of images conveys meaning and point of view. This activity will invite learners to explore images, consider how they convey meaning, theorize the creator's point of view, and share their thinking about how images may be open to different interpretations based on different contexts.

PROCEDURE

Warm-up (3–5 minutes)

1. Begin by showing students the image you selected to begin the activity. (See the Appendix for a list of websites where you can find copyright-free images.)

2. Ask students to start by discussing what they notice about the image. Students may share observations about colors, location of objects within the picture, mood of people in the picture, etc.

3. Use students' observations to guide them to focus on the creator's point of view.

   Example 1: You observed that the people were very far away. Where do you think the creator of this image was standing in order to capture this image?

   Example 2: You observed that the people in the picture seem sad. How do you know this?

4. Invite students to explain their thinking by referring to what they observed in the image.

   Example: I think…because…

5. Explain that the perspective, color, and composition of images provide meaning. They are ways of communicating information or sharing a point of view. For

example, a painter may choose to use dark colors to convey a sense of doom, or a photographer might choose to use a slower shutter speed to increase the blur of a fast-moving object to convey motion.

6. Invite students to consider how the original image you selected might convey a different point of view if changes to the image were made. For example, you might consider what would happen if the creator had chosen different colors or a different position from which to capture the image.

7. Tell students that, similar to this warm-up activity, they will be "reading" the images around them to explore how creators of images share meaning.

Activity: Exploring Images in Our World (20–40 minutes)

1. Tell students that some photographs, like family photos of a vacation or celebration, are used for remembering those moments, while other photographs, like those taken for newspapers or by photojournalists, are there to tell a story.

2. Share an image from a news story that your students may be familiar with. It could be something that happened recently, or something that is iconic and well-known.

3. Invite students to identify the arrangement of colors, objects, or people in the image.

4. Invite students to discuss the journalist's point of view and how they were able to convey that through their choice of subject and composition.

   a. *Example:* What is the photographer trying to say with this image? How do you know that? What do you think their relationship is to the people or things in the photo? How would a different point of view tell a different story?

5. Ask students what they think the main idea of the image is, based on what they have identified.

6. Next, divide students into groups of three to four students, and give each group a different preselected image from newspapers or the internet. Ask groups to discuss the following:

   a. What colors and objects did the creator capture in this image?

   b. Where is the author in relation to the subject(s) in the image?

   c. What effect does this point of view have on the viewer?

   d. What might change if the author had chosen a different viewpoint?

Conclusion: Thinking Critically About the Images Around Us (5 minutes)

As a whole class, elicit what students have learned about how creators use features of visual communication, such as perspective, color, and composition to share different meanings, communicate various messages, or create space for alternative interpretations. Invite students to look out for these features in images they see outside of class or at home and report back.

CAVEATS AND OPTIONS

- Adapt this activity for any proficiency level by choosing your language and images accordingly. Beginners might discuss color, objects, clothing, or emotions, while advanced learners may discuss additional elements or provide additional reasoning for their claims.

- Choose images from recent events carefully. Be respectful of cultural differences and choose images appropriate for your learners' ages, language development levels, and learning contexts.

APPENDIX: *Free Online Image Sources*

In addition to your local newspapers, try these websites to find free images for this activity:

- U.S. National Gallery of Art – www.nga.gov/open-access-images.html
- Metropolitan Museum of Art – www.metmuseum.org/art/collection/search
- Smithsonian Institution – www.si.edu/openaccess
- U.S. Library of Congress – www.loc.gov/free-to-use/

Finally, visit MoMA UK (www.moma.co.uk/public-domain-images/) for links to a collection of open-access and public domain image archives from museums around the world.

Teaching Visual Rhetoric

Wei Xu

Levels	Intermediate to advanced
Ages Suitable for Activity	Adult
Aims	Understand how to analyze and interpret images, with a focus on visual rhetoric
	Apply the guidelines of visual rhetoric for hands-on image analysis
Class Time	75 minutes
Preparation Time	30 minutes
Resources	Images (see Appendixes A–C)
	Access to the internet on laptops or tablets

This activity guides students on how to observe and interpret images from the lens of visual rhetoric. A follow-up activity gives students experience with hands-on image analysis and asks them to produce their own guidelines for image analysis.

PROCEDURE

1. Before the activity, create a shared Padlet (padlet.com) where students can post images and captions in Step 5. In addition, find and select meaningful images for the warm-up exercise (see suggested images in Appendix A).

2. *(10 min)* To begin the activity, hand out your preselected images in printed format or display them on a projection screen. Lead a discussion about each image (or have students talk in small groups) using the following guiding questions:

   a. What aspects of the picture do you find most interesting and why?

   b. How do you make meaning from the image?

   c. How would you analyze these images as meaning-making devices?

   d. Why do you think someone created this image?

3. *(10 min)* After students share their points of view about the guiding questions, introduce the concept of visual literacy (see Appendix B).

   a. Introduce its definition (the ability to discern meaning conveyed through images) and its component (picture reading). Tell students that the analysis and discussion they did in Step 2 was an example of picture reading.

   b. Explain the importance of visual literacy as a method for interpreting the content of visual images, examining their social impact, evaluating arguments about them, and discussing their purpose, audience, and ownership (Alberto et al., 2007).

4. *(25 min)* To better understand images, explain that visual creators sometimes apply visual rhetoric, with the following three components:

a. **Ethos**, which refers to "the persona, or projected character of a speaker/communicator, including their credibility and trustworthiness" (Higgins & Walker, 2012, p. 197)

b. **Logos**, which refers to "the clarity and the integrity of the argument" (Higgins & Walker, 2012, p. 198)

c. **Pathos**, which means "the audience's feelings" (Higgins & Walker, 2012, p. 198).

Demonstrate and discuss how viewers can identify ethos, logos, and pathos in images, using the images provided in Appendix C as examples.

5. Put students in groups of three to four. Ask each group to search online and find at least three images in which they can identify ethos, logos, or pathos. Have groups post their selected images on your Padlet and write a short explanation for each one, explaining which aspect of visual rhetoric is applied.

6. *(15 min)* Conduct a jigsaw sharing activity, and have students share the images they found with their peers in other groups for multiple rounds.

7. *(15 min)* Show students the example guidelines for analyzing images (Appendix D). Then, ask students to produce their own guidelines for visual analysis. Students are allowed to change/critique the example guidelines based on their own visual analysis experience. They should include the aspects that they think are important for analyzing images.

8. If time permits, have students fill in exit cards to show what their takeaway is (i.e., what they learned) from this activity.

CAVEATS AND OPTIONS

- For Step 2, check with the students if they understand the guiding questions before the students begin the activity. Students can also be provided with a space to record the content of the discussion.

- Minimize the use of academic language in Steps 3–4 by paraphrasing the academic definitions provided. Assure the students that it is okay if they still feel confused at this stage, as the following activities will help them better understand the concept.

- In Step 5, check if students understand ethos, pathos, and logos. If not, explain. Also briefly explain how to post on Padlet in case the students are not familiar with it.

REFERENCES AND FURTHER READING

Alberto, P. A., Fredrick, L., Hughes, M., McIntosh, L., & Cihak, D. (2007). Components of visual literacy: Teaching logos. *Focus on Autism and Other Developmental Disabilities, 22*(4), 234–243. https://doi.org/10.1177/10883576070220040501

Higgins, C., & Walker, R. (2012). Ethos, logos, pathos: Strategies of persuasion in social/environmental reports, *Accounting Forum, 36*(3), 194–208. https://doi.org/10.1016/j.accfor.2012.02.003

Gardiner, J. H., Kittredge, G. L., & Arnold, S. L. (1902). *The mother tongue* (Vol. 3). Ginn.

APPENDIX A: *Images for Starter Activity*

Instructor Note

Due to copyright restrictions, not all suggested images can be displayed here. Instructors may look for artful images online and decide on the ones to be used.

Selection of Suggested Images

- Heinz ketchup advertisement (www.julielubbers.com/heinz-1)
- Try Penicillin advertisement (fakescience.org/post/2338593610/try-penicillin)
- Sergeant Frank Praytor looks after a 2-week-old kitten during the height of the Korean War (news.usni.org/2018/01/25/korean-war-marine-made-famous-kitten-photo-dies)

APPENDIX B: *Introducing Visual Literacy*

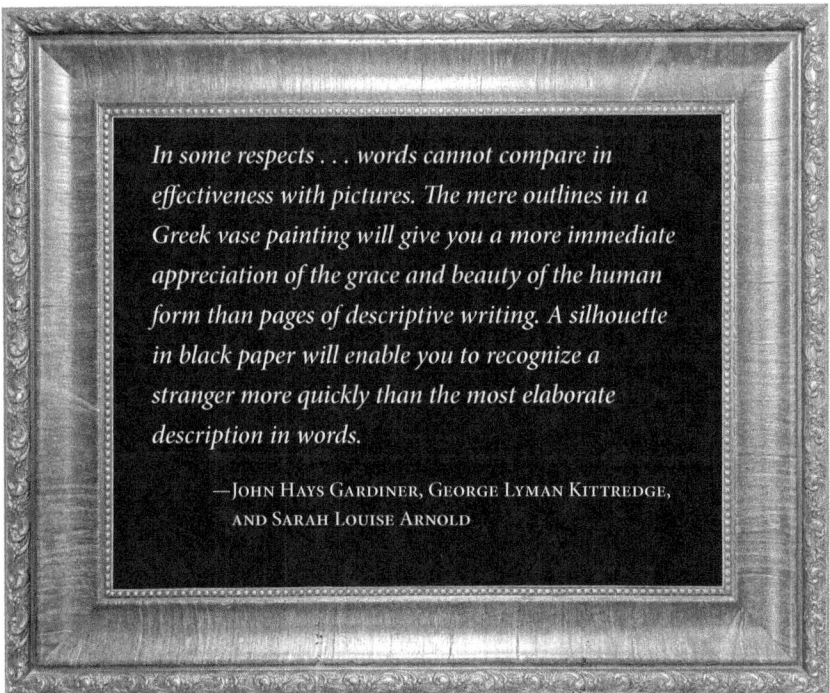

Gardiner, J. H., Kittredge, G. L., & Arnold, S. L. (1902). *The Mother Tongue* (Vol. 3). Ginn.

APPENDIX C: *Images for Introducing Visual Rhetoric*

Ethos

Image source: The Age on Mathew Paul's Flickr photostream (https://www.flickr.com/photos/159358942
%40N07/48526511256/in/photolist-wsY3Lx-2hk3KDV-2gW84ab-2gVirKD-2gVhBWm-2gViCB8-2gViz27-
2nkNkNh-2mWnPxG-2mWXeSf-MjPBp-MjPun)

Logos

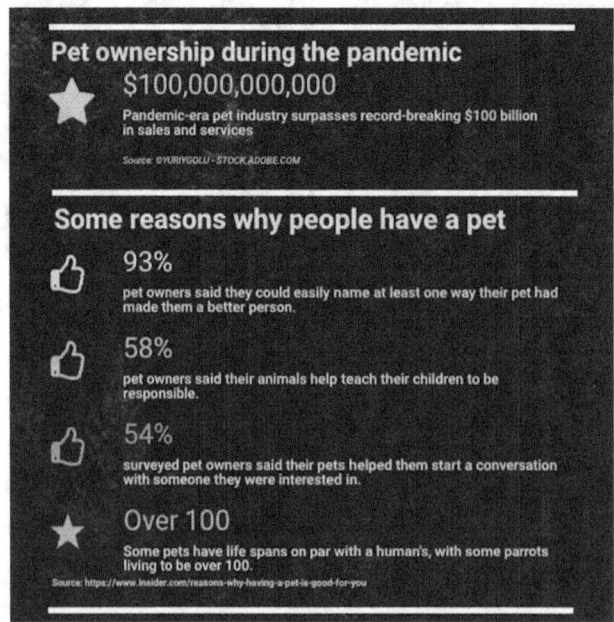

Image source: Wei Xu. Used with permission.

Pathos

Image source: "230426-Z-AL508-1510" by New Jersey National Guard, Public Domain Mark

APPENDIX D: *Guidelines for Visual Analysis*

Design	What does the image look like? Is there text? Special fonts? How are the contents arranged?
Organization	How are items organized? Are there sections? What goes in each section? In what order? What is the focus?
Content	What information is included? What is the message/point? Is there a main claim? What evidence is included?
Style	How is it written/presented/created? What language/visual effect is used?
Rhetoric Effect	How do the images achieve ethos, pathos, or logos?

Using Architecture for Intercultural Reflection

Daniel Costa

Levels	All
Ages Suitable for Activity	Secondary to University
Aims	Develop cultural awareness
	Develop skills in critical thinking and creativity
	Practice deduction through trial and error
	Improve noticing and observation skills
Class Time	10–30 minutes
Preparation Time	10 minutes
Resources	Photographs (see Appendix)
	Access to the internet on laptops or tablets

Photographs of architectural gems can act as useful tools to represent the plurality of the English-speaking world, underlining the cross-cultural power of aesthetics within the scope of the target language. In this activity, using photos of architecture can encourage intercultural reflection while enhancing learners' communicative skills and creative thinking.

PROCEDURE

1. Elicit a list of examples of famous buildings from English-speaking countries (e.g., Big Ben, the White House, Sydney Opera House, etc.).

2. Show learners a picture of a less well-known building from the English-speaking world (see Appendix) and ask general questions about its location. Depending on the level of your learners, you may want to ask open questions for higher level learners (e.g., *Where is this building?*) or closed questions for beginners (e.g., *Is this building in Asia?*). Encourage learners to share which elements in the photo informed their answer.

3. Ask the class more specific questions to stimulate further critical reflection, such as the following, and elicit reasons for their answers:

   a. Open questions: *What is the purpose of this building? When was it likely built?*

   b. Closed questions: *Is it a museum? Is it a residence?*

4. Point out how architecture reflects cultural values, history, and identity. Then, ask learners to research other buildings or monuments in English-speaking countries using an online photo database, such as Pixabay (pixabay.com) or Wikimedia Commons (commons.wikimedia.org). Have students find five photos of different buildings from different English-speaking countries.

5. In pairs, have each learner ask their partner questions to guess the locations of the buildings or monuments in their partners' photos, similar to Steps 2–3. For

more advanced learners, have them identify what visual, cultural, or historical information informed their guesses.

6. Ask each learner to choose their favorite building or monument and show the selected image to the class. Encourage learners to state why they chose this photo and describe what the building tells about the culture that built it.

7. Ask the class what surprised them about the buildings they explored. Ask, "Did anything challenge your assumptions about English-speaking cultures?" Then, if appropriate, have the class vote for their favorite photo giving reasons for their choice.

8. Optionally, ask learners to upload their chosen photos to Instagram or another social network with a short description of the building. For an added challenge, have students include a culturally relevant hashtag or caption.

REFERENCES AND FURTHER READING

Costa, D. (2024). I'm all eyes. *Modern English Teacher, 33*(5), 25–26.

APPENDIX: *Examples of Architecture in the English-Speaking World*

Marina Bay Sands, Singapore
Image credit: Pixabay @cegoh

Hawa Mahal, India
Image credit: Pixabay @dedishari

Using Landscape Photos to Prepare for Description Writing

Jacqueline Nenchin

Levels	High intermediate to advanced
Ages Suitable for Activity	Early secondary to adult
Aims	Practice listening and speaking skills
	Discern important features, perspectives, and details of images
	Write a description using varied and effective language
	Transition from narrative writing to descriptive writing
	Engage with places beyond the immediate community
Class Time	20 minutes
Preparation Time	15–20 minutes
Resources	Landscape photos (8 in. by 10 in. or larger) from calendars or other sources
	Handout (Appendix)
	Paper and pens
	Timer

In this activity, inspired by some ideas from the National Writing Project (Schulten, 2004), students engage with visual images to facilitate the transition from writing narratives to writing descriptions. Students participate in a listening and speaking activity to elicit responses to photos and activate related vocabulary, followed by a freewriting exercise.

PROCEDURE

1. Choose clear, colorful photos of landscapes. The photos should be large (e.g., at least 8 in. by 10 in.) and varied in their perspectives (e.g., subject, time of day, angle, distance). Photos should be from places that may be unfamiliar to learners.

2. Print one photo for each pair of students in your class. Teachers might want to project a sample photo and talk about it before starting the activity, though this may not be necessary for more advanced students or if the class has done this activity previously.

3. Prepare a timer, and ask the students to have a pen/pencil and paper at hand.

4. Divide the students into pairs. If the class has an odd number of students, then there will be one group of three. Hand out the photos.

5. Ask the students to discuss the photos in pairs:

   a. Each student speaks for 1 minute about the photo while the other listens carefully but remains silent. Speakers can say anything they want about the photo, including their observations and their feelings. They can also make guesses about where the place is.

b. Then, partners exchange roles and repeat the activity for another minute.

c. Use the timer to keep the time.

6. Ask students to write a description of their photos:

   a. Instruct them to free-write anything they want to write about the photo. They should just keep writing without worrying about grammar or sentence structure. They do not have to record what they discussed, but they may include the discussion if they like.

   b. Tell them that they have 10 minutes to write, and be sure to time this. The point is for them to generate content.

   c. When the 10 minutes are up, ask them to put down their pens. One pair at a time holds up their photo, and students read some or all of what they wrote to share with the class.

7. End the activity here, or ask the students to use their freewriting as the basis for a well-organized description paragraph, which they can write in class or for homework.

8. Lead a whole-class debriefing discussion with the following prompts:

   a. Do you think it was easier to write the description after listening to one another than it would have been without the activity?

   b. What are some important language features of your description?

   c. How do descriptions differ from the narratives you have written before?

9. Guide students to complete a graphic organizer (see Appendix) that shows some of the differences between narratives and description (e.g., moving through time versus moving through space, verbs of doing and happening versus verbs of being and having). Have students fill in the sections of the organizer with words and phrases from their freewriting.

CAVEATS AND OPTIONS

- Use this activity with students who have at least an intermediate oral proficiency and can speak for 1 minute.

- Choose this activity to help your students move beyond from narrative writing (for which most writers have a strong bias) and introduce them to the features of description.

- Select photos that show scenic areas of the local region or country, because they might be unfamiliar to students who have only lived in urban and suburban environments and have not traveled. It is essential that students experience different environments even in classrooms. In this way, the activity can support equity and social studies standards.

- Use this activity to introduce an essay on the description of setting in a short story.

REFERENCES AND FURTHER READING

National Writing Project. (2025). *National Writing Project: Who we are.* https://www.nwp.org/who-we-are

Schulten, K. (2004). *Teacher to teacher: Ideas that work from the New York City Writing Project.* Institute for Literacy Studies, Lehman College, CUNY.

APPENDIX: *Graphic Organizer*

Write words from your freewriting that fit the appropriate categories in this graphic organizer. You don't have to enter words in all boxes, only the ones that fit.

Differences Between Narrative and Descriptive Writing

	Narratives	Descriptions
Time vs. Space	Words that show a sequence of events	Words related to space/location
Verb Types	Verbs of doing and happening	Verbs of being and having Verbs of feeling
Nouns and Adjectives	The characters involved in the action	Nouns that are being described Words expressing qualities

Using Visuals to Help Brainstorm Arguments

Adelia Mazzella-Chace

Levels	Intermediate to advanced
Ages Suitable for Activity	Any
Aims	Develop noticing and observation skills
	Practice inferring meaning from visuals
	Encourage and promote critical thinking skills
	Recognize the persuasive power of visual arguments
Class Time	30 minutes–1 hour
Preparation Time	15–30 minutes
Resources	Images (see Appendix)

n today's technology-driven world, having the ability to process information critically is essential. Brainstorming different sides to an argument is one critical-thinking activity that is common in teaching both speaking and writing, often used to prepare for popular activities and assignments such as formal debates and persuasive essays. In this activity, learners are presented with various images and are asked to analyze the visual elements of each picture to uncover the different arguments presented.

PROCEDURE

1. Divide the class into pairs or small groups.

2. Ask students what the relationship is between advertisements and arguments. Give learners time to brainstorm their ideas and then have a spokesperson from each group discuss their response.

3. Explain that ads often contain arguments that are conveyed through visual elements to persuade an audience to buy a product or promote an idea or belief.

4. Present each group with a visual (see Appendix). Ask students to first discuss what they see or notice in the visual. You can assign questions such as the following:

    a. What images do you see?

    b. What do you first notice?

    c. What colors are used?

    d. Are there people or animals in the picture? If so, what are they doing?

    e. Is there text? If yes, what does it say?

5. When each group has successfully described their picture, ask the students to look at their assigned visual again and answer the following questions:

    a. What is the tone or feeling of the visual (e.g., happy, sad, angry, cheerful, serious, funny, ironic, objective, subjective)?

b. Can you identify any explicit or implicit arguments the image might be trying to convey?

- *Example Response 1:* "Drinking soda can be harmful to your health and cause diseases such as cancer and obesity."
- *Example Response 2:* "Sugar can be hidden in many beverages we drink."

c. Can you think of a counterargument, or an opposing viewpoint, to this image?

- *Example Response 1:* "Sodas come in many different types of flavors and taste delicious."
- *Example Response 2:* "Sodas contain caffeine, which can boost our energy levels."

6. Have each group present their visuals and findings to the class. They should describe the argument(s) they think their visuals are conveying.

7. Allow other groups to comment, ask questions, and formulate their own opinions for each visual presented.

CAVEATS AND OPTIONS

- Adapt this activity for lower level learners by choosing different visuals and by scaffolding vocabulary.
- Print visuals or project them digitally.
- Ask students to find their own images or create their own.
- Have students record their answers to the discussion questions on a collaborative platform such as Google Docs (docs.google.com) or Padlet (padlet.com).
- Extend learning by turning this activity into a formal debate or persuasive essay assignment:
  — For the debate, present one visual to the entire class at a time. Split the class into two teams, and assign each team one side of the argument. Provide them with debate guidelines and instructions, such as the format, time limits, and expectations.
  — For the persuasive essay, have the students choose a visual and select one side of the argument. Students should create a multiparagraph essay based on that visual, containing a thesis statement that clearly takes one stance and is supported with clear ideas, opinions, and evidence.

REFERENCES AND FURTHER READING

Lunsford, A. A., Ruszkiewicz, J. J., & Walters, K. (2019). *Everything's an argument: With readings* (8th ed.). Bedford/St Martin's.

APPENDIX: *Images*

Image source: Los Angeles County Department of Public Health Division of Chronic Disease and Injury Prevention. Used with permission.

Image credit: Nareeta Martin on Unsplash.

Image credit: Erik Mclean on Unsplash.

Image credit: Jon Tyson on Unsplash.

Image source: The Chronicle of Higher Education; Creative Commons, public domain (https://www.chronicle.com/package/the-distracted-classroom/)

Image source: Abukar Sky on Unsplash.

Image credit: DanielBrachlow on Pixabay.

Part II

Videos

Introduction: Developing Visual Literacy Using Video

In today's media-rich landscape, fostering visual and digital literacies is essential for learners' holistic development. As a multimodal medium that combines visual, auditory, and narrative dimensions, video supports not only language acquisition but also the development of visual literacy, intercultural understanding, and critical media awareness (Goldstein & Driver, 2015; Serafini, 2014). This chapter explores how educators can harness the pedagogical possibilities of video to enrich the English language classroom and cultivate learners' ability to interpret, analyze, and produce meaning through visual and verbal modes.

Valente and King's activity "Developing Young Adolescents' Visual Literacy With Animated Films" centers on the award-winning animated short film *Alike* (Martínez Lara & Cano Méndez, 2015), using a structured creative pedagogy to prompt early secondary learners to examine concepts of conformity and individuality through tasks requiring prediction, discussion, and reflection. Their approach emphasizes learning through multimodal engagement and encourages learners to interpret visual texts from diverse perspectives. Activities such as this one address the interpretive and intercultural dimensions of visual literacy, particularly through learner-centered strategies such as gallery walks and text-exploration tasks.

Furthermore, when learners become video creators—through projects such as vlogs, interviews, or collaborative short films—they engage in authentic language production while developing critical digital competencies. Such tasks promote learner autonomy, agency, and multimodal composition skills (Hafner & Miller, 2011). These practices align with broader educational goals that emphasize 21st-century literacies, including the ability to analyze, evaluate, and create digital media texts.

Jialei Jiang's activity "Fostering Social Awareness Through Digital Storytelling" builds on this by guiding learners to design animated videos that explore socially relevant issues. Using tools like Vyond, learners critically examine sample digital stories before collaboratively scripting and producing their own. This process fosters critical digital literacy and helps learners explore how visual elements convey affective and persuasive messages. Jiang's activity also offers scalable strategies for guiding younger learners through creative, multimodal composition through integrating simplified digital tools or focusing on the planning and storyboarding phases.

From a pedagogical perspective, video can also be integrated flexibly into instruction to meet a wide range of learning goals. It can be used to introduce thematic vocabulary, model conversational structures, prompt critical discussion, or inspire creative production. Activities incorporating video content can address real-world issues and foster media literacy, digital storytelling, and global citizenship.

An example of this is Sean H. Toland's activity "Create an Original Nonprofit Organization Video Plan," which uses viral nonprofit videos as models to inspire learners to create original campaigns. This activity fosters critical thinking, collaboration, and cross-cultural awareness. By analyzing authentic texts and engaging in peer presentation and feedback cycles, learners refine their ability to convey compelling narratives in digital form. The emphasis on social justice themes and real-world application adds a rich layer to the development of visual literacy as learners engage in this performance-based task.

These three activities offer a glimpse into the rich potential for English language educators to scaffold visual literacy instruction through animated and digital texts. Each activity in this section supports learners in interpreting, composing, and sharing videos that foster empathy, social insight, and communicative confidence.

REFERENCES AND FURTHER READING

Byram, M. (1997). *Teaching and assessing intercultural communicative competence.* Multilingual Matters.

Goldstein, B., & Driver, P. (2015). *Language learning with digital video.* Cambridge.

Hafner, C. A., & Miller, L. (2011). Fostering learner autonomy in English for science: A collaborative digital video project in a technological learning environment. *Language Learning & Technology, 15*(3), 68–86.

Herron, C., Dubreil, S., Cole, S., & Corrie, C. (1999). The effectiveness of video-based curriculum in teaching culture. *The Modern Language Journal, 83*(4), 518–533.

Martínez Lara, D., & Cano Méndez, R. (Directors). (2015). *Alike.* [Short film]. Daniel Martínez Lara; La Fiesta. https://www.alike.es/

Mayer, R. E. (2009). *Multimedia learning* (2nd ed.). Cambridge.

Paivio, A. (2007). *Mind and its evolution: A dual coding theoretical approach.* Psychology Press.

Serafini, F. (2014). *Reading the visual: An introduction to teaching multimodal literacy.* Teachers College.

Analyzing Ethos, Pathos, and Logos in Video Commercials

Ilka Kostka

Levels	Low intermediate to advanced
Ages Suitable for Activity	Adult
Aims	Define ethos, pathos, and logos
	Analyze video commercials for elements of ethos, logos, and pathos
	Create a video commercial that incorporates elements of persuasion
Class Time	30–45 minutes
Preparation Time	5–10 minutes
Resources	Video: "Embrace Life" (SussexSaferRoads, 2010; www.youtube.com/watch?v=h-8PBx7isoM)
	Links to additional sample video commercials
	Handout (Appendix)
	Devices for students to create video recordings (e.g., tablets or smartphones)

ritten and oral texts, especially commercials, often contain one or more of the following rhetorical strategies: ethos (an appeal to credibility), logos (an appeal to logic and reasoning), and pathos (an appeal to emotions). This activity focuses on helping multilingual learners of English build critical thinking and media literacy skills by analyzing video commercials and identifying their rhetorical devices.

PROCEDURE

1. Define and explain the following rhetorical strategies for your students:
    a. *Ethos* (an appeal to credibility)
    b. *Logos* (an appeal to logic and reasoning)
    c. *Pathos* (an appeal to emotions)
2. Tell students they will look for elements of ethos, logos, and pathos in a sample video commercial.
3. Play a video commercial of your choice. The example used here is "Embrace Life," a commercial about wearing seatbelts. Project the commercial on a screen or, if an overhead projector is not available, have students watch it on their individual devices (e.g., laptops, smartphones).
4. Ask students to identify how ethos, logos, and pathos are used persuasively in the commercial. Examples from "Embrace Life" include:
    a. **Ethos:** The authority of the video's content creator, Sussex Safer Roads Partnership

b. **Logos:** The implication that seatbelts save lives (The man survives the crash because his family acts as a seatbelt.)

c. **Pathos:** The casting of a young family that evokes a deep emotional connection

5. Discuss the sample commercial as a class, along with students' findings.

6. Divide students into small groups and assign each group a different video commercial to analyze on their own using guiding questions from the handout (see Appendix). Give students 5–10 minutes to discuss their commercials.

7. Invite students to present their findings to the class.

8. In the same small groups, ask students to create their own commercial that includes appeals to ethos, logos, and pathos. To scaffold this step, the topics of their commercials can be linked to course readings or units that they are currently working on.

9. Have students share their videos during the next class session or upload them to your learning management system (e.g., Canvas, Blackboard).

10. Encourage students to watch each other's videos and identify elements of ethos, pathos, and logos. To add an element of fun, students can vote for their favorite commercial.

CAVEATS AND OPTIONS

- Search YouTube for video commercials to share with your students for Step 6.

- Consider the backgrounds of your students and avoid showing commercials that may incorporate unfamiliar cultural references or age-inappropriate content.

- Have students record videos on their smartphones or encourage them to use free screen-recording tools like Screenpal (screenpal.com).

- Review students' choices of commercial topic before they record their videos to ensure that the topic is appropriate and to avoid duplication across groups.

REFERENCES AND FURTHER READING

SussexSaferRoads. (2010, January 29). *Embrace life* [Video]. YouTube. www.youtube.com/watch?v=h-8PBx7isoM

APPENDIX: *Rhetorical Devices Analysis*

Identifying Rhetorical Devices in Commercials

The goal of this activity is to practice critical thinking skills by watching commercials and analyzing them to find elements of ethos, logos, and pathos. After you watch the commercial, answer the following questions with your group members.

- What is the main message in the commercial? In other words, what does the company want you to buy or do? How do you know?

- What rhetorical devices (i.e., ethos, logos, or pathos) are used in the video? Provide examples to explain how any or all of these devices are used.

- What is your reaction to this video? Were you persuaded? Why or why not?

Create an Original Nonprofit Organization Video Plan

Sean H. Toland

Levels	Low intermediate to advanced
Ages Suitable for Activity	Secondary to adult
Aims	Enhance creativity and critical thinking skills
	Foster collaboration
	Cultivate communicative competencies
	Develop cross-cultural awareness
Class Time	90 minutes
Preparation Time	10 minutes
Resources	Access to the internet on mobile devices
	Laptop and projector
	Projector
	Timer/stopwatch
	Handouts (Appendixes A–D)
	Video 1: "Don't Choose Extinction - UNDP" (United Nations, 2021; www.youtube.com/watch?v=3DOcQRl9ASc)
	Video 2: "Millie Bobby Brown: Go Blue on World Children's Day" (UNICEF, 2018; www.youtube.com/watch?v=hGWE2D2Q81U)

In recent years, a growing number of nonprofit organizations (NPOs) have started integrating viral marketing videos into advertising campaigns to spread their messages and connect with younger donors. Through incorporating NPO videos into a classroom, teachers can help multilingual learners of English cultivate creativity, collaboration, critical thinking, communicative competencies, and cross-cultural awareness.

This activity uses the popularity of viral NPO marketing as a springboard for students to discuss important sociocultural issues in an authentic language context. In addition, the activity provides learners with an opportunity to collaborate and harness their creative powers by developing an original NPO video storyboard.

PROCEDURE

1. Divide the class into small groups of three to four learners. Distribute the Key Terms & Mission Statement handout (Appendix A). Assign each group one or two terms. Give them 5 minutes to complete Part 1.

2. Bring the class together. Elicit answers and provide corrective feedback.

3. Ask for volunteers to read aloud the instructions for Part 2 and the example mission statement. Tell the class that each group will have 10 minutes to write a collaborative mission statement for a new NPO. Confirm comprehension and check each team's progress.

4. Bring the class together and ask volunteers to read their answers.

5. Distribute the NPO Video Analysis Chart (Appendix B) and provide the class with an overview of the next task. Tell the students that they are going to watch two NPO videos. During the first viewing, they can relax and enjoy both videos. During the second viewing, they will rewatch and discuss one of the videos. Ask volunteers to read aloud the questions in the chart and check for comprehension.

6. Assign either Video 1 or 2 to each group. Emphasize that they only need to focus on their assigned video. They DO NOT need to complete the chart for both videos.

7. Play Videos 1–2 on a projector or ask students to watch them on their mobile devices. Learners can access the videos by typing the URLs directly into a browser.

8. Give the groups 15 minutes to rewatch their assigned video and complete the chart. When the time is up, ask groups to share their answers.

9. Distribute the Our Original NPO Video Plan handout (Appendix C). Ask volunteers to read aloud the information on the handout. Answer any questions.

10. Put the learners in pairs. (It's important to create an even number of pairs for Step 11; make a group of three if needed). Give the pairs 15 minutes to brainstorm ideas for an original NPO video, making notes on the handout. Remind them that they are the directors and need to be creative so that their video will get millions of hits and likes. Circulate to check progress and provide feedback.

11. Invite the whole class to share their ideas in an interactive mingling session:

    a. Divide the pairs into presenters and listeners. The presenters will mingle to discuss their NPO video plans and answer questions from each pair of listeners.

    b. Before the mingling session starts, model a mini-presentation to the class.

    c. Give the students 5 minutes to organize their presentations. Emphasize that this is a communicative activity and not a read-aloud exercise.

    d. Begin the mingling session: Ask the presenters to pair with the listeners. Set a timer for 5 minutes. Cue groups to switch twice, so that each presenting pair talks with three different listening pairs, for a total of 15 minutes.

    e. At the conclusion of the third presentation cycle, the listeners and presenters change roles and repeat the previous step. Circulate to check progress and provide feedback.

    f. When the presentations are finished, bring the class together. Tell them that the ideas they just talked about will be used in a homework assignment.

12. Distribute the Our NPO Storyboard handout (Appendix D). Ask a volunteer to read the instructions aloud. Tell the students that they will make a storyboard for their NPO video that is based on their mind map. This activity will be done individually for homework. Each of the 10 scenes must have an image and brief written description. The images can be drawn by hand or downloaded from the internet. Have the students share their storyboards during the next class.

CAVEATS AND OPTIONS

- Modify the activity for different proficiency levels. For example, lower-level students might need more time to analyze the videos and practice their presentations.

- Flip the classroom by assigning Steps 5–8 as homework before the activity.
- As a follow-up, have advanced students write a persuasive email to the teacher or a classmate requesting funding to make another NPO video.

REFERENCES AND FURTHER READING

New York Public Library. (2025). *NYPL's mission statement.* https://www.nypl.org/about/mission

UNICEF. (2018, November 15). *Millie Bobby Brown: Go blue on world children's day* [Video]. YouTube. www.youtube.com/watch?v=hGWE2D2Q81U

United Nations. (2021, October 28). *Don't choose extinction–UNDP* [Video]. YouTube. www.youtube.com/watch?v=3DOcQRl9ASc

APPENDIX A: *Key Terms & Mission Statement*

Part 1: Match Key Terms

Work in a small group. Match the words/phrases with their definitions. Write the appropriate number next to each word or phrase.

Word or Phrase	Definition
A) nonprofit organization (NPO) ___	1) situation in which something no longer exists
B) mission statement ___	2) group that is formed to benefit the public or promote a social cause; it has tax-exempt status because it does not earn profits for its owners
C) extinction ___	3) fuel (e.g., coal, oil, natural gas) formed in the earth from plant or animal remains
D) viral marketing ___	4) money paid by the government to help an organization or industry reduce its costs so that it can provide goods or services at a lower cost
E) fossil fuel ___	5) business strategy that promotes a product on different social media platforms
F) social issue ___	6) formal summary of the aims and values of a company or organization
G) government subsidies ___	7) problem that affects a large group of people in a society

Part 2: Write an Original Mission Statement

Work in a small group. Your team has been asked to start a new NPO. You must do the following:

1. Create an original name for your NPO.
2. Write a mission statement for your NPO (one or two sentences). Read the following mission statement before you start (New York Public Library, 2025):

   The mission of The New York Public Library is to inspire lifelong learning, advance knowledge, and strengthen our communities.

APPENDIX B: *NPO Video Analysis Chart*

Part 3: Watch the Videos

Work in a small group. Watch your assigned video and complete the chart for ONLY that video. Discuss your answers with your group.

Video A: "Don't Choose Extinction - UNDP" (United Nations, 2021; www.youtube.com/watch?v=3DOcQRl9ASc)

Video B: "Millie Bobby Brown: Go Blue on World Children's Day" (UNICEF, 2018; www.youtube.com/watch?v=hGWE2D2Q81U)

Question	Video A	Video B
1. What happened in the video?		
2. Who were the major characters in the video? Who were the minor characters?		
3. Describe the setting of the video. (Where does it take place? Country? City? Locations?)		
4. What was the most surprising or interesting part of the video?		
5. What was the main message of the video?		
6. What social issue(s) did you notice?		
7. How much money do you think it cost to make this video? Why?		
8. Did you enjoy watching this video? Which video did you prefer? Why?		

APPENDIX C: *Our Original NPO Video Plan*

Part 4: Create Your Video Plan

Work with a partner. The two of you are going to create and direct an original video for your own NPO. Your video must get viewers to think critically about a social issue.

Take 15 minutes to brainstorm your ideas. You will discuss your NPO video plan with your classmates during a mini-presentation mingling session. Use the graphic organizer to record your ideas.

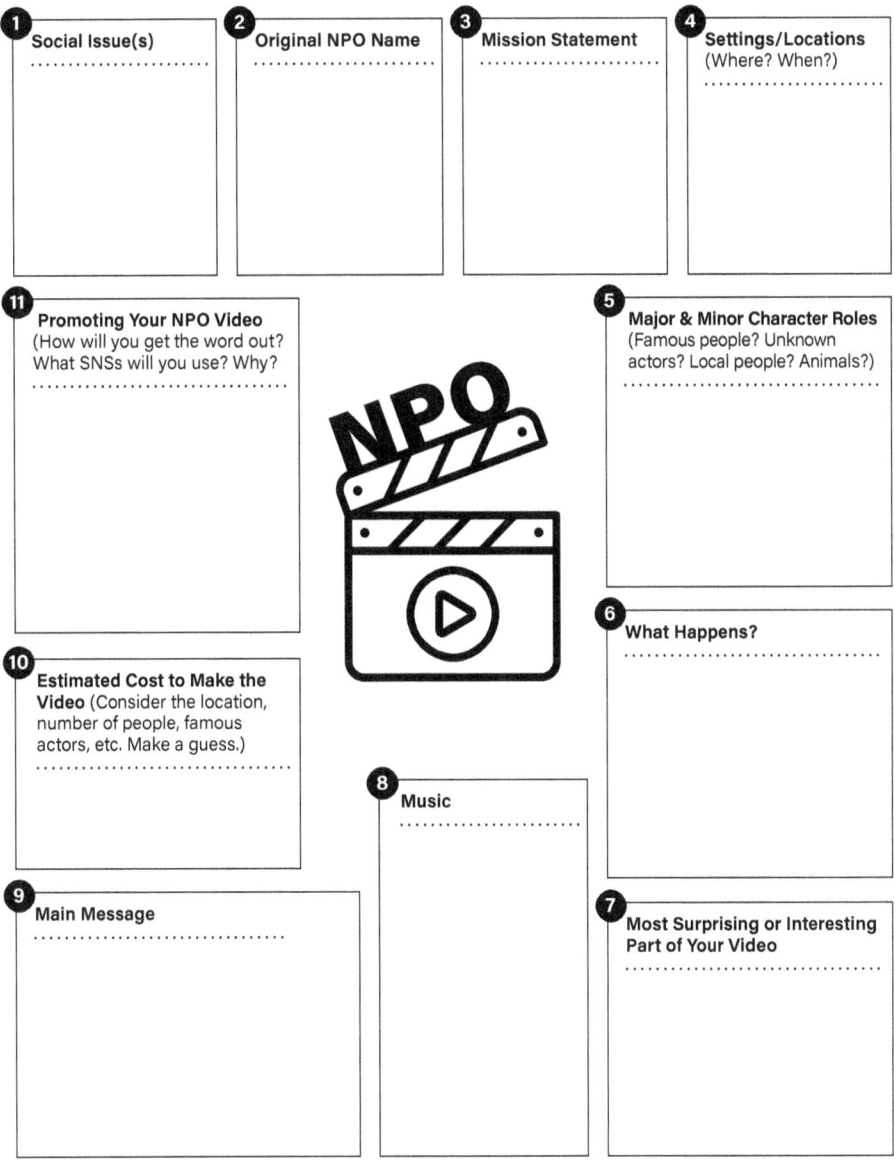

II

1 Social Issue(s)
....

2 Original NPO Name
....

3 Mission Statement
....

4 Settings/Locations
(Where? When?)
....

11 Promoting Your NPO Video
(How will you get the word out? What SNSs will you use? Why?)
....

5 Major & Minor Character Roles
(Famous people? Unknown actors? Local people? Animals?)
....

10 Estimated Cost to Make the Video (Consider the location, number of people, famous actors, etc. Make a guess.)
....

6 What Happens?
....

8 Music
....

9 Main Message
....

7 Most Surprising or Interesting Part of Your Video
....

APPENDIX D: *Our NPO Storyboard*

Part 5: Draw Your Storyboard

Take the ideas from your graphic organizer in Part 4 and put them onto a 10-slide storyboard. For each scene, make a sketch and provide a brief written description.

Sketch	Description
Scene 1:	
Scene 2:	
Scene 3:	
Scene 4:	
Scene 5:	

Sketch	Description
Scene 6:	
Scene 7:	
Scene 8:	
Scene 9:	
Scene 10:	

Connecting Audio and Visual Elements to Words

Defne Akıncı Midas

Levels	Intermediate to advanced
Ages Suitable for Activity	Secondary to adult
Aims	Identify different types of media (audio, visual, and textual) presented in a documentary video
	Recognize how verbal, auditory, and visual elements work together to convey meaning
Class Time	45–50 minutes
Preparation Time	50 minutes
Resources	Laptop and projector
	Board and board markers

Audio and visual elements add depth and meaning to the narration of documentary videos. This activity encourages learners to become familiar with and identify different media elements commonly used in documentary videos and link them to narration, enhancing their acquisition of new vocabulary.

PROCEDURE

1. Select a documentary video appropriate to your learners and their level.

   Sample Video: "The Entire History of Africa in Under 10 Minutes" (Made in History, 2021; www.youtube.com/watch?v=6wiTZZ5EbQ4)

2. Elicit types of documentary films from the class. Possible answers could include history, science, nature, and/or mystery.

3. Elicit what one can see in a documentary film and make a list on the board. Possible answers could include pictures, dramatizations, animations, simulations, maps, pictures, scenes from nature, scenes from settlements, cartoons, subtitles, narration, and/or interviews.

4. Elicit what one can hear in a documentary film and make a list on the board. Possible answers could include the narrator's voice, interviewees' voices, sounds of animals, sounds of nature, background music, traditional music, and sounds of crowds, cities, or machines.

5. Divide the class into two groups. Play 3 minutes of your selected video.

   a. Students in Group A identify as many different audio elements as they can.

   b. Students in Group B identify as many different visual elements as they can (besides the narrator's voice).

   c. Students in each group compare their answers.

d. As a whole class, elicit their answers and put a check mark on the board next to the names of the elements as they say each one they have identified.

6. Replay the first 3 minutes of the video to check the answers with the whole class.

   a. Ask the students to raise their hands if they see or hear any other element that has not been added to the list as they watch the video the second time.

   b. Pause the video each time the students raise their hands and add a new element (if any) to the list on the board.

7. Tell the students that they will watch the same 3-minute segment of the video again. This time, ask Groups A and B to pay attention to when an audio or visual element matches a word or phrase spoken by the narrator and clap when they notice that.

   a. Stop the video and elicit the word/phrase that they heard and the audio or visual element that matches it.

   b. Write the word/phrase and the audio or visual element that matches it on the board.

8. Replay the same 3-minute segment of the video. Pause at the scenes when the students clapped and check if the audio or visual elements actually match. If so, elicit the word/phrase and the audio or visual element in the scene from the students.

   a. If students cannot immediately produce the word/phrase, rewind slightly and play again. If necessary, provide the word/phrase and write it on the board.

9. Tell the students that they will now watch the next 3-minute segment of the video. Repeat Steps 4–9 with the next segment.

10. Compare the two lists that emerge on the board elicited from Group A (audio elements) and Group B (visual elements). Establish that the reason for the difference in the two lists is due to the fact that not all audio and visual elements are accompanied by words/phrases of the narrator, and not all words/phrases match the audio/visual elements in documentaries (see Appendix B for an example).

11. Divide the class into three new groups. Assign one of the following questions to each group to discuss for 3 to 4 minutes.

    a. *Question 1:* How do the audio and visual elements affect the meaning and emotion of the narrator's words in the video?

    b. *Question 2:* How would different audio and visual elements change the meaning of the words?

    c. *Question 3:* How do the audio and visual elements contribute to or hinder your comprehension of the message of the video?

12. When the time is up, display the questions on the board, ask each group to share their answers for their respective question. Finally, elicit any further comments from the students in the other two groups, as well (see Appendix A for possible answers).

13. Wrap up the activity by eliciting what students remember from this activity:

    a. What are the elements that we can see in a documentary?

    b. How can language learners benefit from documentaries?

CAVEATS AND OPTIONS

- Prepare for your students to understand little from the content of the video, not only because it is dense and the narration is fast, but also because they will be focusing on identifying specific elements in the videos rather than following the storyline of the video.

- Do not expect full comprehension or retention of the content of the video after completing the tasks in this activity plan.

REFERENCES AND FURTHER READING

Goldstein, B., & Driver, G. (2015). *Cambridge handbooks for language teachers: Language learning with digital video*. Cambridge.

Made in History. (2021, September 25). *The entire history of Africa in under 10 minutes* [Video]. https://www.youtube.com/watch?v=6wiTZZ5EbQ4

APPENDIX A: *Possible Answers for Steps 11–12*

Question 1

How do the audio and visual elements [in a documentary] affect the meaning and emotion of the narrator's words in the video?

The audio and visual elements may set the tone, making it fun, sad, serious, or scary. Also, the music or background noises and sounds allow the viewers to feel they are experiencing the story or the events.

Question 2

How would different audio and visual elements change the meaning of the words?

They could add a positive or negative meaning, or alternative meanings, to a word/ phrase. They would add a specific context as well as a specific atmosphere in which the word/phrase is used, helping the word/phrase come alive.

Question 3

How do the audio and visual elements contribute to or hinder comprehension of the message of the video?

They contribute to comprehension by providing the meaning in visual form as well as illustrating the surrounding context in which the word/phrase is used. However, they may hinder comprehension sometimes because they may not always direct the viewer to the meaning of the word/phrase. Learners may need to check meaning by referring to subtitles and/or dictionaries.

APPENDIX B: *Video Analysis Activity*

Part 1. First 3-Minute Segment

Based on the sample video, "The Entire History of Africa in Under 10 Minutes" (Made in History, 2021; www.youtube.com/watch?v=6wiTZZ5EbQ4), students may identify the following elements, in order of appearance.

Group A: Audio Elements

African traditional music, Egyptian traditional music

Group B: Visual Elements

Nature (land), people at a birthday party, world map, illustration/picture, pictures of animals, map, nature (land and animals), fossils/bones, animation/simulation of ancient man, dramatization of first man, map, nature (forest and desert), map, animal pictures, map, pictures, view of pyramid, paintings/illustrations, animation, map, animation, map, illustration, map

Chart of Words/Phrases That Match Audio/Visual Elements

Items in the table are presented in order of appearance in the video:

Narrator says...	We see...	We hear...
20 years old	the number 20	African traditional music
over 30	the number 30 on the birthday cake	African traditional music
the second largest continent	the map	African traditional music
the tallest	a giraffe	African traditional music
the fastest	a cheetah	African traditional music
the largest	an elephant	African traditional music
Africa	map of Africa with different countries	African traditional music
fossils	a hand with a brush going over bones in the soil	African traditional music
our own species, homo sapiens	animation and dramatization of ancient humans	African traditional music
50,000 years ago—migration	map with years and migration routes	African traditional music
once lush and green	green forest seen from above	African traditional music
becoming a desert	view of desert	Egyptian traditional music
move to the Nile Valley	view of the Nile Valley from above	Egyptian traditional music
domesticate cattle, donkeys, and goats	picture of cattle, donkeys, and goats	Egyptian traditional music
a writing system	illustration of papyrus with ancient script	Egyptian traditional music
Alexander the Great	illustration of Alexander the Great and his army in Egypt	Egyptian traditional music
based in Carthage	Carthage on map	Egyptian traditional music
sea traders	boats on sea	Egyptian traditional music
Romans destroying North African civilization	animated illustration of Roman soldiers attacking from the sea	Egyptian traditional music
new name of Africa—Proconsularis	the word *proconsularis*	Egyptian traditional music
first Roman emperor of African descent	illustration of a man on a horse fighting	Egyptian traditional music

Part 2. Second 3-Minute Segment

Group A: Audio Elements

Egyptian traditional music, African traditional music, Western classical music

Group B: Visual Elements

(Items are listed in order of appearance.) Map, illustrations, map and script, pictures, nature (animal and land), drawings, map and pictures, map and illustrations, map and statues/figurines, nature (animal and land), map, people hunting, maps, coast with boar, scene with walking people, map, maps with dates, illustrations, map pictures, map, illustrations, paintings and drawings of the old lifestyles, video of people, illustration, drawing and map.

Chart of Words/Phrases That Match Audio/Visual Elements

Items in the table are presented in order of appearance in the video:

Narrator says...	We see...	We hear...
in the 600s	map with dates, title with dates	Egyptian traditional music
urban center	picture of Dhar Tichit and Oualata	African traditional music
Djenne-Djeno	the name Djenne-Djeno	African traditional music
present-day Nigeria	map with name Nigeria on it	African traditional music
Nok culture	Nok appears on map	African traditional music
terracotta figures of humans and other animals	figurines	African traditional music
living hunter–gatherer lifestyles	man shooting an arrow	African traditional music
in central Africa	middle of the map appears	African traditional music
eastern coast	seaside with boat	African traditional music
on the Sahara	map of Sahara	African traditional music
the Mali Empire	the title of Mali Empire	African traditional music
Mansa Musa	picture of Mansa Musa	African traditional music
Sunni Ali	picture and name of Sunni Ali	African traditional music
Songhai Empire	map with name of Songhai Empire	African traditional music
in North Africa	map of North Africa	African traditional music
migrated westwards	man on horse moves to the left of the map	African traditional music
slavery	picture of African captives	Western classical music

Deconstructing Physical Delivery in Videoconferencing

Hale H. Kızılcık

Level	Intermediate to advanced
Ages Suitable for Activity	University and adult
Aims	Develop awareness of how physical delivery contributes to establishing a positive impression and enhances verbal messages in video interviews
	Facilitate the development of effective physical delivery in video interviews
Class Time	50 minutes
Preparation Time	5 minutes–1 hour
Resources	Video: "Do you have a weakness?" (Hale Hatice Kızılcık, 2025; youtu.be/_ynV9ztpo-c)
	Interactive Video: "Do you have a weakness?" (Hale Hatice Kızılcık, 2025; edpuzzle.com/media/686f95da3599a21ff30d835a)
	Laptop and projector
	Access to watch videos on individual mobile devices

Videoconferencing has become prevalent in many contexts, including job interviews. The lack of physical presence and low information richness in video-mediated communication are two fundamental features distinguishing it from in-person communication (Croes et al., 2018). Furthermore, interviewers may form different impressions about a person, such as their likeability, trustworthiness, and intelligence, when mediated by video (Fullwood, 2006). In this activity, learners will practice noticing and improving physical aspects of their communication delivery, including mainly appearance, facial expressions, eye contact, posture, and setting.

PROCEDURE

1. Select an appropriate video, from YouTube or another online source, of a person being interviewed for a job. An example is provided in the Resources; alternatively, you can record your own video for this activity.

    a. If recording your own clip, use Edpuzzle (edpuzzle.com) to create an interactive version with open-ended questions, as in the provided example.

    b. Sample question prompt: "Describe the applicant's posture and facial expressions here. What impression do they form?"

2. Tell the class that they will assume the role of recruiters in a job interview and evaluate an applicant. Introduce a position that the interviewee applied for and explain that the person will answer the question, "Do you have a weakness?"

3. Tell the class you will play the video multiple times. Each time, ask students to concentrate on a different aspect of the applicant's performance.

4. Show the video and ask the class to make note of their first impressions by writing down three adjectives to describe the applicant (e.g., *confident, positive, professional, smart, immature, uninterested, distracted*).

5. Elicit answers from the whole class. Tell students that as they continue to watch the video, they will look for different aspects of the applicant's performance that contribute to these first impressions.

6. Play the video again, this time asking students to focus on the content (i.e., what the interviewee says to answer the question). Provide the following criteria to guide students' evaluation:

   a. Does the applicant address the question directly and include only relevant information?

   b. Does the applicant seem to have the necessary skills for the position?

   c. Does the applicant use time effectively?

7. Ask the class to discuss their evaluations in small groups. Then, initiate a whole-class discussion about the strengths and weaknesses of the content.

8. Play the video again, this time asking students to focus on the applicant's physical delivery.

   a. Elicit elements of physical delivery (e.g., appearance, facial expressions, eye contact, posture).

   b. Discuss how physical delivery in videoconferencing is different from in-person communication. For example, in videoconferencing, applicants are typically viewed from the chest up, the camera angle impacts eye contact, and arranging the setting is like choosing a suitable attire.

9. Ask the class to discuss their evaluations in small groups. Then, initiate a whole-class discussion about the strengths and weaknesses of the physical delivery.

10. Assign the class to watch the interactive version of the video on their own devices. During the video, students are prompted to reflect individually on some key visual cues.

11. Watch the interactive video again together and initiate a whole-class discussion on how physical delivery enhances or impedes the formation of positive impressions.

12. Finally, ask the class what they have learned about how to conduct themselves in video interviews.

CAVEATS AND OPTIONS

- Depending on your learners' proficiency level, introduce specific vocabulary to describe physical delivery (e.g., *looks to upper corner, rolls eyes, purses lips, frowns, nods, squints*). If necessary, create a (picture) glossary for these terms.

- Encourage students to mimic the body language of the applicant while sharing their comments in Step 9.

- Extend the discussion to the applicant's clothes and the setting of the video (e.g., she is wearing a T-shirt with the logo, "I need my space").

- Remind students that there may be cultural differences in the interpretation of body language.

- Explore other paralinguistics aspects of the applicant's performance (e.g., tone, pitch of voice, and similar).

REFERENCES AND FURTHER READING

Croes, E., Antheunis, M., Schouten, A., & Krahmer, E. (2019). Social attraction in video-mediated communication: The role of nonverbal affiliative behavior. *Journal of Social and Personal Relationships, 36*(4), 1210–1232.

Fullwood, C. (2006). The effect of mediation on impression formation: A comparison of face-to-face and video-mediated conditions. *Applied Ergonomics, 38*(3), 267–273.

APPENDIX A: *Sample Reflections*

00:09	00:40	00:47
Observations: leaning on her hand, avoiding eye contact, looking sideways, rolling eyes, hair band around her wrist, unmotivated, bored.	Observations: pulling a face, raised eyebrows, eyes bugging out, a mocking smile, seems to be engaged but to show dislike and disapproval, unkind.	Observations: grimacing, sneering, expressing dislike and disapproval again.

Developing Young Adolescents' Visual Literacy With Animated Films

David Valente and Wendy King

Level	High intermediate
Age Suitable for Activity	11–13 years old
Aims	Explore similarities and differences through visual stimuli
	Make and check predictions based on visual clues
	Interpret an animated film in depth
	Reflect on a visual text from multiple perspectives
Class Time	90 minutes–2 hours
Preparation Time	20–30 minutes
Resources	Printed photographs
	Sticky tack adhesive
	Film: *Alike* (Martínez Lara & Cano Méndez, 2015; www.alike.es)
	Laptop and projector
	Text Explorers cards (Appendix B)
	4 laptops or tablets for students
	Poster paper
	Marker pens

This activity fosters young adolescent learners' development of critical visual literacy. The activity sequence is underpinned by reading for in-depth learning, a creative pedagogical framework developed as a collaboration between teacher educators at Nord University, Norway, and Bishop's University, Canada (ELLiL Project Partners, 2023). The graphic in Appendix A outlines the framework's main points.

PROCEDURE

1. Before the activity, select 10 diverse photographs of young teens and print them out. (Ideas for databases to search online include Wikimedia Commons [commons.wikimedia.org] and Pixabay [pixabay.com].)

2. Stick the photographs around the classroom walls and put learners into pairs for a gallery walk. Have learners walk around as if they are visiting an art gallery and suggest to each other how the photographs are alike. Before students begin, clarify the meaning of *to be alike* using examples and the learners' home languages, if necessary.

3. Bring the learners together as a class and elicit their ideas about ways they think the people in the photos are alike. Elicit additional ways the people in the photographs might be alike that we cannot see, such as they might all like gaming or they might all be concerned about the environment, etc.

4. Ask the learners why we often focus on differences between people rather than similarities (or the ways that they are alike). Use the learners' language(s) and recast to clarify. Accept learners' responses in any language(s) they prefer.

5. Show learners the cover image from the award-winning animated Spanish short film *Alike* (see Resources for link). Draw learners' attention to the title and the two characters. Then use think, pair, square (i.e., have students work individually, then with a partner, then as groups of four) and ask learners to predict what the film might be about and why. Monitor to prompt their ideas and provide language support.

6. Bring the learners together and collect their ideas from Step 5 by writing them on the board. Use these ideas for the initial viewing task:

   a. The learners should watch the film to see which scenes are like their predictions and note the differences.

   b. Remind the learners to note the differences they see as they watch. Play the film and monitor unobtrusively.

   c. After watching, ask the learners to first share their notes in groups and then in plenary. Elicit their thoughts on the meaning of the title, Alike, and whether it is positive or negative and why. Provide language support to help expand their ideas as necessary.

7. As a whole class, discuss if they enjoyed the film, what surprised them, and what the messages might be. Encourage the learners to contribute reasons for their opinions and emphasize that there are no right or wrong answers.

8. Next, explain that the learners will work in groups to watch the film again as text explorers. Clarify that this is a jigsaw activity and that they will share their ideas with the other groups afterward.

   a. Allocate four groups with the following themes: 1) tell me more, 2) connect to the text, 3) go beyond the text, and 4) make a difference. Then distribute the Text Explorers cards (see Appendix B).

   b. Ask each group to work in a different area of the classroom with a laptop or tablet. Share the URL for groups to open the video on their devices.

   c. Give learners time to read their cards and monitor comprehension. If needed, clarify the language in the prompts.

   d. When they are ready, have the learners watch the film again, pausing it whenever a member of the group wants to discuss a prompt from one of the cards. Monitor to provide ideas and language support.

   e. After they have finished watching, have the learners share their ideas about each prompt in their groups. Monitor to help them expand their ideas and recast into English if necessary.

   f. Set a time limit and distribute poster paper and marker pens for the learners to record and visualize their group's ideas. Each member of the group should create their own poster notes or mind map. Circulate to monitor and support.

   g. When time is up, reallocate the learners into new groups and ensure that each group has one representative from Groups 1, 2, 3, and 4 and that each student has completed a poster.

h. In their new groups, learners should take turns to share their posters. Encourage them to ask each other questions. Monitor unobtrusively and identify ideas to share during the plenary feedback.

9. In plenary, elicit what the learners have learned from their classmates' ideas about being alike and being different. Encourage several contributions and recast as necessary.

10. Finally, as a class, reflect on the benefits of exploring a text with "different glasses" or from different perspectives. Use the learners' own languages to clarify and support their reflections. Close the activity by summarizing the learning outcomes.

REFERENCES AND FURTHER READING

Martínez Lara, D., & Cano Méndez, R. (Directors). (2015). *Alike*. [Short film]. Daniel Martínez Lara; La Fiesta. https://www.alike.es/

ELLiL Project Partners (2023). *Reading for in-depth learning (Ridl) framework*. https://site.nord.no/ellil/reading-for-in-depth-learning/

APPENDIX A: *Reading for In-Depth Learning (RIDL) Framework*

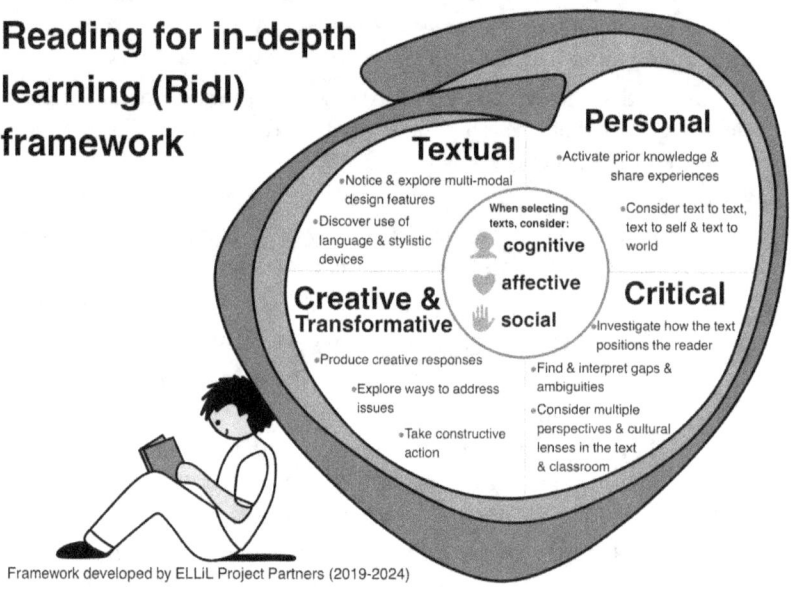

Reading for in-depth learning (Ridl) framework. Used with permission of Eltonix IDEVELOPELT Ltd, UK, © 2023 ELLiL Project Partners

APPENDIX B: *Text Explorer Cards*

Text Explorer Card 1: *Tell me more...*

- Talk about the objects in *Alike* (e.g., the schoolbag, the tie, the violin, the briefcase). Explain what they might represent and why.
- Listen to the music from the film and think about the ways that it creates different moods. Discuss your ideas as a group.
- How do the colors in *Alike* reflect the routines of school and work?
- How do contrasts help you to understand the story in *Alike*? Here are some examples:
  — The child's enthusiasm / the father's boredom
  — Black and white images / colorful images
  — The father's discipline / the child's love
  — The musician's island / the ordinary street

Text Explorer Card 2: *Connect to the text...*

- Talk about how important you think the music is in *Alike*. Discuss the ways you use music in your daily life.
- Notice how the images of school life are black and white in *Alike*. What would you like to change about your school life to make it more colorful?
- What job do you think the father wants the child to do in the future? How does this change during the film? Talk about the differences between the jobs children might want to do and their families' ideas.

Text Explorer Card 3: *Go beyond the text...*

- In *Alike*, who decides how the child spends their time? Who do you think should decide? Do children have to agree with their families and teachers on ways to spend their time? Explain why or why not.
- What are the similarities between the father's routine at work and the child's routine at school? Do we need routines in our daily lives? Explain why or why not.
- In the film, where is the child's mother? Do you think the child's mother might act differently from the father? Do you think a female teacher might act differently from a male teacher? Explain why or why not.

Text Explorer Card 4: *Make a difference...*

- How do art and music help the characters in *Alike*? Brainstorm five ways that you could use art and music for learning English.
- How does the child tell the father about their hopes and dreams? Brainstorm creative ways that teenagers can tell their families about their hopes and dreams. One example might be a TikTok dance!
- By the end of *Alike*, the father celebrates the child's love of creativity. Suggest and agree on three changes your school could make to celebrate students' creativity.

Fostering Social Awareness Through Digital Storytelling

Jialei Jiang

Levels	High intermediate to advanced
Ages Suitable for Activity	Adult
Aims	Develop observation skills
	Encourage critical thinking and creative response
	Practice speaking and communicating with multimodalities
	Develop critical social awareness
Class Time	45–75 minutes
Preparation Time	10 minutes
Resources	Video: "Why Water" (charity: water, 2015; www.youtube.com/watch?v=womlxQqO2tE)
	List of suggested social issues (Appendix A)
	Storyboard template (Appendix B)
	Devices for students to create video recordings (i.e., tablets or smartphones)

Digital storytelling projects offer a dynamic and interactive learning experience that involves multiple modes of communication. This activity promotes learners' creative thinking and critical digital literacy (Jiang, 2024; Kendrick et al., 2022) by asking them to develop animated videos and tell their stories. In this activity, learners work in groups to design an animated video about a socially relevant topic that interests them.

PROCEDURE

1. Before this class session, help students create accounts at Vyond (www.vyond.com), a beginner-friendly online animated video creation platform. Vyond has a free 30-day trial for which students can sign up without requiring a credit card.

2. Elicit the meaning of *digital stories*, accepting all possible answers. Explain to students the definition of digital storytelling (Jiang, 2024), which involves the creation of a 2- to 3-minute short film for the purpose of promoting public awareness around a social issue.

3. Ask learners to analyze the language use and multimodal design in a sample digital story. One example is charity: water's animated video, "Why Water," which tells the story of the water crisis in Africa and raises awareness of the need to save water.

4. Put learners in small groups to discuss why they think this animated video is particularly effective in storytelling and multimodal design. Accept all possible answers.

5. In small groups, ask students to collaboratively brainstorm ideas for a short film focusing on a social issue, such as racial profiling, poverty in education, or animal protection. (To help students brainstorm, you could project or print copies of Appendix A).

6. Hand out the template in Appendix B. Tell groups to design a storyboard that maps out each scene in the short film.

7. Ask each group to log into Vyond on a tablet and start designing a 2- to 3-minute animated video based on their storyboard. Guide students on ways to select an appropriate background, design the visual appearance of a few characters, and animate the characters' actions using the animation design resources available in Vyond. Encourage students to focus on mapping ideas for a few scenes of their Vyond animation.

8. As a class, preview each group's video and discuss what is effective or thought provoking about the draft of their animated video.

9. Give groups time to reflect on what can be added to their videos to make them more engaging for their audience. Elicit answers from the groups. Write them on the board. Comment on students' drafts.

10. Wrap up the class by discussing how certain visual elements communicate messages that cannot be communicated through speech alone. Assign students to complete their animated videos after class.

CAVEATS AND OPTIONS

- Adapt this activity to a younger age or lower proficiency level by asking students to tell a simpler story or by shortening the minimum length requirement.

- Use this activity as a 10-minute warm-up by asking students to analyze sample animated videos. Extend the activity for a full-length class by asking students to collaboratively produce a digital story.

- Extend the learning by having groups share their drafts of animated videos and comment on each other's drafts.

- Ask students to add voiceover and/or captions to their animated videos as homework or during the next class meeting.

REFERENCES AND FURTHER READING

Jiang, J. (2024). "Emotions are what will draw people in": A study of critical affective literacy through digital storytelling. *Journal of Adolescent & Adult Literacy, 67*(4), 253–263.

Kendrick, M., Early, M., Michalovich, A., & Mangat, M. (2022). Digital storytelling with youth from refugee backgrounds: Possibilities for language and digital literacy learning. *TESOL Quarterly, 56*(3), 961–984. https://doi.org/10.1002/tesq.3146

Lambert, J. (2013). *Digital storytelling: Capturing lives, creating community* (4th ed.). Routledge.

APPENDIX A: *List of Suggested Social Issues*

- Food issues: food deserts, local foods, access to farmers' markets, food sustainability, fast food versus healthier food options
- Poverty and its relationship with education (especially as it relates to local schools)
- Revitalization of depressed areas
- Increased cost of tuition and textbooks
- Education spending
- Environmental issues: oil spills and their aftermath, deforestation, local waste and recycling, air quality, local mining's effect on ecosystems, urban farming
- Oil pipelines and fracking, energy sustainability
- Public transportation (and the lack thereof)
- Rates of illiteracy and access to education
- Police militarization, police force racial profiling
- Accessibility of campus spaces to individuals with disabilities and other minority groups
- Issues of racism and sexism on campus
- Sexual violence/rape among college students (which could be addressed locally or nationally)
- Animal protection, euthanasia of animals
- Issues of immigration and homelessness

APPENDIX B: *Storyboard Template*

TITLE _____ NAME _____

SCENE 1:	SCENE 2:	SCENE 3:
MOVEMENT:	MOVEMENT:	MOVEMENT:
SCRIPT:	SCRIPT:	SCRIPT:
MUSIC/SOUND:	MUSIC/SOUND:	MUSIC/SOUND:

SCENE 4:	SCENE 5:	SCENE 6:
MOVEMENT:	MOVEMENT:	MOVEMENT:

Our Dream Trip Vlogs

Sean H. Toland and Tony Cripps

Levels	High beginner to advanced
Ages Suitable for Activity	Secondary to adult
Aims	Develop skills in research and information technology
	Practice brainstorming and planning
	Foster collaboration and cross-cultural awareness
	Improve presentation and communication skills
	Cultivate visual literacy
Class Time	90 minutes (Activity 1)
	60 minutes (Activity 2)
Preparation Time	10 minutes
Resources	Laptop and projector
	Timer/stopwatch
	Devices for students to create video recordings (i.e., tablets or smartphones)
	Handouts (Appendixes A–D)
	Video: "Around the World in 3 Minutes" (GQ Trippin, 2013; www.youtube.com/watch?v=CkOwDiab29E)
	Video: "Make It Count" (Neistat, 2012; www.youtube.com/watch?v=WxfZkMm3wcg)

here are numerous globetrotting social media content creators who wander around exotic destinations, vlogging about their adventures. Integrating travel vlogs into your English language classroom can foster multilingual learners' communicative competencies and expand their cultural horizons. This activity draws on the popularity of travel vlogging and uses it as a stepping stone for learners to discuss a 1-week dream trip plan, practicing their speaking and presentation skills in an authentic language context.

PROCEDURE

Activity 1: Vlog Introduction and Planning

1. Divide the class into small groups. Write the following on the board: *vlog, vlogger, hits, likes,* and *dream trip*. Elicit students' ideas on the meanings of these terms and provide corrective feedback.

2. Distribute the Video Viewing and Discussion Questions handout (Appendix A). Ask volunteers to read the instructions and questions. Tell the class they will watch two dream trip vlogs, then talk about vlogging in a small group.

   a. Play the two vlogs, "Around the World in 3 Minutes" and "Make It Count," on a projector or have students access them on their smartphones.

   b. Give the groups 15 minutes to discuss their ideas about the questions on the handout. Afterward, ask volunteers to share their answers.

3. Distribute the Our Dream Trip Mind Map handout (Appendix B). Ask volunteers to read the information on the handout. Answer any questions that arise.

   a. Pair students up and tell them that they will have 15 minutes to brainstorm ideas for a 1-week dream trip. Remind them to visit three countries and make their plan exciting!

   b. When the brainstorming is finished, tell the class that they will share their ideas in a mingling session. Each pair will make three 5-minute presentations and listen to three 5-minute presentations. Emphasize that this is a communication activity and not a read-aloud exercise.

   c. Model a mini-presentation to the class. Divide the pairs into presenters and listeners. Give the partners 5 minutes to organize their presentations, then pair with another set of students and begin their presentations.

   d. When the third presentation cycle is finished, the presenters and listeners change roles and repeat the previous step. Monitor the students' progress and provide any necessary feedback.

4. Distribute the Our Dream Trip Vlog—Instructions handout (Appendix C). Ask for volunteers to read Parts 1–3. Answer any questions that arise.

5. Distribute the Our Dream Trip Vlog—Outline handout (Appendix D). Tell the class to work in pairs, and that each partner must complete 50% of the chart. Partners must prepare the following before the next class session:

   a. complete schedule outline (for a 6-day trip)

   b. a photo slide for each day (see Appendix E), as digital files or color prints

   c. a vlog description for each day

6. Give the partners 5 minutes to divide the tasks. Remind students that they must bring their completed charts and digital images (or color prints) to the next class session.

Activity 2: Vlog Recording and Viewing

7. Check the students' homework as assigned in the previous activity. Ask volunteers to read Part 4 of the instructions (Appendix C). Emphasize that when recording their vlogs, students must look at the camera and talk about their dream trips. They should not read or try to memorize their descriptions. Both partners will be on camera at the same time. (*Note*: The nonspeaking partner will hold the slides.)

8. Ask volunteers to read Part 5 of the instructions (Appendix C). Emphasize the importance of privacy and remind students to be careful handling others' smartphones.

9. Give the partners 15 minutes to check their descriptions, practice, and time their vlogs.

10. Match partners up with another pair. Tell the class that they will have 15 minutes to record both teams' vlogs. Students will only get one take, so they need to keep talking even if a mistake occurs.

11. Write these two questions on the board:
    a. How did the images you selected make you feel?
    b. How can travel vloggers use images and visual media effectively?

12. After all pairs have finished recording their vlogs, tell partners to circulate, share their vlogs with other teams, and answer questions for about 20 minutes total. Refer students to the questions written on the board. Each team should watch two other teams' vlogs.

13. When the video viewing session concludes, give the groups 5 minutes to discuss these two questions. Then, ask volunteers to share their thoughts with the whole class.

CAVEATS AND OPTIONS

- Give students more time to practice their vlogs before leading the second activity, rather than having students record immediately in the next class session.
- Modify the activity for different proficiency levels. For example, three students can work together instead of pairs in a lower proficiency class, or more advanced students can work individually.
- Have students explain their dream trip schedule in a mini-presentation session instead of making a video if recording devices are not available. This can also reduce any potential problematic privacy issues.

REFERENCES AND FURTHER READING

GQ Trippin. (2013, January 31). *Around the world in 3 minutes* [Video]. YouTube. https://www.youtube.com/watch?v=CkOwDiab29E

Neistat, C. (2012, April 9). *Make it count* [Video]. YouTube. https://www.youtube.com/watch?v=WxfZkMm3wcg

APPENDIX A: *Video Viewing and Discussion Questions*

Instructions

Work in a small group. Watch the two videos and complete the chart. Discuss your answers with your group.

Questions	Vlog 1: Make It Count Source: https://www.youtube.com/watch?v=WxfZkMm3wcg	Vlog 2: Around the World in 3 MInutes Source: https://www.youtube.com/watch?v=CkOwDiab29E
1. What activities did the vloggers do on their trip?		
2. How did the bloggers get around? (What type of transportation did they use?)		
3. Which travel vlog did you enjoy the most? Why?		
4. What skills does a person need to be a successful travel vlogger?		
5. What are the advantages and disadvantages of working as a full-time travel vlogger?		
6. Have you ever uploaded a travel vlog to a social media site? Why or why not?		

APPENDIX B: *Our Dream Trip Mind Map*

Instructions

Work with a partner. A famous company is sponsoring your team to make a 7-minute travel vlog about a 1-week dream trip to three countries. Make your trip EXCITING and INTERESTING! Do NOT worry about the cost.

Use the mind map to brainstorm ideas. Your team will make a mini-presentation to other pairs.

1 COUNTRIES AND CITIES:

A

B

C

2 SETTING(S):
Where does it take place?

3 ACTIVITIES:
What will you do in your vlog?

4 WHO: Local people, celebrities, character roles?

5 MUSIC:
Genre, famous songs?

6 MOST SURPRISING/ INTERESTING PART OF YOUR VLOG?

7 AUDIENCE AND SOCIAL MEDIA PLATFORMS: Who will watch your vlog? What social networking sites will you use?

8 EQUIPMENT:
What equipment do you need to travel and make your vlog?

APPENDIX C: *Our Dream Trip Vlog—Instructions*

Part 1: Create Your Dream Trip Vlog Outline

Instructions

With your partner, fill in the chart in Appendix D to help you organize your dream trip vlog. Remember, you must visit three countries in 6 days. Day 7 is a travel day.

Make sure you include the following for each day:

- your location (country and city)
- places to visit (e.g., beach, temple, museum)
- four activities (e.g., bungee jumping, hiking, traveling)

Here is an example to get you started:

Morning	Afternoon / Evening
Day 1: Kyoto, Japan	Day 1: Kyoto, Japan
Sannenzaka historical street—drank green tea and ate Japanese sweets	Arashiyama bamboo forest—participated in a walking tour
Hokanji temple—took photos and talked with a monk	Fushimi Inari shrine—climbed the hiking trail

Part 2: Select Images for Your Vlog

Instructions

With your partner, find and organize the photos that you will use in your vlog:

- Use Microsoft PowerPoint or a Word document (in landscape orientation) to create your slides. Another option for this is Apple Keynote.
- You MUST have a total of six slides—one per day. Each partner is responsible for three slides. You do NOT need to find photos for all of the activities on your outline.
- Each slide can have up to four photos.

Review the following design principles before you create your slides.

Slide Design Principles and Tips

- Use high-resolution images.
- Do NOT use images with a copyright stamp.
- Do NOT use clipart.
- Do NOT use colourful backgrounds behind your photos. Use a white background.
- Do NOT leave empty space. Your image(s) should cover the entire slide.
- Think about balance. Arrange your images in an attractive manner.
- Do NOT use much text (simply include the day, city, and country).

Part 3: Write Your Vlog Description

Instructions

With your partner, write a description for each day. Use your OWN WORDS. Read the following example before you begin:

Part 4: Review the Parts of a Vlog

Instructions

With your partner, review and discuss the following parts of a vlog:

1. Introduction
   a. Greet the audience.
   b. Introduce yourselves and your vlog topic (dream trip).
   c. Give a short overview. What three countries did you visit?
2. Body
   a. Describe your itinerary for each day.
   b. For Day 7, you can just say "We flew back home!"
3. Conclusion
   a. Thank the audience for watching.
   b. Ask them to send you their questions and comments.
   c. Ask them to please hit the Like button and subscribe to your channel.

Part 5: Practice and Record Your Vlog

Instructions

Read the recording guidelines. Practice what you are going to say a few times before you record your vlog. When practicing, time your vlog to make sure it is under 7 minutes long. After you complete recording, you will share your dream trip vlogs during a class mingling session.

IMPORTANT: This is a communication exercise. Look at the camera and TALK about your trip. DO NOT READ your notes.

Vlog Recording Guidelines

1. A classmate from another pair will record your vlog on your smartphone (or tablet).
2. Handle your classmates' smartphones very carefully. We don't want any damaged devices.
3. Do NOT record anything or anyone other than the vlog.
4. Record the smartphone videos horizontally. Do NOT record vertically.
5. Make sure your finger does not cover the lens or microphone.

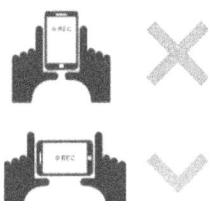

6. Each partner must talk 50% of the time (e.g., Student A gives the introduction and Days 1–3, Student B does Days 4–6 and the conclusion).

7. When the sharing activity is finished, delete the video files from your smart-phone. Do NOT upload video files to any social networking sites. Respect everyone's privacy.

APPENDIX D: *Our Dream Trip Vlog—Outline*

Morning Locations & Activities	Afternoon/Evening Locations & Activities
Day 1: (city, country)	Day 1:
Vlog Description: Day 1 Image(s):	
Day 2: (city, country)	Day 2:
Vlog Description: Day 2 Image(s):	
Day 3: (city, country)	Day 3:
Vlog Description: Day 3 Image(s):	

Morning Locations & Activities	Afternoon/Evening Locations & Activities
Day 4: (city, country)	Day 4:
Vlog Description: Day 4 Image(s):	
Day 5: (city, country)	Day 5:
Vlog Description: Day 5 Image(s):	
Day 6: (city, country)	Day 6:
Vlog Description: Day 6 Image(s):	

Spinning a Story With Reels

Daniela Dascalita Ortiz

Levels	High intermediate to advanced
Ages Suitable for Activity	Secondary to adult
Aims	Identify and understand relationships based on visual input
	Make inferences based on visual input
	Create dialogue that shows empathy and respect for others
	Use oral language structures in context
Class Time	20–50 minutes
Preparation Time	15 minutes
Resources	Nonverbal reel and sample dialogue (Appendix A)
	Additional video links (Appendix B)
	Laptop and projector
	Devices for students to create video recordings (i.e., tablets or smartphones)

Several studies (Ansari & Khan, 2020; Ghounane, 2020; Sarangapani & Hashim, 2022) have shown the positive impact of social media platforms on language learning. One of the most popular features of social media is watching and/or creating short video clips ranging from 30 to 60 seconds. With many different names (TikToks, reels on Instagram and Facebook, or shorts on YouTube), these videos' main purpose is the same: to entertain and connect with an audience. These videos represent an effective resource for engaging students in oral storytelling and using language in context. In this activity, students will watch several nonverbal or low-verbal reels, and through collaboration, they will develop and record a dialogue to match a reel.

PROCEDURE

1. Ask learners about memorable reels or short videos they have watched recently on social media. What were they about?

2. Play one reel for the class ("How your kids wash the car," from Appendix B). Elicit brief information about its message. Then, ask students how the dialogue helped convey that message. You can focus on stressed or repeated words, intonation, and gestures.

3. Divide learners into groups and ask them to create a specific list of things that could make a reel impactful (e.g., images, objects, storyline, music). Ask them to reflect on the video they have just watched and/or reels they have previously watched online.

4. Elicit their answers and create a master list together on the board based on the discussion.

5. Discuss why some reels can be socially offensive. Create another master list, this time of things to avoid. Discuss how reels can show empathy and respect for others—or the opposite. You can ask questions such as the following:

   a. How did the characters show respect for each other?

   b. Were there any words or gestures that you found offensive?

   c. Was there a socially awkward situation?

   d. Would you say things differently in your culture or in your family?

   e. What expressions did you find uplifting or encouraging?

   f. What would you have done differently to show more empathy?

   g. Play a nonverbal reel for the class ("Assistance dog sigma 🥺," from Appendix A). Tell students they will create a monologue or dialogue to accompany this reel.

   h. A monologue could represent the inside voice of the main character telling the story from their perspective.

   i. A dialogue could be a conversation between characters. (As in the sample dialogue given in Appendix A, the conversation could be between the dog and its instructor, or between the dog and a peer.)

6. Put learners in groups of two or three and tell them to brainstorm and write a possible narrative and dialogue accompanying the nonverbal reel they have just watched.

7. Ask groups to perform their dialogues using words, gestures, and objects. You can ask them to record the dialogue themselves, or you can record each group as they present to their classmates.

8. As homework, ask students to create a reel themselves from scratch with a short dialogue/monologue. Alternatively, assign students to create a monologue or dialogue for another existing reel.

CAVEATS AND OPTIONS

- Choose video shorts or reels that fit the age of your students. For example, animal-themed reels represent a good choice for younger students, middle school students might enjoy magic tricks, and teenagers and adults may enjoy short videos about relationships and sports (see Appendix B for more suggested reels).

- As an alternative to nonverbal reels, use videos with dialogue and ask students to create a similar video themselves.

- Adapt the activity to expand on a particular topic discussed in class by having students create a short dialogue to go with a chosen reel.

- Adapt the activity for a grammar class by asking students to incorporate a certain structure in their dialogues, such as imperative verbs, *if* clauses, or past tense.

- Adapt the activity to focus on pronunciation elements such as intonation, word stress (i.e., contrastive/emphatic), and other features of spoken language.

- Ask students to peer review their classmates' performance or to self-assess their performance by watching it later and finding elements they can improve.

REFERENCES AND FURTHER READING

Ansari, J. A. N., & Khan, N. A. (2020). Exploring the role of social media in collaborative learning the new domain of learning. *Smart Learning Environments, 7*(1), 1–16. https://doi.org/10.1186/s40561-020-00118-7

FOYSAL VLOG YT [@foysalvlogyt7546]. (2023, February 4). *Assistance dog sigma* 👀 [Video]. Instagram. https://www.youtube.com/shorts/DuqNHbCpXOc

Ghounane, N. (2020). Moodle or social networks: What alternative refuge is appropriate to Algerian EFL students to learn during COVID-19 pandemic. *Arab World English Journal, 11*, 21–41. http://dx.doi.org/10.31235/osf.io/hzs3r

LaBelle, D. (2022, August 30). *Don't let the ball touch the ground* [Video]. YouTube. https://www.youtube.com/watch?v=MdYUb7CTSl4

Sarangapani, S., & Hashim, H. (2022). "InstaGrammar!" Incorporating Instagram reel to enhance English as a second language learners' grammatical accuracy. *Creative Education, 13*(6), 1965–1980. http://dx.doi.org/10.4236/ce.2022.136122

Therrien, TJ. (2022, July 29). *How your kids wash the car* [Video]. YouTube. https://www.youtube.com/shorts/IKsddIGXixQ

Zach King Compilations. (2023, February 11). *He didn't see this coming* [Video]. YouTube. https://www.youtube.com/shorts/QgF4PafuJJE

Zach King Compilations. (2023, February 13). *If only it was this easy to start the morning* [Video]. YouTube. https://www.youtube.com/shorts/9TiUML4YTP8

APPENDIX A: *Reel With Invented Dialogue*

Nonverbal Reel

"Assistance dog sigma 👀" (FOYSAL VLOG YT, 2023; www.youtube.com/shorts/DuqNHbCpXOc)

Sample Dialogue Created in Class

Trainer:	Let me measure you.
Dog:	Yes, ma'am.
Trainer:	Oh, your height is not good enough.
Dog:	I can lift my ear.
Trainer:	I guess. You can go in.
Storyteller:	This is how Buddy, our dog, starts training at the Canine University.
Dog:	I hope I can help her through the obstacles. Oh, no. She fell. How embarrassing.
Trainer:	Time to eat.
Dog:	Oh, I pressed the wrong button. I made a mess. It's so mortifying.
Storyteller:	The dog repeatedly fails during training, making his teacher fall. But despite this, he wants to succeed and is determined to work harder. He learns how to serve himself and help his trainer through the obstacles. Finally, exam day arrives.
Examiner:	Buddy, it's your turn.
Dog:	I am determined to do my best.

Trainer:	Oh, I'm hurt again.
Examiner:	Get out. You are not fit for this job.
Storyteller:	Buddy was crying when suddenly he saw a blind woman walking through a construction site. He ran, grabbed her purse around his neck, and helped her cross the street safely.
Woman:	Thank you, doggy. You saved my life.
Other dogs:	Buddy, come here! We saw you! You did an amazing job!
Examiner:	You deserve to be an assistance dog. Congratulations, graduate!

APPENDIX B: *Examples of Reels or Short Videos Based on Age Groups*

Middle School

- "How your kids wash the car" (Therrien, 2022; www.youtube.com/shorts/IKsddIGXixQ)
- "Don't Let the Ball Touch the Ground" (LaBelle, 2022; www.youtube.com/watch?v=MdYUb7CTSI4)

Primary School

- "He didn't see this coming" (Zach King Compilations, 2023; www.youtube.com/shorts/QgF4PafuJJE)

Secondary School

- "If only it was this easy to start the morning" (Zach King Compilations, 2023; www.youtube.com/shorts/9TiUML4YTP8)

Using a Queer-Themed Television Ad for Sexuality and Visual Literacy Engagement

Cris Delatado Barabas

Levels	High intermediate to advanced
Ages Suitable for Activity	Secondary
Aims	Identify basic features of a television ad
	Infer an ad's messages and themes
	Evaluate an ad's effectiveness and target audience responses
Class Time	90–100 minutes
Preparation Time	15–20 minutes
Resources	Video: "How Long Can You Keep a Secret?" (Bench, 2018; www.youtube.com/watch?v=Mw_gHMNs5iE)
	Laptop and projector

There are now various calls (Barabas & Jiang, 2022; Moore et al., 2024) to incorporate queer sexuality literacies in language and literacy education classes. One of the best ways to do this is to take advantage of mass media, particularly television ads that promote inclusivity and gender diversity. Conversations on queer inclusivity are evident in the global north context, but these topics are rarely addressed in the global south. For this activity, students will engage with a television ad produced in the Philippines that embraces gender inclusivity. Students will acquire the skills to critically and actively decode the messages of the ad, reflect and argue on the relevance of the ad's message in today's social and political climate, and understand how corporations leverage social issues and calls for inclusion in order to market their brands.

PROCEDURE

1. Ask learners to talk about a recent television ad that caught their attention or has created an impact on viewers. Elicit why they thought the ad was effective, guiding the discussion to factors like the ad's striking features, intended audience, clear message, and context of production.

2. To induce critical thinking, ask learners to think of certain social issues they think are embedded in the ad, especially when talking about its message or content.

3. Tell learners the title of the ad you will be showing them. Describe the ad or show the opening thumbnail image.

4. Before viewing, ask learners if they have seen this particular ad before, and if so, what their impression of the ad was. For classes outside the Philippines, you may ask the students to infer what the content of the ad is, based on the title given.

5. Discuss story elements as a class (i.e., plot, characters, setting, conflict, and emotions).

6. Play the ad. Then, divide the class into pairs and have them identify and discuss how the various story elements are shown in the ad.

7. As a whole class, ask learners what the most significant part of the ad was. Also, ask them why this part was important in conveying the message of the ad.

8. Return learners to their pairs and ask them to focus on the ad's language use. Play the ad again for this part of the activity.

   a. The ad's language is bilingual, a mixture of English and Filipino. Instruct learners to infer why the producers opted to use these two languages.

   b. Ask the students to identify words and phrases that were striking and ask them to explain how these conveyed emotions.

   c. *Note*: If an ad from another context is used, ask students to discuss the language(s) used, the varieties of tones, and code-mixing, if any.

9. Draw the learners' attention to notice how at the end of the ad, the father wrote *Amoy kita*, which can be literally translated to *I smell you*. The note was placed under the perfume bottle. Ask the students to explain its significance and how this choice is important to the product being advertised. Teachers should also point out that the phrase *amoy kita* indicates the father's awareness that his son is queer.

   a. For mixed-language groups, learners could be asked to create phrases to go with selected scenes.

   b. For ads from different contexts, perhaps you may ask students if there are any phrases or utterances that seem to imply knowledge of one's sexuality.

10. Provide the YouTube link to the students and ask them to open the ad on their devices and read the comments. Ask them to deduce how the ad was perceived by the commenters and prompt them to judge or evaluate the effectiveness of the material based on these comments.

11. To close the activity, divide learners into small groups to discuss the following higher level questions:

    a. How does the ad convey or defy perceived cultural values? What can we learn about the nature of values based on this ad?

    b. How do companies leverage social issues to market their brands and products? How is this done in this particular ad?

    c. How is queerness portrayed in this ad? Are there any stereotypes shown?

    d. How is masculinity portrayed by the three male characters? How do you think culture shaped these portrayals?

CAVEATS AND OPTIONS

- Adapt the activity for your learning context and your learners' backgrounds via your choice of television ad.

- Adapt the discussion questions, for example, by asking for personal responses from the students such as their own attitudes toward queerness.

- Extend the activity by having learners write an elevator pitch about the role of companies in promoting inclusivity, providing examples from their own local context. If assigning this, introduce or scaffold the elevator pitch text type to help learners develop genre awareness.

- Extend the activity by organizing a debate. Divide the class into two groups to debate the following motion: "The portrayal of queerness in advertising is not a genuine reflection of inclusion but rather an exploitation of identity."

- Assign students to write a reflection paper discussing the topic of queerness. They can be specifically asked to express their views on queer identities, issues of inclusion, diversity, and representation of these identities in media.

- Extend the activity by showing another ad from a different company (and product) that includes a portrayal of queer identity. In the discussion, ask students to compare how the same issue is conveyed similarly or differently.

- Show a similar ad from the Global North context for comparison. Anchor the discussion and further activities on cultural differences and similarities in messaging.

REFERENCES AND FURTHER READING

Barabas, C. D., & Jiang, Q. (2022). Queering a high school literature class in China: Teacher's and student's reflections. *TESOL Journal*, *13*(4). https://doi.org/10.1002/tesj.671

BENCH. (2018, February 19). *How long can you keep a secret?* [Video]. YouTube. www.youtube.com/watch?v=Mw_gHMNs5iE

Moore, A. R., Coda, J., Spiegelman, J. D., & Cahnmann-Taylor, M. (2024). Queer breaches and normative devices: Language learners queering gender, sexuality, and the L2 classroom. *International Journal of Bilingual Education and Bilingualism*, *27*(5), 675–688. https://doi.org/10.1080/13670050.2024.2306398

Visual Collaborative Boards

Daniela Dascalita Ortiz

Levels	All
Ages Suitable for Activity	Secondary to adult
Aims	Integrate visual elements to present steps in a process
	Offer clear oral explanations that align with the visual content
	Use word connectors to show transitions from one step to another
	Develop video production skills
	Provide and receive constructive feedback from peers
Class Time	2 class periods of 20–50 minutes
Preparation Time	15 minutes
Resources	Video: "How to Change a Tire" (How To, 2022; www.youtube.com/shorts/5ypnZDl7whc)
	Devices for students to create video recordings (i.e., tablets or smartphones)
	Assessment rubric (Appendix)
	Laptop and projector

This activity transforms written discussion boards into visual collaborative boards where students can engage with peers' speeches and provide constructive feedback. This taps into the popularity of visual content creation, mirroring social media platforms which are full of instructional and explanatory videos. By integrating visual elements with words, students can learn to communicate processes clearly and creatively, enhancing both their visual literacy and oral proficiency. The process of selecting the best shots and rehearsing multiple times encourages students to refine their speaking and presenting skills. Adding a peer feedback component can also foster a supportive class environment.

PROCEDURE

1. Before this class session, create an account at Padlet (padlet.com), a visual collaboration platform. Padlet has a free subscription level for which teachers can sign up without requiring a credit card.

2. Introduce the concept of a visual collaborative board to students. Explain that it is a digital space where students can upload their videos and benefit from feedback from their peers and instructors.

3. Explain to students that they will create videos explaining steps in a process, then upload their videos to a collaborative board online.

4. Divide students into groups and ask them to brainstorm possible ideas they could use for their videos. After 2–3 minutes, compile a list on the board of the different ideas. Here are a few ideas:

    a.   how to cook a traditional recipe

    b.   how to fix something in a car (i.e., change a tire)

    c.   how to do a hobby or play a sport

    d.   how to spot a liar

    e.   how to have fun without money

5. Play the video ("How to Change a Tire") to exemplify what you would like them to create. (If you choose a different sample video, make sure that it is no longer than 2–3 minutes.) Ask students to comment on the video:

    a.   What elements did they like?

    b.   What would they change to make it better?

    c.   How did the visual aspect help understand what was being said?

6. Pair up students who expressed similar interests during brainstorming. Ask them to collaborate in creating their own video. Although they will create this as homework, offer class time for them to agree on the tools, space, and time they need to record their videos. Be clear about the components the video-recorded speech needs to have:

    a.   Give an introduction.

    b.   Explain why this process is important.

    c.   Demonstrate a step-by-step explanation with connectors (e.g., first, next, finally).

    d.   Use visual supports, such as simple props, diagrams, or images, to convey information clearly.

    e.   Give a summary or share final thoughts on the process.

7. Offer students the flexibility to record their videos in one single shot or to film several clips they can edit together into a final video. Explain that you don't expect perfection, but that the images should be clearly combined with oral explanations of what is presented.

8. Introduce students to Padlet and demonstrate how they will upload their videos to your visual collaborative board.

9. After all videos are uploaded, assign each student to watch one or two peer videos to watch and provide feedback, as homework. Ensure each video will receive peer feedback. Offer clear guidelines on how to provide constructive feedback. Have students use the structure of praise, question, suggest:

    a.   Give a positive comment about a specific part of the video.

    b.   Ask a clarifying question about something you might not have understood well.

    c.   Suggest one aspect for improvement.

10. During the next class period, celebrate your students' work by watching all the videos together. You could even give awards by highlighting what students did best or by asking the class to vote for different categories. Here are some ideas: the funniest video, the best edited one, the best explained one, the most creative presentation, the most liked overall, etc.

CAVEATS AND OPTIONS

- Adapt this activity for various themes or genres of video relevant to your learning goals, such as research presentations, inspirational speeches, or explanations of grammar points.

- Ask students to incorporate certain grammar structures in their presentations: imperative, present perfect, modal verbs.

- Adapt this activity as a quick 15-minute warm-up: Have students use their smartphones to record a simple process on the spot and then upload the videos for all to see.

- Offer students a scoring rubric (see Appendix) before they record their videos so that students understand your expectations.

REFERENCES AND FURTHER READING

Alharbi, M. (2015). Effects of Blackboard's discussion boards, blogs and wikis on effective integration and development of literacy skills in EFL students. *English Language Teaching, 8*(6), 111–132.

Ho, E. (2022). Online peer review of oral presentations. *RELC Journal, 53*(3), 712–722.

How To. (2022, May 27). *How to change a tire* [Video]. YouTube. www.youtube.com/shorts/5ypnZDI7whc

Li, F., & Liu, Y. (2018). Can using a discussion-board enhance writing practice for EAP/ESL students? *Theory and Practice in Language Studies, 8*(5), 467–474.

Mendoza, L. E. (2019). Discussion boards as a culturally responsive tool in the ESL classroom. *Research on Education and Media, 11*(2), 29–37.

Razawi, N. A., Zulkornain, L. H., and Razlan, R. M. (2019). Anxiety in oral presentations among ESL students. *Journal of Academia, 7*(1), 31–36.

Tazijan, F. N., Ab Rahim, S., Abdul Halim, F. S., Abdullah, A., Ismail, I. N., & Cochrane, T. A. (2012). Implementing a virtual presentation program in ESL classrooms. *International Journal of e-Education, e-Business, e-Management and e-Learning 2*(3), 218–222.

APPENDIX: Rubric for Describing Steps in a Process

Criteria	Excellent (5)	Proficient (4)	Adequate (3)	Needs Improvement (2)	Inadequate (1)
Language Mechanics	The presenter shows an exceptional command of English, using advanced vocabulary and accurate grammar.	The presenter shows a strong command of English, using varied vocabulary and mostly accurate grammar. The minor errors do not hinder understanding.	The presenter has some grammar and sentence structure but remains understandable. Vocabulary is basic but sufficient.	Frequent grammar and sentence structure errors make parts of the presentation unclear. Vocabulary is limited or repetitive.	Significant grammar errors make the presentation difficult to follow. Vocabulary is limited or incorrect, leading to confusion.
Content	The steps of the process are articulated with exceptional clarity, making it easy for the audience to follow. The presenter effectively uses transition words and sequencing language.	The steps of the process are explained clearly, with good use of transition words and sequencing language, ensuring a coherent and understandable presentation.	The explanation of the steps is generally clear, but there may be occasional lapses in clarity due to a lack of transition words or sequencing language.	The explanation lacks clarity, with limited use of transition words and sequencing language, making it challenging for the audience to follow.	The presentation is confusing and the steps of the process are not effectively communicated, leading to significant comprehension issues.
Visual Support	The visuals are exceptionally well chosen and effectively enhance the understanding of the steps. Visuals are clear, relevant, and thoughtfully integrated into the presentation.	The visuals are well chosen and contribute to the understanding of the steps. They are generally clear and relevant but may lack some detail.	Visuals are present and provide basic support for the explanation, but they may be somewhat generic or lack clarity.	Visuals are limited, unclear, or irrelevant, providing minimal support for the explanation of the steps.	Visuals are absent or completely irrelevant, hindering rather than aiding in the understanding of the process.
Pronunciation	The student's pronunciation is clear and accurate with excellent use of stress and intonation.	Pronunciation is generally clear with minor errors that do not impede comprehension. Intonation and stress are mostly correct.	Pronunciation is understandable but contains several noticeable errors. Intonation and stress are inconsistent but do not greatly affect understanding.	Frequent pronunciation errors make some parts of the presentation hard to understand. Intonation and stress are often incorrect or missing.	Pronunciation is unclear, with many errors that significantly hinder understanding. Intonation and stress are largely absent or incorrect.

Part III

Social Media

Introduction: The Role of Social Media as a Gateway to Visual Literacy

In the modern world, social media has become an essential tool not just for social interaction, but also for language learning. For multilingual learners of English (MLEs) of all ages, social media platforms offer authentic, engaging, and interactive resources that support the development of both linguistic knowledge and visual literacy. These platforms are a rich source of multimodal content. Combining text, images, and video, they allow MLEs to immerse themselves in real-world language usage while enhancing their understanding of how language and visuals work together.

Social media's role in fostering visual literacy is crucial in today's media-saturated environment. Visual literacy (the ability to interpret, negotiate, and create meaning from images, videos, and other visual media) has become essential for effective communication. Platforms like Instagram, TikTok, and Twitter incorporate images, videos, and memes, all of which convey meaning through both verbal and nonverbal cues. By engaging with these types of content, MLEs gain a deeper understanding of how visuals complement and reinforce language. For instance, memes—one of the key elements discussed in the activities ahead—serve as a perfect example of how visual and textual elements work together to convey humor, cultural context, and social commentary.

This connection between social media and visual literacy is explored further in the activity "Creating a Digital Multilanguage Meme" by Alexandra Krasova. Memes, defined by Shifman (2014) as multimodal texts, reflect cultural jokes and messages that can be transmitted through the internet. Krasova's activity encourages students to create memes that blend multiple languages, thus promoting multilingualism, translanguaging, and cultural expression. Through this creative process, learners not only develop their language skills but also enhance their ability to decode and create meaning from visual content.

Moreover, activities that engage with social media can help to foster critical thinking and empathy, such as in "Deconstructing Physicality" by Zhi Qi Wendy Chen. This activity examines media portrayals of body image and encourages students to reflect on the ways in which social media can shape perceptions of physical attractiveness. By creating and analyzing TikTok videos with and without filters, learners are prompted to engage critically with visual media and explore its impact on societal norms. This activity not only enhances MLEs' ability to interpret media messages but also encourages them to recognize the power dynamics embedded within digital platforms.

In "Create a Graph Meme" by Katherine Miller, learners use humor and visual content to interpret and represent numerical data, connecting the language of graphs with the humor found in memes. This activity highlights the potential of memes as tools for language learning, helping students practice vocabulary and conceptual understanding while engaging in a fun, creative activity that reinforces both linguistic knowledge and visual literacy.

Through these and the other activities in this section, social media serves as a dynamic and multifaceted tool for English language teaching. The activities provide opportunities to engage with authentic language and multimodal content, fostering both language acquisition and visual literacy. By integrating platforms like TikTok, Instagram, and meme creation apps into language instruction, educators can create immersive learning experiences that prepare students for a world where language and visuals are inseparable components of communication.

REFERENCES AND FURTHER READING

Davidson, P. (2012). The language of internet memes. In M. Maniberg (Ed.), *The social media reader* (pp. 120–134). New York University.

Learning for Justice. (2009). *Beauty is skin deep.* https://www.learningforjustice.org/classroom-resources/lessons/beauty-is-skin-deep

Shifman, L. (2014). *Memes in digital culture.* MIT.

Create a Graph Meme

Katherine Miller

Levels	All
Ages Suitable for Activity	Secondary to adult
Aims	Understand how graphs display information
	Read and interpret information presented in a graph
	Use target vocabulary
Class Time	30–45 minutes
Preparation Time	10 minutes
Resources	Example memes (Appendix)
	Paper
	Markers

emes are the currency of shared humor in a digital landscape. Though many multilingual learners of English may not yet be proficient in reading and writing academic paragraphs, the short and comical nature of memes lends itself to quick, digestible bites of information that can be created and understood in a short time. Here, learners work independently or in pairs to create a meme from a graph to show their understanding of 1) how graphs display numerical data and 2) how data can be interpreted to humorous effect.

PROCEDURE

1. Ask the class if they know what a meme is and if they can share an example. In case they cannot, be prepared with a few of your own to share. Choose three to four memes appropriate for your students' age and level from your own social media feed or from an online search.

2. Next, review how different types of graphs are used to display information visually.

   a. Elicit from learners the different types of graphs they know about (e.g., pie, line, bar, Venn) and elicit what kind of information each type can display.

3. Discuss the examples of graph memes (see Appendix):

   a. Hand out printed copies of the example memes, or project them on a screen.

   b. Have learners read the captions out loud. Explain any references or vocabulary that might be unfamiliar to the class.

   c. Working in pairs or as a whole class, ask learners to explain why each graph is funny or silly.

   d. Discuss how each graph uses scale to make its point (e.g., the height of the bars, the size of the slices of the pie, the shape of the line).

   e. Have learners rate each meme on a scale of 1 to 5 by holding their fingers up in the air: One finger means the meme is not funny at all, and five fingers means it's hilarious.

4. Give the learners paper and markers, and have them draw and caption their own graph meme. They can describe a silly situation in their everyday life, a topic in the news, or a connection to the course content.

5. Conduct a gallery walk where students display their finished memes and the classmates walk around the room to have a look. After the gallery walk, ask students to give feedback on what they liked about each one.

CAVEATS AND OPTIONS

-   You can adapt the activity as follows:
    -   For beginners, use this activity to support vocabulary for daily routines, for example, and ask students to use a humorous example from their own life.
    -   For an advanced English literature class, have students create graphs about a book or short story they are reading, including the characters, conflict, or the author's style choices.
-   Use example memes that are age-appropriate in both language and content.
-   Instead of paper and markers, have students use a computer program such as Microsoft Excel or Google Slides to create their graphs digitally.

APPENDIX: *Example Graph Memes*

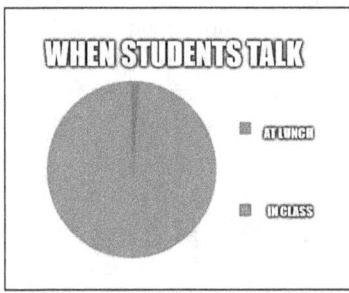 

Image credit: Katherine Miller. Used with permission.

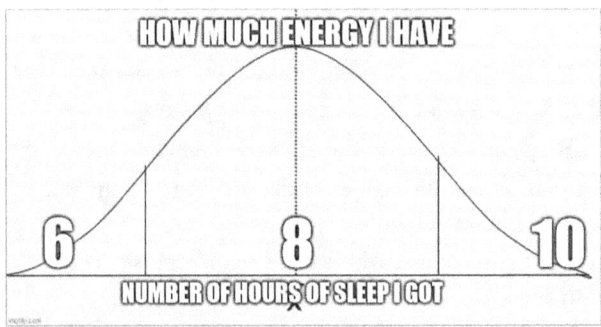

Image credit: Katherine Miller. Used with permission.

Time spent as a mother

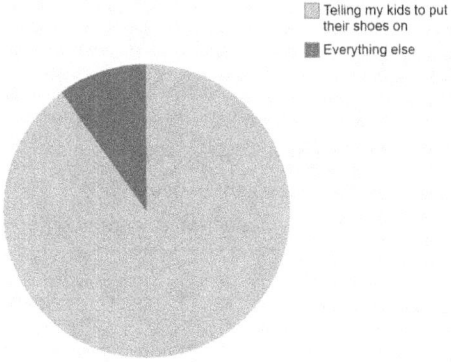

Image credit: Katherine Miller. Used with permission.

Watching TV

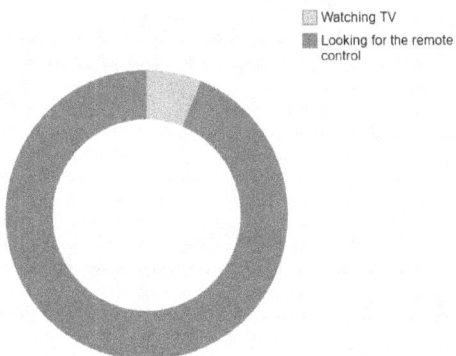

Image credit: Katherine Miller. Used with permission.

Creating a Digital Multilanguage Meme

Alexandra Krasova

Levels	All
Ages Suitable for Activity	Any
Aims	Develop multimodal digital literacy
	Encourage multilingualism
	Promote translanguaging
	Facilitate multicultural understanding
Class Time	45–50 minutes
Preparation Time	5–10 minutes
Resources	Example of a meme (Appendix)
	Access to the internet on laptops or tablets
	Laptop and projector

Shifman (2014) defines memes as multimodal texts that "reflect deep social and cultural structures" (p. 15). From another lens, Davidson (2012) describes memes as cultural jokes that can be transmitted through the internet. This activity promotes learners' creativity and helps to construct multilingual identity by asking students to mix the languages they know and express their cultural backgrounds. Students can work individually, in pairs, or groups to create a meme.

PROCEDURE

1. Discuss what kind of memes students like and what their favorite ones are. Ask them to share popular memes from their countries and explain their meaning.

2. Show students an example of a meme without a caption (Appendix A).

3. Put students in small groups or pairs to discuss the following questions:

   a. What is their first impressions of the image?

   b. What do they see in the picture?

   c. What message is the meme is trying to convey?

   d. Can they relate to the message?

4. Lead an open class discussion about why this picture is funny, who the target audience is, and what might the purpose of this meme be.

5. Ask groups/pairs to create a short caption to accompany the image. Students may use their home languages or other languages they know. Let them mix those languages.

6. Ask groups/pairs to share their captions. Discuss students' responses and allow groups/pairs to explain the meaning of the text they added.

7. Now ask students to create their own memes online using Make a Meme.org (makeameme.org). They can work in pairs or individually. Students must mix

the languages they know, including their home languages, in their captions. This promotes their self-expression and provides an opportunity to demonstrate their cultural backgrounds.

8. Allow students to present their memes to the class. You can have learners post their memes to a shared discussion blog, upload to your learning management system, or contribute to a shared Google Doc.

9. Project each meme for the whole class. As each group presents their meme, ask the other students if they can determine the meaning of memes captioned in unfamiliar languages. Ask if (and how) the image helps them determine the meaning of unknown words. Let the creators of the memes confirm or explain.

10. Ask the class to vote on their favorite meme and discuss the reasons.

CAVEATS AND OPTIONS

- For lower level students, adapt this activity by doing the activity together as a class.
- For higher level students, use this as a prewriting activity for a written reflection on multimodal experiences.
- For a shorter class, use only the first part of the activity or ask students to create memes at home.

REFERENCES AND FURTHER READING

Davison, P. (2012). The language of internet memes. In M. Maniberg (Ed.), *The social media reader* (pp. 120–134). New York University.

Shifman, L. (2014). *Memes in digital culture.* MIT.

APPENDIX: *Sample Meme Image*

Image credit: Alexandra Krasova. Used with permission.

Creating a Meme

Susan Iannuzzi

Levels	All
Ages Suitable for Activity	Any
Aims	Develop noticing and observation skills
	Encourage critical thinking and creative response
	Respond verbally to visual input
	Develop cultural and social awareness
Class Time	10–45 minutes
Preparation Time	0–10 minutes
Resources	Sample meme images (Appendix)

According to Davison (2012), a meme is "a piece of culture, typically a joke, which gains influence through online transmission" (p. 122). Memes appeal to different users because they draw on different resources, such as references to pop culture, current events, and political issues (Wells, 2018). When memes contain both image and text, individuals must connect their meanings, which may be contradictory. This activity promotes learners' creativity by asking them to develop text to accompany an image that could become a meme. Learners work individually or in groups to craft a meme that comments on something they find interesting or humorous.

PROCEDURE

1. Ask the class to share some of their favorite memes. Be prepared with examples from your own social media feeds or other websites, such as Giphy (www.giphy.com).

2. Elicit the meanings of your example memes, accepting all possible answers.

3. Ask learners to explain the relationship between the visuals and the text of your example memes.

4. Elicit why learners think these memes are funny or thought provoking. Accept all possible answers.

5. Show the meme art of the monkeys in the car (see Appendix) to the class.

6. Put learners in groups to discuss what they can see in the photograph. Ask them to be as descriptive as possible.

7. Elicit their descriptions, continuing discussion until there are no new observations. For example, students could respond with any of the following:

   a. There are two different kinds of apes.

   b. The chimpanzee is in the driver's seat, but it seems to be confused or worried about something.

   c. The other ape in the passenger seat appears to look confused or sleepy.

   d. The car appears to be an old model. Its windshield wipers and mirror do not look modern.

   e. The background is an urban environment.

8. As a class, discuss what is funny, strange, or thought provoking about the photograph.

9. Give groups time to think of a short text to accompany the image. Elicit answers from the groups. Write them on the board.

10. Check that all learners understand the meanings of the texts on the board. Allow other groups to explain or correct for their classmates.

11. Ask the class to vote on their favorite caption.

CAVEATS AND OPTIONS

- Adapt this activity for a younger age or lower level by doing the activity as a whole class.
- Use this activity as a 10-minute short warm-up.
- Extend it to a full-length class by using all the meme photographs provided in the Appendix.
- Extend the learning by having groups share their memes and comment on each other's ideas.
- Ask students to find their own image and add text to it to create a new meme.

REFERENCES AND FURTHER READING

Davison, P. (2012). The language of internet memes. In M. Maniberg (Ed.), *The social media reader* (pp. 120–134). New York University.

Wells, D. (2018). You all made dank memes: Using internet memes to promote critical thinking. *Journal of Political Science Education, 14*(2), 240–248.

APPENDIX: *Sample Meme Images*

Image credit: Sam Williams from Pixabay.

Image credit: Sam Williams from Pixabay.

Image credit: Sam Williams from Pixabay.

Image credit: Sam Williams from Pixabay.

Deconstructing Gender Stereotyping, Expectations, and Demands

Zhi Qi Wendy Chen

Levels	High intermediate to high advanced
Ages Suitable for Activity	Secondary, adult, preservice teachers
Aims	Understand how gender stereotypes are perpetuated in the media
	Communicate and collaborate in a confident and creative way
	Develop skills in interpretation, analysis, and evaluation
	Develop an understanding of relationships between media texts and a variety of perspectives, cultural contexts, and global issues
Class Time	1 hour 50 minutes
Preparation Time	10–20 minutes
Resources	Video shorts displaying gender stereotypes, expectations, and demands (Appendix A)
	Discussion prompts (Appendix B)
	Think, pair, share prompts (Appendix C)
	Google Docs for brainstorming (see Step 1)
	Laptop and projector
	Access to the internet on laptops or tablets

ender stereotype theory suggests that men are generally perceived as more masculine than women, whereas women are generally perceived as more feminine than men (Kachel et al., 2016). Gender is also one of the first social categories that children learn in today's societies. Thus, knowledge of gender stereotypes is evident early on, and it continues to be learned from childhood into adulthood. In this activity, students will analyze concepts of self in line with internalized gender stereotypes.

PROCEDURE

1. Before the activity, prepare six different Google Docs to share with student groups. Title each document with one of the following questions:

   a. **School:** How do schools set expectations/demands on gender?

   b. **Workplace:** How does the workplace set expectations/demands on gender?

   c. **Family:** How do families set expectations/demands on gender?

   d. **Partner:** How do romantic partners set expectations/demands on gender?

   e. **Friend:** How do friends set expectations/demands on gender?

   f. **Society:** How does society set expectations/demands on gender? *Note:* This includes media, the internet, and people/places that aren't schools, workplaces, families, romantic partners, or friends.

2. To begin the activity, play several short video clips from social media that portray gender expectations (see Appendix A for suggestions).

   a. After each video, give students 5 seconds to decide whether the artifacts shown in the videos represent masculine or feminine stereotypes.

   b. Poll students by asking them to raise one hand for "masculine" or two hands for "feminine," or through an online polling app if all students have access to mobile devices. (It's likely that students will agree on most of the videos.)

3. Put students into small groups, and have groups consider the following prompts:

   a. Why do you think there was so much agreement?

   b. Where do these ideas come from?

   c. Is it true that these are just feminine or masculine things?

   d. Where are these answers coming from?

4. After 10–15 minutes of discussion, tell groups to brainstorm the different expectations toward and demands on girls/young women and boys/young men in contemporary society.

5. Divide students into six groups. Share one Google Doc from Step 1 with each group and ask them to list as many demands/expectations on girls/young women and boys/young men as they can think of in their given contexts (i.e., school, workplace, family, partner, friend, or society).

6. After completing their list on the Google Doc, hand out or project the discussion prompts from Appendix B.

   a. Tell groups to read the questions, then use them to examine and analyze their list of demands/expectations.

   b. Explain that their discussion will be guided by the following two concepts. Give examples of each and check for comprehension:

      i. *Figured world*: A *figured world* is a shared way of understanding how things work in a certain setting. It reflects what people see as normal or typical, and it is based on culture, background, and experiences. Consider how a person's figured world would affect the gender demands/expectations they experience.

      ii. *Conceptual Understanding #4 from the Critical Media Literacy Framework*: "Media have embedded values and points of view."

   c. Explain that they will have 30 minutes and that one person will report back on their discussion to the whole class.

   d. Circulate to monitor and support.

7. After 30–40 minutes, or when groups have finished their discussions, bring all students to sit in a big circle. Ask each group to report briefly on their discussion. Invite students to take notes on their thoughts and emotional responses to their classmates' presentations.

8. As a final debriefing and evaluation, put students in pairs and have them complete four rounds of think, pair, share conversations using the prompts from Appendix C.

CAVEATS AND OPTIONS

- Please take the time to answer the question prompts in this activity yourself before guiding students through this inquiry process.

- Practice and nurture a spirit of self-reflection to heighten self-awareness of your own pedagogies and political assumptions as a critical media literacy educator. This self-reflection prepares you to face complex situations that may arise during/after this activity, such as unexpected meaning-making from students, a shift in social roles in the classroom (i.e., the teacher becoming the learner), or heightened scrutiny from parents or administrators due to community context around gender expectations.

- To adapt this activity for a shorter class period, ask students to answer the prompts in Appendix C individually at home in a reflective journal activity. Alternatively, to retain the benefit of having students reflect together as a group, assign them to answer the prompts asynchronously in your class's online discussion forum.

REFERENCES AND FURTHER READING

ActuallyRandomPerson. (2022, January 7). *How to use Tumblr* [Video]. YouTube. https://www.youtube.com/watch?v=K-svwX764-g

FutureProofTV. (2022, December 30). *The TRUE COST of a hydro flask #shorts* [Video]. YouTube. https://www.youtube.com/shorts/WpOfa8nDb3g

Gee, J. P. (2010). *How to do discourse analysis: A toolkit.* Routledge.

He Spoke Style. (2019, May 23). *3 different types of suits | off the rack, made to measure, bespoke* [Video]. YouTube. https://youtu.be/MxucYV17jeo

Howfinity. (2020, December 16). *How to use Pinterest - complete beginner's guide* [Video]. YouTube. https://www.youtube.com/watch?v=QVWDeIfYOK4

Joy of Gaming. (2022, April 30). *(PS5) gran turismo 7 is beautiful - ferrari 458 italia gameplay | realistic graphics [4K HDR 60FPS]* [Video]. YouTube. https://www.youtube.com/watch?v=s1NENhRDb6c

Joy of Gaming. (2022, July 20). *(PS5) stray is the best game of all2022... | ultra realistic graphics gameplay [4K HDR 60 FPS]* [Video]. YouTube. https://www.youtube.com/watch?v=-ogpWD5BZc8

Kachel, S., Steffens, M. C., & Niedlich, C. (2016). Traditional masculinity and femininity: Validation of a new scale assessing gender roles. *Frontiers in Psychology, 7,* Article 956. https://doi.org/10.3389/fpsyg.2016.00956

Ridge [@ridge]. (2023). *Not a reenactment #ridgewallet #dailyessentials #dailyaccessories #fyp* [Video]. TikTok. https://www.tiktok.com/@theridgewallet/video/7214268668035976494

Share, J., & Thoman, E. (2007). *Teaching democracy: A media literacy approach.* National Center for the Preservation of Democracy. https://www.academia.edu/26709676/Teaching_Democracy_A_Media_Literacy_Approach

Taquero [@taquero10]. (2023, January 29). *Taquero* [Video]. TikTok. https://www.tiktok.com/@taquero10/video/7193745493439106347

Throneful. (2019, December 22). *SUPERHOT gameplay (PC HD) [1080p60fps]* [Video]. YouTube. https://www.youtube.com/watch?v=9KDxMbKWw5g

TikTok Finds. (2022, March 8). *Beautiful dresses on TikTok* [Video]. YouTube. https://www.youtube.com/watch?v=OqC4XtGhNeU

APPENDIX A: *Example Gender-Biased Video Clips*

- "How to use Tumblr" (ActuallyRandomPerson, 2022; www.youtube.com/watch?v=K-svwX764-g)
- "The TRUE COST of a hydro flask #shorts" (FutureProofTV, 2022; www.youtube.com/shorts/WpOfa8nDb3g)
- "3 different types of suits | off the rack, made to measure, bespoke" (He Spoke Style, 2019; youtu.be/MxucYV17jeo)
- "How to use Pinterest - complete beginner's guide" (Howfinity, 2020; www.youtube.com/watch?v=QVWDelfYOK4)
- "(PS5) gran turismo 7 is beautiful - ferrari 458 italia gameplay | realistic graphics [4K HDR 60FPS]" (Joy of Gaming, 2022; www.youtube.com/watch?v=s1NENhRDb6c)
- "(PS5) stray is the best game of all2022... | ultra realistic graphics gameplay [4K HDR 60 FPS]" (Joy of Gaming, 2022; www.youtube.com/watch?v=-ogpWD5BZc8)
- "Taquero" (Taquero [@taquero10], 2023; https://www.tiktok.com/@taquero10/video/7193745493439106347)
- "Not a reenactment #ridgewallet #dailyessentials #dailyaccessories #fyp" (Ridge [@ridge], 2023; www.tiktok.com/@theridgewallet/video/7214268668035976494)
- "Beautiful dresses on TikTok" (TikTok Finds, 2022; www.youtube.com/watch?v=OqC4XtGhNeU)

APPENDIX B: *Discussion Prompts*

1. Do the items on your list of gender demands/expectations relate to each other? Why or why not?
2. Do the items listed belong to one figured world, or multiple? Describe the figured world of each member of your group and categorize the items on your list accordingly.
3. After categorizing the items on your list, how are people portrayed in each category? What kinds of behaviors or consequences are depicted?
4. Are there any political or economic ideas that come through in each group of items?
5. What judgements or statements are being made about how to treat other people?
6. What perspectives are left out? How can you add to each category?
7. What did you learn from the experience of the other members of your group?

APPENDIX C: *Questions for Think, Pair, Share*

Round 1

- How did you find the exercise? How did you feel during the exercise?
- Was it easy to identify gender expectations in the first part of the activity?
- Where do people's gender expectations come from? Who establishes them?

Round 2

- Is it easy for boys and girls (or young men and young women) to fulfill these expectations? If not, what are the difficulties?
- Who helps to promote these expectations?
- How do we ourselves promote them (whether consciously or unconsciously)?

Round 3

(Optional. Students may feel uncomfortable sharing the following with a classmate. If so, have students reflect on the following questions individually.)

- Have you ever felt pressured by gender expectations? If so, how did it feel? How did you react?
- Have you ever pressured others to conform to gender expectations? If so, how do you think it made those others feel?
- Have you ever challenged gender expectations or norms? If so, how was your challenge taken? Were there any consequences?

Round 4

- Can gender expectations or demands violate human rights? In what way?
- How can individuals work to address damaging gender stereotypes and expectations?
- What could be done to promote gender equality among young people?

Deconstructing Physicality

Zhi Qi Wendy Chen

Levels	High intermediate to high advanced
Ages Suitable for Activity	Teens and adults, including preservice teachers
Aims	Demonstrate media literacy and critical thinking skills
	Take action to look beyond appearance as a dominant force in their social lives
	Create media to explore the effects of assumptions
Class Time	65 minutes
Preparation Time	10–20 minutes
Resources	Video: "What do you think? If you need help manifesting physical appearance changes," (Wong, 2022; www.tiktok.com/@manifestwithken/video/7175594371360853253)
	Video: "How to manifest an appearance change	Law of assumption + Robotic affirmation	Dream body" (Station Jaya, 2024; www.youtube.com/watch?v=d7lzfaaYVcw&t=155s)
	Prompts (Appendixes A–B)
	Smartphones
	Laptop and projector
	Timer/Bell

This activity is designed to help students examine various forms of media messages about physical appearance and take action to look beyond appearance as a dominant force in their social lives (Learning for Justice, 2009). In this activity, after creating their own short videos with and without beauty filters, students will engage in a series of reflections and discussions to explore their own biases and reflect on the influence of (social) media. Students will strengthen their critical thinking skills and ultimately shift their perspectives to recognize, accept, and celebrate differences that exist within our global society.

PROCEDURE

1. Before the activity, prepare a shared online platform where students will be able to upload video files, such as a Padlet (padlet.com) or a Google Slides presentation. Write the link to this platform on the board or share it digitally with students.

2. Open the class by showing two short-form social media videos on "manifesting" your physical appearance. Examples are provided in the Resources section of this activity. It is best to find videos presented from more than one perspective (i.e., masculine, feminine, nonbinary) to emphasize that people of all genders care about their physical attractiveness.

3. After seeing the example videos, tell students that a *figured world* is a socially constructed cultural model, a distillate of reality, a thinking tool that relates to

social practice. Give examples to confirm understanding of this concept. Discuss the following as a whole class:

    a. What figured world do you live in?

    b. What participants, activities, ways of interacting, forms of language, people, objects, environments, institutions, and values are in your figured worlds?

4. After the class discussion, explain that students will be reflecting on the influence of social media on our perception of physical attractiveness. Encourage them to consider how much the media projects society's pressure on us to conform to a certain standard of beauty.

5. Tell students to open TikTok (or another social media app) on their smartphones and take two 15-second videos of themselves—one with the Bold Glamour filter (or a similar filter, if not TikTok) and one without any beauty filters.

    a. They can pair their footage with a song or sound bite from another video or stitch it with a video by another creator.

    b. Students will have 10–15 minutes to create both videos.

    c. Hand out or project the questions found in Appendix A, and tell students to consider these questions while they are producing the two videos.

    d. Give students the link to upload their videos to your shared platform, prepared in Step 1.

6. After students have uploaded their videos, commence a virtual gallery walk.

    a. Tell students to browse all of their classmates' videos silently, with their headphones on, and to take notes about the videos.

    b. Provide students with copies of Appendix B and ask them to answer five of the questions for each video. These answers will serve as "assumptions," which the creators will have the chance to eliminate in the next activity.

7. Have students form an inner and outer circle. Students in the inner circle will face the students in the outer circle.

    a. Tell the students in the inner circle that they will be the interviewers and the ones in the outer circle will answer questions. Interviewers lead the discussion based on one of the questions in Appendix B.

    b. Have students ask and answer one question per round, which will probably take 5 minutes. After 5 minutes, ring a bell to signal students in the inner circle to switch to the next person.

    c. As stated previously, have students phrase their question as a statement, except for "What questions come to mind as you watch the videos?" The reason for this is so that the creators of the videos can understand how others perceive their work and then explain to their viewers their intentions for creating the videos.

8. Once the inner circle has gone five times around the circle, have the students in the outer circle switch to being the interviewers. If students need more time to discuss the assumptions, they can meet in person after class or discuss via email.

9. For homework, ask students to write a reflection essay or journal entry, answering the following questions:

    a. What messages does the media usually send out about people and their physical appearances?

b. How does the portrayed physical appearance of a person affect the message they are sharing?

c. What might be the result of the media's tendency to portray people who are a certain size and appearance?

d. Reflect on your experience today in class.

CAVEATS AND OPTIONS

- Note that this activity follows dialogic pedagogy, which emphasizes equality between the teacher and students.

- Be sure to emphasize three key points throughout the activity:

  — The media generally presents images of people who are a certain size and have a certain appearance—reflecting society's pressure on people to conform to those gendered expectations of sizes and appearances (Learning for Justice, 2009).

  — People often have unrealistic expectations of appearance, body size, and physical attributes for themselves and others, which lead them to judge others unfairly based on those expectations (Learning for Justice, 2009).

  — Body/appearance dissatisfaction is experienced when someone perceives that their body/facial features fall short of the societal ideas in terms of size, shape, and facial structures, regardless of that person's objective appearance (Mills et al., 2017).

- Consider the videos that are uploaded onto your chosen digital platform as a formative assessment that can help you assess student understanding and provide feedback.

- Assess student understanding by reviewing their reflections from Step 9.

REFERENCES AND FURTHER READING

Gee, J. P. (2010). *How to do discourse analysis: A toolkit.* Routledge.

Kellner, D., & Share, J. (2019). *Critical media literacy framework: Conceptual understandings and questions* [Poster]. ResearchGate. http://dx.doi.org/10.13140/RG.2.2.32448.79360

Learning for Justice. (2009). *Beauty is skin deep.* https://www.learningforjustice.org/classroom-resources/lessons/beauty-is-skin-deep

Mills, J. S., Shannon, A., & Hogue, J. (2017). Beauty, body image, and the media. In M. P. Levine (Ed.), *Perception of beauty.* IntechOpen. https://doi.org/10.5772/intechopen.68944

Share, J., Thoman, E. (2007). *Teaching democracy: A media literacy approach.* National Center for the Preservation of Democracy. https://www.academia.edu/26709676/Teaching_Democracy_A_Media_Literacy_Approach

Station Jaya. (2024, August 25). *How to manifest an appearance change | Law of assumption + robotic affirmation | Dream body* [Video]. YouTube. https://www.youtube.com/watch?v=d7IzfaaYVcw&t=155s

Wong, K. [@manifestwithken]. (2022, December 10). *What do you think? If you need help manifesting physical appearance changes* [Video]. TikTok. https://www.tiktok.com/@manifestwithken/video/7175594371360853253

APPENDIX A: *Guiding Questions for Video Recording*

Question	Corresponding Question from Discourse Analysis
What am I creating?	Which of my social identities do I want to emphasize?
What techniques should I use to attract attention to my video?	Which of my audience's social identities do I want to attract with my video?
How might different people understand my message?	How would my audience's social identity influence the way they interpret my message?
What lifestyles, values, and points of views are represented in, or omitted from my message?	How am I manipulating my audience's social identity?
Why do I want to send this message?	What *figured world* do I want to portray? What ideas do I want to sell?

APPENDIX B: *Reflection and Discussion Questions*

1. What questions come to mind as you watch the videos?
2. What type of person is the viewer invited to identify with?
3. How are the people portrayed in the videos? What kinds of behaviors or consequences are depicted?
4. Are there any political or economic ideas that come through in the message?
5. What judgements or statements are made about how to treat people?
6. What would be the most important things in life for the people portrayed in the video?
7. What view of the world do the creators of the videos assume the viewer holds? How did you come to this conclusion?
8. What ideas or perspectives are left out? How can you tell what is missing?
9. What would the story be like if the main character of the videos were of a different gender?
10. What historical events have been left out that can provide important information about the present?
11. What is implied about large concepts such as competition/cooperation, consumption/conservation, etc.?

Developing Awareness of Negative Bias Toward Indigenous Peoples

Adriana Marin-Herrera

Levels	High intermediate to advanced
Ages Suitable for Activity	Secondary
Aims	Increase awareness of negative biases toward Indigenous peoples in social media
	Critically assess how social media can create bias toward a particular group of people
Class Time	60 minutes
Preparation Time	5 minutes
Resources	Supplemental materials (Appendix A)
	Video: "The animals are telling me... you shouldn't interrupt" (UNILAD, 2021; www.facebook.com/uniladmag/videos/804649956895599; see Appendix B)
	Article: "Mapping Indigenous Languages in Canada" (Canadian Geographic, 2017; canadiangeographic.ca/articles/mapping-indigenous-languages-in-canada/)
	Handout (Appendix C)
	Laptop and projector
	Access to the internet on laptops or tablets

Countries with Indigenous populations continue to struggle to build awareness toward Indigenous peoples among the majority of their populations. This has many social repercussions, and also affects ongoing efforts to maintain Indigenous languages. This activity promotes self-reflection about and social awareness of biases against Indigenous people. Through critical discussion and analysis of a meme video by an Indigenous content creator, students are challenged to take on different perspectives, critically assess their society's biases, and understand the role of social media in perpetuating (or subverting) those biases.

PROCEDURE

1. *Before the Activity*: Share basic background information about the Indigenous populations of a specific country (e.g., the number of Indigenous languages, the colonizing languages, the location of reservations or areas governed by Indigenous populations).

2. *Introducing the Activity*: Use the following warm-up activities to activate learners' background knowledge and prepare them to engage:

   a. Survey learners about their experiences interacting with Indigenous peoples and cultures. For example, how many students have spoken with an Indigenous person, visited their lands or reservations, or noticed their presence in towns or cities?

b. Ask if there are any learners who might want to share their Indigenous heritage with the class. It's important to give learners choice in how they want to use their voices; do not pressure students to represent their heritage if they are uncomfortable.

c. Ask learners how many Indigenous languages they think are spoken in their countries. For example, Colombia is home to 65 Indigenous languages, as well as Castilian Spanish and other languages.

d. Choose a country and explore the geographical distribution of Indigenous languages in that country. Find language maps online by searching the internet for "geographical distribution of Indigenous languages in [specific country]." See Appendix A for an example from Canada.

3. *Introducing Memes:* Use the following steps to raise students' awareness of memes before watching the video clip:

a. Ask learners if they know what a meme is.

b. Elicit a definition of a meme and write it on the board.

Note: According to one dictionary, a meme is "an image, a video, a piece of text, etc. that is passed very quickly from one internet user to another, often with slight changes that make it humorous." It is also described as "an idea that is passed from one member of society to another, not in the genes but often by people copying it" (Oxford Learner's Dictionaries, n.d.)

c. Discuss what a meme is supposed to do and what defines it.

4. Ask the learners if they have seen memes on social media involving Indigenous people. Ask them to describe the memes and their impressions of them.

5. Show selected memes featuring Indigenous people or cultures.

a. Elicit learners' opinions about each meme. Point out that some memes can be offensive and some memes can be empowering to the Indigenous people whose lives they reflect.

b. Elicit what might make a meme offensive and what might make a meme empowering. (Offensive memes may depict religious beliefs or traditional practices out of context or in a negative way. Empowering memes may portray the traditional features of Indigenous cultures in a respectful, positive way.)

6. *Group Discussion and Analysis:* Introduce the video by explaining that it is a compilation of meme clips created by Brett Mooswa, a member of the Makwa Sahgaiehcan First Nation in Canada. (See Appendix B for the video link and more information.) Play the video.

7. Divide the class into eight groups. (If you don't have enough students for eight pairs/groups, it's better to have pairs discuss fewer clips than to have students work individually.) Assign each group one of the eight clips from the video and give them the discussion and writing prompts from Appendix C that align with each clip.

8. Tell groups to watch their assigned clip on their devices and discuss the given questions about that clip. Circulate to monitor and support understanding.

9. After the discussion, have learners individually write a description of the clip they watched and summarize their group discussion in response to the clip. (This can be completed in class or as homework.)

10. In the next class, have each group present their video clip and their group's response to it.

CAVEATS AND OPTIONS

- Adapt this activity for a younger age or lower level by doing the activity as a class and using just one clip from the video (e.g., the clip of the person going through the forest).

- Extend the activity by having groups brainstorm possible memes from the perspective of Indigenous people. Learners can research a specific nation, people, or tribe to learn about the group's history and culture, helping learners infer what might be offensive or not. Encourage learners to reflect on their biases. Ask them to report how hard it was to come up with ideas and why.

- Ask learners to find an image online and add text to it to create a new photo meme that is empowering to Indigenous people.

- If there is any student in the class who might have a background of Indigenous heritage, ask if they feel comfortable sharing their background, culture, and/or language knowledge with the class. This also brings awareness of lacking or having this voice in the class.

REFERENCES AND FURTHER READING

Betancourt Sabatini, N. (2016). Discriminación al indígena a través de los memes: Un análisis pragmático [Discrimination against Indigenous people through memes: A pragmatic analysis]. *Expedicionario Revista de Estudios en Antropología. 2*(4), 34–37.

Darvin, R. (2017). *Language, ideology, and critical digital literacy.* Springer International. https://doi.org/10.1007/978-3-319-02328-1_35-1

Frazer, R., & Carlson, B. (2017). Indigenous memes and the invention of a people. *Social Media + Society, 3*(4), https://doi.org/10.1177/2056305117738993

Oxford Learner's Dictionaries. (n.d.). *Meme.* In Oxford Advanced Learner's Dictionary. https://www.oxfordlearnersdictionaries.com/us/definition/english/meme

Pangrazio, L. (2016). Reconceptualising critical digital literacy. *Discourse: Studies in the Cultural Politics of Education. 37*(2), 163–174. https://doi.org/10.1080/0159630 6.2014.942836

PBS News. (2021, October 1). *How Indigenous creators are nurturing a space on TikTok to educate and entertain.* https://www.pbs.org/newshour/arts/how-indigenous-creators-are-nurturing-a-space-on-tiktok-to-educate-and-entertain

UNILAD. (2021, August 11). *"The animals are telling me... you shouldn't interrupt."* - *This guy's Indigenous skits are too much* 😂 [Video]. Facebook. https://www.facebook.com/uniladmag/videos/804649956895599/

Vargas Franco, A. (2019). Prácticas letradas, identidad y resistencia en Facebook: Un estudio de caso de un estudiante indígena colombiano [Writing practices, identity and resistance on Facebook: A case study of a Colombian Indigenous student]. *Polyphōnía: Revista de Educación Inclusiva, 3*(1), 47–65.

Walker, N. (2017, December 15). Mapping indigenous languages in Canada. *Canadian Geographic.* https://canadiangeographic.ca/articles/mapping-indigenous-languages-in-canada/

APPENDIX A: *Supplemental Materials for Discussion*

Map of Indigenous Languages in Canada for Step 2d

You can find a helpful map and infographic within the following article:

"Mapping Indigenous Languages in Canada" (Walker, 2017; canadiangeographic.ca/articles/mapping-indigenous-languages-in-canada/)

Sample Memes for Step 5

Ideally, search for examples of meme images and videos featuring the Indigenous Peoples in your country. This connects the activity more closely with your educational context.

APPENDIX B: *Video Short by Brett Mooswa*

Link to Video

UNILAD. (2021, August 11). *"The animals are telling me... you shouldn't interrupt." - This guy's Indigenous skits are too much* 😂 [Video]. Facebook. https://www.facebook.com/uniladmag/videos/804649956895599/

Video Description

In this video, Brett Mooswa, a popular influencer on TikTok and a member of the Makwa Sahgaiehcan First Nation in Canada, challenges stereotypes against Indigenous people by showing his knowledge of his Indigenous language and his awareness of stereotypes. He takes the power out of the stereotypes by making fun of a person who is asking him stereotypical questions. This questioning person does not appear in the video, so it is left for the viewer to guess who this is.

APPENDIX C: *Discussion and Writing Prompts*

There are eight different clips in the video we have just watched, which was created by Brett Mooswa, a member of the Makwa Sahgaiehcan First Nation in Canada.

Instructions

1. As a group, watch your assigned part of the video.
2. Discuss the questions on this handout that correspond to your clip.
3. Write a summary of the clip and your group's discussion of it.
4. Prepare a brief presentation for the class in which you will present the clip and summarize your group's response.

Clip 1: Indigenous Person Waving Hello to Another Person

- Who do these two people represent in society?
- How can you tell who is who in society?
- Why does one person view it as an honor that the other is supposedly blessing the land?
- What is the person waving really doing?
- Is there a difference in the way they speak?
- How would you call the attention of another person from far away?

Clip 2: Indigenous Person Eating

- Where is this person? What is in the background?
- What is he wearing? Is there anything Indigenous in the way he dresses?
- Why is he eating like he does? How does this compare to where and how you eat?
- Do you know of other cultures that also eat near the floor?
- What does it mean in your society to eat near the floor, and what could this mean for other people in terms of what the ground/Earth means to them?

Clip 3: Person Interrupting to Ask About Animal Talk

- What is the Indigenous person talking about with his friend?
- Is it okay to call a person by their race? Why or why not?
- Why do you think Brett does not show the person who is asking him a question? How is the person who interrupts portrayed? Why?
- Is animal wisdom valued in your society? What is valued in your society?
- What is the assumption shown in the video about talking to animals in relation to Indigenous people versus "civilized" people?
- Do you notice a change in accent/tone and body language? Why is this?

Clip 4: Cooking Indigenous Food

- Would you associate pancakes with Indigenous food in your country? Why or why not?
- Have you ever made your own pancakes? Why is it important to check on the pan's heat level when making pancakes?
- How is this person dressed? What is in the background?
- Who do you think asks the questions?
- Do you have a routine to bless your food at home? What does it look like?
- What is the effect of hearing Brett reply, "Just kidding," and listening to him explain in English?

Clip 5: Dressing Up

- What is the first person wearing? What brand is his cap?
- What is the second person wearing in the beginning? What does his shirt say?
- Why do you think some people are annoyed by how others dress?
- What is the sequence of dressing up for the Indigenous person?

- What is the effect of saying *bro* or *just chillin'*? Which groups are this vocabulary typically associated with?
- What happens to the Indigenous person as the meme progresses in terms of voice and vocabulary to convey what he is doing? What effect does this have?

Clip 6: Wisdom From the Sky
- What is the effect of interrupting by saying *Indigenous man*, *shaman*, or *mystical guy*? What would be something similar that you would not like to be called in his place?
- Which place is the Indigenous person talking about before being interrupted? Would most people in your society expect to see Indigenous people at this place? Why or why not?
- What is the effect of the Indigenous person joking by replying "Just kidding, I can't do that!"?
- Does your family or community believe in the power of nature or energy in bringing wisdom?

Clip 7: Baby Talk
- What is the assumption shown by the baby talking in this meme?
- Why does the baby acknowledge respect for his parents?
- How do you acknowledge respect for your loved ones? How would you say it?
- What is the effect of this person and his baby talking and singing the way they do to each other?
- Does your name have a story behind it? Do you have a nickname?
- The name "Ben" (son of my right hand, in Hebrew) is very common in the United States. Do you know any specific names used by Indigenous communities? What do they mean? Why do you think they are chosen by parents in Indigenous communities?
- Why does the father say "Cry for the people"? Which people is he talking about? What happened to the people?
- *Bonus:* How do you say *go to sleep, speak, hello, I see you, yes,* and *just wait, father* in the Indigenous language spoken in this video (Plains Cree)?

Clip 8: Nature Walk
- Where is the person? What is he wearing?
- Do you often take walks in nature? How does it feel?
- What is the meaning of "being one with nature"?
- Do you think Indigenous people always like to be in nature?
- Does being Indigenous imply the person knows all animals and they know him? Why or why not?
- This person says their ancestors are "watching him having a good life." Do you believe your ancestors (grandparents, aunts, uncles, etc.) are watching your life? How do you keep their memory?
- Have you been camping? What would you do if you saw a bear?
- What is the Indigenous person trying to convey by being afraid?

III

Purposeful Social Media: Images for Advocacy

Nicholas J. Santavicca

Level	Any
Ages Suitable for Activity	Secondary to adult
Aims	Enhance the power of imagination, creativity, and critical thinking
	Create a notion of advocacy for social issues and support ways to express advocacy
	Develop writing and speaking skills for social media platforms to increase awareness of digital literacy
	Engage in writing using visual images and descriptive language conventions
Class Time	10–30 minutes (regularly for 4–6 weeks)
Preparation Time	15 minutes
Resources	Social media accounts
	Internet access

In this activity, students confront environmental issues by documenting landscapes, weather, animal/human biomes, and other natural phenomena to make meaning of the evolving world around them. In the age of climate change, biodiversity loss, and weather extremes, students will develop visual and written literacies by investigating images and writing about the world around them.

PROCEDURE

5. Ask students to find photos, videos, or images that illustrate natural settings, urban landscapes, issues of climate change, weather phenomena, animal/human habitats, biomes, or related visual realia. Some of these items collected will be placed on the class social media site. Students may also produce their own images, art, comics, and/or photography. Collecting photos/media can be completed as prework or used as a complementary activity. Let students know that the objective is to find photos that highlight environmental phenomena and human involvement. Be sure their content complements advocacy by asking questions like:

    a. Are there active people in the images?

    b. Are the images evoking a feeling?

    c. Do they tell the story of what you're advocating for?

6. Have students then upload and create a post using their visual content on a class social media account. Optimal platforms include Instagram, TikTok, and Facebook.

7. Have students work on writing assignments and tasks throughout the term using the photos and pictures that they have chosen related to raising social awareness and advocacy. The assignments can include grammar/vocabulary-related writing tasks on word order, syntax, and adjectives/adverbs (depending on the images) and writing tasks linking the students' lives to current issues related to environmental issues and advocacy surrounding the biological/natural world.

8. Task students with understanding in oral and written form the "language of advocacy" by asking students to complete the following in written form as a script to produce social media posts in oral form:

    a. Name the problem

    b. State why it matters

    c. Propose a solution

9. Highlight specific vocabulary and word choice for linguistic practice related to advocacy for 4a, 4b, and 4c.

    a. **Name the problem:** may include specific syntactical adverbs of time/description (first, second, lastly, then, next, etc.).

    b. **State why it matters:** may include specific preposition phrases to express opinion (*in my opinion, in this scenario, on the other hand, above all, due to this situation* etc.).

    c. **Propose a solution:** may include specific phrases to highlight cause and effect. (hence, therefore, since, as a result, because, etc.).

10. Have students submit the images and oral videos using the framework from Step 4 via the newly created social media class site. The social media site will become a visual portfolio, a social networking site, a postcard for global friends, and an imaging journal for advocacy.

11. At the end of the semester or session, have students interview and record each other for a 4- to 5-minute video reflection describing the images they collected as a call to action to be shared on the social media platform. Students should richly describe their hopes, dreams, and desires for the future regarding the environment to create a visual postcard to the Earth. Sample Guiding Questions for the interview could include (using the framework from Step 4):

    a. In a few words, explain the environmental issue you're advocating on behalf of. What is the call to action?

    b. Why does this issue matter to you?

    c. Who or what is being affected?

    d. In your opinion, what needs to change to make the Earth a better place for the future based on what you have learned?

CAVEATS AND OPTIONS

- This project is adaptable to any level of English and integrates all language skills (reading, writing, listening, and speaking). This project may be used for any content or academic area to enhance vocabulary and promote advocacy from a visual perspective. Students may write from varied points of view and post. Students can imagine being a scientist, an animal, a weather system, a person from another biome, etc.

- Students may also advocate for any issues related to classroom content, academic standards, and/or student interests. Students can generate or create a combination of their own art, visual imagery, comics, or photography for the activity. Students can creatively describe the images in writing using the varied discourses of the respective social media platforms.

- Students could write corresponding hashtags, poems, haiku, hokku, or simple descriptive sentences. Students may link the images through the writing to create a gallery or flipbook of images posted on the class social media sites. Students also may interact with other students, activists, scholars, scientists, teachers, etc., who are connected to global issues and the environment.

- This activity can be adapted for newcomer learners of English because students can use images to express their advocacy ideas without needing an expansive vocabulary to participate.

- Students may showcase their work as a final project/visual gallery of advocacy.

REFERENCES AND FURTHER READING

Cooper, M. (2019). *The animal who writes: A posthumanist composition.* University of Pittsburgh Press.

Gries, L. E. (2015). *Still life with rhetoric: A new materialist approach to visual rhetorics.* Utah State University Press.

Kanno, Y., & Norton, B. (Eds.). (2003). Imagined communities and educational possibilities (Special Issue). *Journal of Language, Identity, and Education, 2*(4).

APPENDIX A: *Sample Image With Suggested Post Content*

This image, with a text component, can then be linked to other posts from various classmates in the same classroom to create a large effect for advocacy and social change.

Suggested post content:

- Headline
- News story for advocacy
- Multiple hashtags with rich descriptors
- Haiku/poem
- Weather forecast caption
- Call for action

APPENDIX B: *Questions to Ponder*

1. Are there any noticeable changes in language skills specifically related to advocacy and the ability to express attitudes of social responsibility from the first weeks of the visual project to the last (specifically related to the linguistic practice in Step 4)?

2. Do you or the students visually see how their site can be used for social change and advocacy for the environment and other issues in society?

3. Have the students developed a deeper understanding of social media discourse and connections to others? Are students able to use the conventions of the social media platform to express themselves orally?

4. How have you integrated specific vocabulary related to advocacy into the students' activity?

Part IV

Student-Generated Art

Introduction: Building Visual Literacy Through Student-Generated Art

A key component of visual literacy is the ability to produce visual media. Through the creation of visual media, students engage in both the interpretation and production of visual meaning (Association of College & Research Libraries, 2011). By participating in productive visual activities, learners explore color, form, composition, and symbolism while reflecting on personal and social influences. They also foster deeper intercultural understanding, engage in self-expression, and develop essential 21st-century communication skills.

In alignment with the aims of this volume, the activities in this section provide students with opportunities to become both critical consumers and competent contributors of visual media. Student-generated art tasks position learners as active producers of meaning. Through a wide variety of media—including drawing, painting, sculpture, collage, photography, infographics, comics, mood boards, paper collage, and digital artworks—students communicate personal, cultural, and social messages. These activities provide a valuable platform for learners to develop vocabulary, grammar, speaking, listening, reading, and writing skills in meaningful communicative contexts (Donaghy & Xerri, 2017).

The pedagogical approaches represented in this section reflect the versatility of student-generated art across language levels and educational settings. Activities range from playful explorations of color and shape with young learners to more complex, reflective projects such as storytelling through tableaux, analyzing processes through infographics, and mapping personal aspirations through visual roadmaps. Learners engage in collaborative and individual projects that promote creativity, critical thinking, empathy, and autonomy.

These activities are designed with adaptability in mind. Teachers working in both high- and low-resource environments will find options to implement activities with traditional art materials or digital tools. Regardless of the medium, the consistent objective is to enhance language learning through the intentional integration of student-created visual representations.

By incorporating student-generated art into the language classroom, educators can empower learners to become visually and linguistically literate participants in a multimodal world. These experiences support students in developing the life skills needed to interpret, evaluate, and contribute meaningfully to the visual culture that surrounds them, preparing them to navigate and communicate effectively in an increasingly image-saturated global landscape (Kress, 2003).

REFERENCES AND FURTHER READING

Association of College & Research Libraries. (2011). *ACRL visual literacy competency standards for higher education.* American Library Association. https://www.ala.org/acrl/standards/visualliteracy

Donaghy, K., & Xerri, D. (Eds.). (2017). *The image in English language teaching.* ELT Council.

Kress, G. (2003). *Literacy in the new media age.* Routledge.

AI Belongs to You: Your Words, Your Art

Gökçe Gök

Levels	Intermediate to advanced
Ages Suitable for Activity	Secondary to adult
Aims	Develop descriptive writing skills
Class Time	30 minutes
Preparation Time	5 minutes
Resources	Access to the internet on laptops or tablets
	Laptop and projector
	Shared platform for students to upload their work

W riting detailed descriptions is a valuable skill for multilingual learners of English. Experimenting with artificial intelligence (AI) art generation makes practicing descriptive writing more motivating and engaging. In this activity, students enhance their descriptive writing abilities by creating visual artwork with AI tools—a practice that merges language learning with creative expression.

PROCEDURE

1. Before the activity, prepare a shared platform for students to upload their work for peer feedback. This could be a forum on your learning management system, a Padlet (padlet.com), or a shared Google Doc.

2. To begin, introduce AI-generated art to the class. If possible, show some examples of AI-generated art. Demonstrate the use of an AI image-generation platform, such as DALL·E (openai.com/index/dall-e-3/).

3. Explain that in order for an AI tool to generate art, someone must provide a description as a prompt.

4. Discuss what makes a good description (i.e., lots of detail, being specific, using adjectives and adverbs). Show learners some examples of descriptions and the art generated by those descriptions.

5. Practice the activity as a whole class:

    a. Choose a theme (e.g., sea, forest, holiday, tourism, home, hotel, cooking) and, as a class, collaboratively write a description that could be used to generate art related to that theme.

    b. Demonstrate how to generate the art by opening an AI art generator and inserting the description created by the class.

    c. Compare the generated image to the written description and discuss the results as a class.

6. Divide the class into pairs. Tell learners to imagine a scene related to their chosen theme. Then, have them work together to write a detailed description of the scene they imagined.

7. Instruct students to insert their description into an AI art generator.

8. Ask students to anonymously share their art and description with the class on the shared platform you prepared in Step 1.

9. For homework, instruct students to read the descriptions and match them to the artworks.

CAVEATS AND OPTIONS

- Adapt the activity for contexts without access to the internet:
  — Put students in pairs. One writes the description and gives it to their partner, who generates the art.
  — Then, have pairs discuss how the art generated was different than what the describer imagined.
  — Have the art generator offer suggestions on how the writer could have provided a better description.

IV

Art Makes Me Feel

Cynthia Ramírez Pérez

Levels	All
Ages Suitable for Activity	Secondary to university
Aims	Express likes and dislikes
	Express feelings and emotions inspired by a song
	Share ideas and thoughts about their own and others' work
Class Time	60–100 minutes
Preparation Time	20–30 minutes
Resources	A song that elicits strong emotion (selected by the teacher)
	Laptop and projector or speakers
	Paper
	Crayons, colors, markers, pencils, etc.
	Post-it notes

This activity is based on the principles of task-based learning, which foster meaningful communication in language learning. By emphasizing real-world tasks and authentic contexts, this activity aims to promote language acquisition and engage learners in purposeful language use. This activity enables students to connect with others by sharing their pictures and drawings while developing their language skills and building vocabulary related to art.

PROCEDURE

1. Ask students to watch or listen to your selected song.

2. Engage students in a brainstorming session to share their thoughts and emotions evoked by the song.

3. Provide students with a piece of paper and art materials. Play the song several times, encouraging students to create a drawing that expresses their feelings and thoughts inspired by the song. The drawing can be as concrete or abstract as students would like.

4. Once students have completed their drawings, ask them to write a description of their artwork and give it a name or title. Have students focus on describing the emotions they felt while listening to the music and how those emotions are represented in their artwork.

5. Create an art gallery in the classroom by having students post their drawings and descriptions on the walls. Alternatively, for older students or online classes, have students post their work in a digital space for their classmates to see.

6. Distribute Post-it notes to each student. Instruct them to write comments about their classmates' artworks on the Post-it notes. Encourage them to express how the artwork makes them feel and identify any personal connections.

7. Ask students to stick their Post-it notes on their classmates' drawings, providing feedback and appreciation.

8. In the end, have students collect the notes they received on their artwork and reflect on how they feel about others seeing their creations.

CAVEATS AND OPTIONS

- Establish a respectful and inclusive environment at the beginning of the activity. Emphasize that every work will be treated with respect, and negative or offensive comments are not allowed. This ensures a positive and supportive atmosphere for students to share their artwork.

- Adapt the task for higher levels by requiring students to use more complex language for expressing opinions. Provide additional vocabulary or sentence frames to support lower level learners in articulating their thoughts and feelings about the artwork.

- Extend and enhance the language learning experience by offering students the opportunity to share their written descriptions with a more advanced class. This allows for peer correction and feedback, providing an additional learning opportunity for both groups of students.

FURTHER READING

Nunan, D. (2004). *Task-based language teaching*. Cambridge.

IV

Artful Writing: Arctic Habitat

Svetlana V. Nuss

Levels	All
Ages Suitable for Activity	Any
Aims	Develop Arctic nature–themed vocabulary and language structures
	Use specific details in description writing
	Create a piece of art with basic painting techniques and use related vocabulary
Class Time	3 (1-hour) sessions
Preparation Time	15 minutes
Resources	Short informational video about life in the arctic
	Video: "Arctic Habitat" (Svetlana Nuss, Language Pedagogy, 2020; www.youtube.com/watch?v=LSpg2jhhegE)
	Laptop and projector
	Painting supplies (paper, paints, brushes, water, and crayons)
	Optional: art stands and backing material

This is a scaffolded descriptive writing activity in which students paint an Arctic habitat with watercolor, discuss it in a gallery walk, and then metaphorically paint their picture with words. This activity is suitable for Montessori and other nature-related and content-based educational contexts.

PROCEDURE

Artmaking (60 minutes)

1. Raise learners' interest in the Arctic by showing them a short video about life in the Arctic in general or about an Arctic animal, such as a polar bear or a whale.

2. *Optional*: Have students fill out a Venn diagram (see Appendix A) comparing the climate features of the location where they currently are to the Arctic. Students can work in pairs or small groups, or you can elicit responses to complete the diagram as a whole class.

3. *Optional*: Have students use a bubble map (see Appendix B) to brainstorm vocabulary for natural features of the Arctic. For a basic activity, ask learners to fill the bubbles with nouns (e.g., Arctic Ocean, habitat, snow, ice, chunks); for higher levels, or as an extension, ask learners to write descriptions with adjectives.

4. Explain that students will make watercolor paintings of Arctic habitats (see Appendix C). Demonstrate the watercolor and crayon resist painting technique by either modeling it in person or showing learners the video "Arctic Habitat."

5. Give students time to make their art. Encourage students to make more than one art piece (if time allows) so they have choices for the gallery walk.

Gallery Walk (30-60 minutes)

1. Have one group of students (the artists) display their work while the rest of the students (the audience) attend the exhibit and ask questions about the art:
   a. Does the artist like making art with watercolors?
   b. Was this the artist's first experience in making watercolor art?
   c. Why did the artist choose certain colors or include certain features?
   d. What is the artist's personal experience with the Arctic?
2. After a certain period of time, have the groups switch roles.
3. This works well as a semistructured activity. Tell the learners to visit a certain number of artists and collect some specific information from them by asking questions.
4. Bring the class together for a debrief activity. Have individual students "read" their painting by describing it to their peers (in small groups or as a whole class). The teacher may want to model by describing their own or a sample art piece (see Appendix C).

Descriptive Writing (30-50 minutes)

1. Tell students they are going to create their picture anew, this time with words. Give students 15–20 minutes for individual descriptive writing about their paintings.
2. Have students read their written art piece (the text they wrote) to their partner and then listen to their partner's reading. Students are encouraged to use this opportunity to proofread and fine-tune their writing.

CAVEATS AND OPTIONS

- Adapt for lower levels by providing sentence/paragraph stems for Step 4 of the Gallery Walk.
- For higher level learners, provide less scaffolding and ask them to create additional art along with more writing. Assign them to combine their watercolor paintings with "word pictures" (text they write based on their art) into artful albums (perhaps for the classroom library, to be read by younger grades, or to be shared with families).
- If the teacher chooses to personally model the painting technique, it is best to gather learners around the table where the teacher makes the painting. Quality watercolor paper is recommended but optional, and wider brushes work best for blending.
- Instead of, or in addition to, a gallery walk, create a teacher-led community word picture. As a result of this group activity, the learners create a community word wall (using the classroom board or on poster paper) which then serves as a scaffold for their independent descriptive writing.
- For online teaching contexts, have learners watch the video and prepare their art ahead of time, then participate in synchronous group activities (e.g., gallery walk and community word picture).
- As an extension activity, students can add a polar bear to their Arctic habitat (see Appendix C).

REFERENCES AND FURTHER READING

Nuss, S., & Language Pedagogy. (2020, May 27). *Arctic habitat* [Video]. https://www.youtube.com/watch?v=LSpg2jhhegE

Nuss, S., & Language Pedagogy. (2020, June 9). *Polar bear* [Video]. https://www.youtube.com/watch?v=X1FbBtwX1is

APPENDIX A: *Venn Diagram*

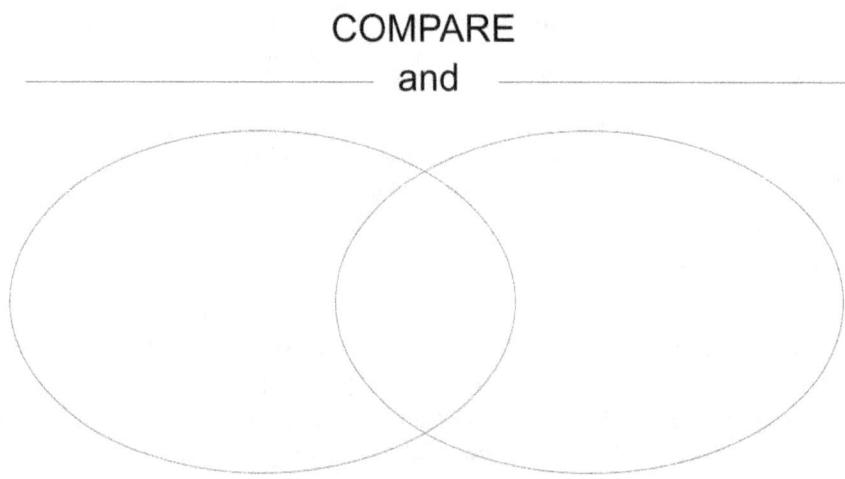

Created by Svetlana Nuss for TESOL Press Series *New Ways of Teaching*

APPENDIX B: *Bubble Map*

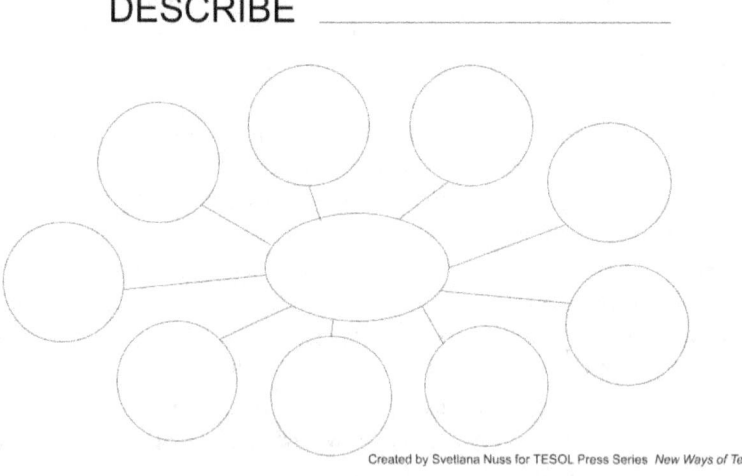

Created by Svetlana Nuss for TESOL Press Series *New Ways of Teaching*

APPENDIX C: *Sample Art Piece*

For guidance on painting techniques, watch or show students the following videos:

- "Arctic Habitat" (Svetlana Nuss, Language Pedagogy, 2020; www.youtube.com/watch?v=LSpg2jhhegE)
- "Polar Bear" (Svetlana Nuss, Language Pedagogy, 2020; www.youtube.com/watch?v=X1FbBtwX1is)

Arctic Ocean art piece created by the teacher and "read" to students in class. Art techniques used: crayon resist (white crayon) and blending (with watercolors).

Image credit: Svetlana V. Nuss. Used with permission.

Collaborative AI Art Generation

Sasha Wajnryb

Levels	Beginner to intermediate
Ages Suitable for Activity	Elementary to adult
Aims	Work collaboratively
	Write notes on key features of desired AI artwork
	Design a detailed piece of art
Class Time	20–40 minutes
Preparation Time	5 minutes
Resources	Whiteboard and markers
	Access to the internet on laptops or tablets
	Laptop and projector

his activity combines the use of new technology and groupwork to create a fun activity where students work collaboratively to design a piece of artificial intelligence (AI)-generated art. Engaging with new technology encourages teamwork and creativity, creating strong bonds among classmates.

PROCEDURE

1. Use one of the following AI art generators to create some sample art before the class:
   a. Hotpot (hotpot.ai/art-generator)
   b. Picsart (picsart.com/ai-image-generator)
   c. Artimator (artimator.io)
   d. Cutout.pro (www.cutout.pro/ai-art-generation)
2. Warm up the students to today's topic by showing the students the art, as well as the AI prompt used to create it. Discuss with the class how the prompt compares to the results.
3. Divide learners into groups of two to four. Tell learners they are going to make AI art as a team and that they will work together to make the most interesting, creative, and detailed piece of art possible.
4. Write *Who, Where, What, When, Why* on the board. Explain that if they include all of this information and write a detailed prompt, the AI art generator will create their unique art. The more detailed the prompt, the more customized the art.
5. Give the teams 10 minutes to brainstorm what their art will contain. Remind them to use the five *wh-* question words to add details to their idea.
6. One student in each group writes notes in a list format, focusing on the who, where, when, what, and why. As learners brainstorm, circulate and encourage students to create detailed prompts.

7. Next, ask each group to turn their list into a short descriptive paragraph—the prompt used to generate the AI art.

8. Write the websites for AI art generators listed in Step 1 on the board. Instruct learners to open one of these websites (or other AI art generators) on their computer or smartphone and write in their detailed prompt that uses all of their notes from their group's brainstorming session.

9. Tell learners to generate their art. They can copy and paste the same prompt into the other AI art generators to create other images, compare the results, and then choose their favorite image.

10. Have groups exchange paragraphs. Tell groups to review the other group's paragraph and deconstruct it into the answers to the five *wh-* questions.

CAVEATS AND OPTIONS

- As technology develops, more and more (and better) options for free AI art generators will appear. Continue to explore other websites.

- In the warm-up activity (Step 2 of the procedure), the discussion about AI art can easily move to other relevant topics (e.g., traditional art versus AI art, ethical considerations about using AI art). Explore these topics in a postactivity discussion.

- Before the activity, show your current class the AI-generated art from previous classes to inspire their creativity.

- If your learners have recently focused on particular lexical sets (e.g., animals, transportation, household items), encourage learners to use these words in their paragraph prompt.

- After all the groups have created their own art, students can swap art and then write a short story (or another type of creative writing, such as a letter from one character to another) using another group's art as inspiration.

- After the activity is finished, post some AI art from a previous class on one side of the classroom, and their written prompts on the other side. One learner from each team needs to run from side to side to match the art to the prompt.

- If you are teaching in a low-resource context, adapt this activity so that a pair of students work together, with one student writing the prompt and the other student generating the art with pen/pencil or other art supplies.

IV

Conveying Meaning With Words and Images

Suzan Stamper

Levels	All
Ages Suitable for Activity	Secondary to adult
Aims	Identify and communicate meaning and feeling with images and words
	Distinguish between images that students have the right to use (their own) and those copied from the internet
	Establish the habit of citing multimodal sources (e.g., using captions with images)
Class Time	15 minutes
Preparation Time	10 minutes
Resources	A shared online discussion space
	Access to the internet on laptops or tablets
	Laptop and projector

In preparation for a larger multimodal assignment, this is an introductory activity in which students explore possible meanings associated with images and how meanings change when images change.

PROCEDURE

1. Set up the activity in a shared discussion space or learning management system where students can upload still photos and reply to classmates. Options could include Google Docs, WhatsApp, Padlet, Canvas, or Moodle.

2. Before or during class, post prompts like the following to guide students as they upload and caption a photo before commenting on classmates' photos:

    a. Select a photo you have taken of scenery, an animal, or an object (not people). This should be an original photo and not from the internet.

    b. Upload your photo and add a caption in APA format.

    c. *Example*: Figure 1: Footprints in snow (Stamper, 2022)

    d. Select photos by two or three classmates and answer the following questions:

        i. What words best describe this photo?

        ii. What is going on in this photo?

        iii. What do you see that makes you think that?

        iv. How does the photo make you feel?

    e. Be prepared to discuss your answers in the next class.

3. In the class discussion, ask students to share their impressions of the original photos and discuss their answers to the questions about the photos. What words

were used to describe the photos? Were the guesses about the photos accurate? What clues did students notice? What feelings did students have about the photos? Were the student photographers surprised by any of the responses?

4. Next, ask students to imagine how the feeling or meaning of a photo would change if one thing in the photo changed. Have students reply to their original post with a new image (e.g., a new photo, a drawing) that includes one change and then comment on the new feelings or meaning. (See example in the Appendix.)

CAVEATS AND OPTIONS

- For a low- or no-tech option, have students post their images on classroom walls or whiteboards and tell classmates to write their responses on paper or sticky notes.

- Images of people are not included. If included, introduce students to the topic of getting permission from others to use their image, in writing or in a release.

- Choose words for students to illustrate with an original photo or drawing with the following directions:
  — Choose one of the following words: *creativity, nonconformity, collaboration, intelligence, perseverance, team*.
  — Take a photo or draw an image representing the word and post it in the shared discussion space. (This should be an original photo/picture and not something copied from the internet.) Do not tell your classmates what word you have chosen.
  — Reply to postings from two or three classmates by guessing the word and explaining in one or two sentences the reason for your guess. Be prepared to discuss your guesses in class.

APPENDIX: *Example Photos and Responses*

Sample Photo and Caption	Sample Classmate's Responses
Figure 1. Footprints in snow (*Image credit:* Suzan Stamper. Used with permission.)	*What words best describe this photo?* A cold walk *What is going on in this picture?* It looks like someone went for an evening walk in new snow. *What do you see that makes you think that?* There are shadows in the snow. I see only one set of footprints in the snow. *How does the photo make you feel?* I feel cold, but I also feel peaceful. I can imagine the sound of walking in the snow. Crunch crunch crunch.

Sample Changes After Discussion	
Change 1 – Change the snow to sand.	Change 2 – Add many footprints in the sand.
Does this change make you think of something new? Does it give you a different feeling?	Does this change make you think of something new? Does it give you a different feeling?

Figure 2. Footprints in sand	**Figure 3.** Footprints in sand
(*Image credit:* Suzan Stamper. Used with permission.)	(*Image credit:* Suzan Stamper. Used with permission.)

Creating a Comic

Alexandra Krasova

Levels	All
Ages Suitable for Activity	Any
Aims	Engage with cultural content
	Develop visual literacy skills
	Synthesize information
Class Time	45–50 minutes
Preparation Time	5–10 minutes
Resources	Examples of multipanel comics found online or in print
	Laptop and projector OR printed copies of Appendixes A–C

ccording to Merriam-Webster (n.d.), a comic strip is defined as a group of drawings in narrative sequence. Comics help learners develop multimodal literacy skills and are thus regarded as a valuable resource for English language classrooms (Ravelo, 2013). This activity promotes creativity, develops visual literacy skills, and encourages critical thinking by incorporating comics into teaching.

PROCEDURE

1. Ask students if they ever read comics. If they do, discuss the kind of comics they read and ask about their favorite ones. If not, explain what comics are; then, show and read one or two sample multipanel comics with the whole class to clarify they understand the medium.

2. Show students the comic page with blank speech bubbles (Appendix A). Put learners in pairs or groups to discuss what they can see in the pictures. Ask them to be as descriptive as possible while focusing on the visuals.

3. Have an open class discussion about the images of the comic. Ask learners to explain the order of images on the comic page and elicit the idea of the story. Continue the discussion until no new information can be elicited.

4. Show students the speech bubbles with text included (Appendix B). Return students to their pairs or groups and ask them to match each bubble with the appropriate panel from the comic strip.

5. After students complete the task, have the groups share their answers by reading the comic aloud. Let other groups agree or disagree with their answers and provide their reasons.

6. Then, show the students the original comic (Appendix C). Read the comic with the class. Discuss how analyzing the images helped them understand where each speech bubble belonged.

7. Return students to their pairs or groups and ask them to create their own original dialogue for the speech bubbles of the same comic. Provide printed copies of Appendix A, or simply tell students to write their dialogues in their notebooks.

8. Let groups exchange their comics so that everyone has a chance to read all the new versions.

9. Ask the class to vote on their favorite version of the comic. Discuss the reasons for their choice.

CAVEATS AND OPTIONS

- Adapt this activity for younger learners by
  — choosing speech bubbles with simple and familiar vocabulary,
  — letting students color the images,
  — using a familiar newspaper or magazine comic,
  — asking learners to create their own comic page on paper, and/or
  — doing the activity together as a class.
- Adapt this activity for a higher level by providing learners with a new comic without dialogue for Step 7.
- Extend creativity by asking learners to draw images for the comic.
- Extend learning by having learners provide peer feedback in Step 8.

REFERENCES AND FURTHER READING

Merriam-Webster. (n.d.). Comic strip. In *Merriam-Webster.com dictionary*. https://www.merriam-webster.com/dictionary/comic%20strip

Ravelo, L. C. (2013). The use of comic strips as a means of teaching history in the EFL class: Proposal of activities based on two historical comic strips adhering to the principles of CLIL. *LACLIL Latin American Journal, 6*(1), 1–19. https://doi.org/10.5294/laclil.2013.6.1.1

APPENDIX A: *Blank Comic Page Example*

Image credit: Alexandra Krasova. Used with permission.

APPENDIX B: *Speech Bubbles*

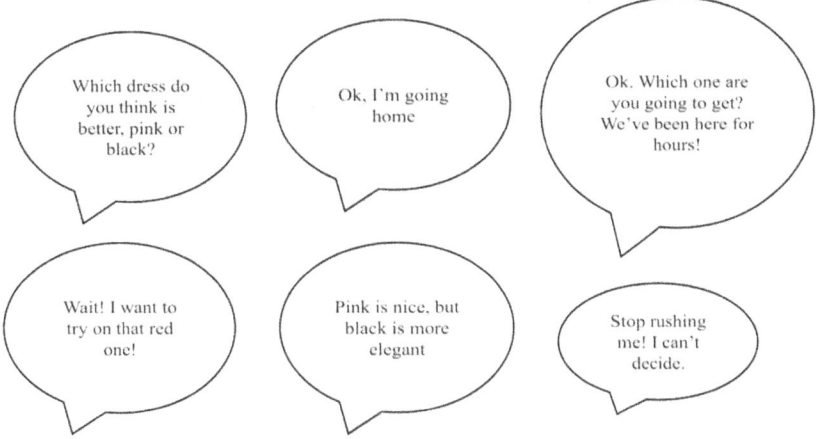

APPENDIX C: *Original Comic Page Example*

A Difficult Choice

Image credit: Alexandra Krasova. Used with permission.

Creating Language and Visuals With Pieces of Paper

Ana Luisa Lado

Level	Beginner to high beginner and low intermediate
Ages Suitable for Activity	Primary to adult
Aims	Read the book aloud fluently
	Reflect and write about drawings
	Read, retell, rewrite, and visually represent an original allegory
Class Time	30 minutes x 4
Preparation Time	10 minutes
Resources	Copy of *Perfect Square* (Hall, 2011)
	Video: "Story Time in the Galleries: "Perfect Square," by Michael Hall" (Milwaukee Art Museum, 2021; www.youtube.com/watch?v=8epgVp5YrUg)
	Red squares of paper
	Paper, pencils, glue, and scissors
	Assessment (Appendix A)
	Progress Tracker (Appendix B)

Perfect Square (Hall, 2011) provides the perfect backdrop for teaching vocabulary in a visual and experiential context. In this activity, students use their creativity to make something new from scraps of paper. This picture book, as well as the book-specific resources online, prompt activities that develop a full complement of oral, written, and visual literacy skills. Written with patterned sentences at a Lexile level of ADL 470L, the book is an allegory demonstrating ways to withstand adversity by creatively transforming challenges into new beginnings.

PROCEDURE

Presentation

1. Teach the nouns from *Perfect Square* (i.e., *square, corner, side, smile, piece, hole, scrap, strip, kite, fountain, garden, bridge, mountain, park, river, window*).

2. Conduct a picture walk and note what is done to the square each day (the verbs) and what the square makes: *square, fountain, garden, bridge, mountain, park, river, window.* Check the comprehension of nouns by focusing students' attention to each object.

3. Conduct another picture walk, this time saying each noun and having the class repeat after you.

4. Divide students into eight groups. Have each group make a vocabulary card for one of the following key nouns (listed in order of appearance): *square, fountain, garden, park bridge, river, mountain, window.*

....

a. Collect the cards from each group and redistribute them randomly among groups so each group has a new card.

b. Conduct another picture walk. Pause at each key noun to give groups time to match their word card to its corresponding illustration in the book.

c. Write cloze sentences from the book on the board, leaving blanks for the nouns.

   Example: So it made itself into a _____.

d. Read each cloze sentence, and as you read, invite volunteers to insert their cards in the correct blanks.

e. Ask students to write a parallel sentence substituting any of these nouns.

5. Select an appropriate number of verbs from the book to teach according to the age and ability level of the students.

   a. Assign each group a verb and ask groups to make vocabulary cards for each verb.

   b. Say each verb and gesture to demonstrate the meaning of each. Together with the students, repeat a second time by saying and demonstrating the meaning.

   c. Conduct a Total Physical Response (TPR) activity. Say a verb and encourage them to mime the verb as you say it (see Lado, 2012; Lado, n.d.).

   d. Demonstrate the verbs (*poke, tear, shred, crumple, rip*) with a square piece of paper. Hand out squares of paper to each student and have them do the same actions on their own squares of paper along with you.

   e. Write on the board the cloze of a patterned sentence with a blank for the verb and underline the object.

      Example: On Tuesday, the square was _____ into scraps.

   f. Ask students to insert verb cards into the cloze.

   g. Ask students to write a parallel sentence substituting any of these verbs. In addition, allow students to substitute in their sentences the object and the day of the week of their choice.

   h. Read each of the students' sentences. As you read, invite students to stand and demonstrate an action. Have their classmates identify the action.

6. Teach the verbs introduced in the last pages of the book (i.e., *waited, made, looked out, gave birth to, crossed, lead, had*).

   a. Make additional verb cards for these.

   b. Conduct another TPR activity for these verbs.

7. Check mastery of the verbs (hand out the Assessment in Appendix A) and track progress (see Appendix B).

Guided Practice

1. Give students more square pieces of paper and have them reenact all of the scenes from the book (or their favorite scenes) by poking, crumpling, cutting, etc., their paper.

2. Gather groups of up to seven students and take dictation of their experience. Transcribe what they say onto a language experience approach (LEA) chart. See Appendix C for an example of an LEA chart.

3. Read this chart together in a variety of ways until students are able to read it on their own.

Fluency Practice

Have students read and reread the book and the LEA chart.

Application

Either together or independently, have students make books using another shape.

CAVEATS AND OPTIONS

- For early-level beginners and younger students, limit the cloze activity to four nouns first, then four verbs, and complete the book's activities across a week of class sessions.
- In pairs, have learners ask and answer these questions: "What happened on Monday? What happened on Tuesday?" Continue for each day of the week.
- In pairs, have learners ask their partner to demonstrate each of the verbs (e.g., "Show me *bubbled*").
- Adapt the activity for older students by discussing the allegory itself—a tale not just of resilience but of creative transformation. The square is not defeated by what is done to it, whether that is being ripped, shattered, or poked. It withstands the assaults by quickly creating something out of this adversity. Each day, it makes something beautiful—and in the end, after the bullying stops, the square makes itself into a window that reveals the resulting beauty it created.
- Adapt the activity for higher levels by drawing attention to the utility of this type of sentence structure to reflect the passivity of the square. It does not focus on who did the bullying.
- To adapt the activity for students with limited formal schooling, see Appendix D.

REFERENCES AND FURTHER READING

Feldman, J. (n.d.). *Language experience charts*. Literacy Connections. https://www.literacyconnections.com/drjeanlecharts-php/ (Reprinted from *Ready, set, read: Hundreds of exciting, skill-appropriate activities, pre-K–1*, by J. Feldman, 1999, Crystal Springs Books).

Hall, M. (2011). *Perfect Square*. Greenwillow Books.

Lado, A. (n.d.) *ELL Teaching Strategies Guidebook*. Marymount University. https://marymount.edu/academics/wp-content/uploads/sites/3/2023/02/ELL-Teaching-Strategies-Guidebook.pdf

Lado, A. (2012). *Teaching beginner ELLs with picture books: Tellability*. Corwin/Sage.

Lado, A. (2015). Teaching beginner ELLs with picture books: Tellability. *GATESOL Journal 24*(2). https://doi.org/10.52242/gatesol.19

Milwaukee Art Museum. (2021, October 2). *Story time in the galleries: "Perfect square," by Michael Hall* [Video]. https://www.youtube.com/watch?v=8epgVp5YrUg

Nessel, D. D., & Dixon, C. N. (2008). *Using the language experience approach with English language learners: Strategies for engaging students and developing literacy*. Corwin.

APPENDIX A: *Assessment*

Distribute a sheet of paper to each student with drawings of the action words that were taught. Give commands for them to match the word to the correct drawing, such as the following:

- put an X on the paper that is *torn*
- put a circle on *poked*
- underline *waited*
- put an X on *looked*
- put a circle on *crumpled*

Student Name _____

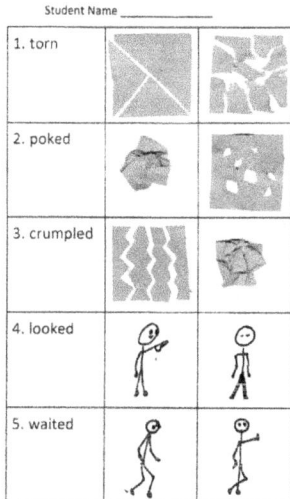

1. torn		
2. poked		
3. crumpled		
4. looked		
5. waited		

APPENDIX B: *Progress Tracker*

Create a Tracking Chart

1. Make a list of student names in the left column. In the top row, make columns for the set of words you taught (see the example checklist).

2. Assess students individually by marking the columns with different letters depending on whether a student demonstrates the ability to understand, express, or read it.

   a. Say the action word and, when a student demonstrates their understanding when listening, mark the column with the letter *L*.

   b. Mime the action or show an illustration of the action and, when a student demonstrates their ability to orally recall the word, mark the column with the letter *O* to indicate that they can orally express it.

   c. Show the written word and mark the column with the letter *R* to indicate that the student can read it.

IV

Sample Checklist: Words With Initial Blends

Perfect Square	clapped	crossed	shredded	crumbled	cramped	snipped	square
student #1	L	L	L	L			
student #2		L O	L O	L O	L	L	
student #3	L O R	L O R	L O R	L O R	O	O	O

APPENDIX C: *Sample Language Experience Approach Chart*

An LEA chart is a sample of sentences that students dictated to the teacher, as in the following example.

> *Perfect Square* (Hall, 2011)
>
> *Maria said, "I like this book."*
>
> *Shay said, "I gave red papers to everyone." Ayshm said, "I poked my square."*
>
> *Shahan said, "I cut my paper."*
>
> *Iqbal said, "I ripped my square so it made itself into a mountain." Shahan said, "I crumpled my paper and it is a ball."*
>
> *Esteban said, "We made a book about a square."*

APPENDIX D: *Simultaneous Oral Written Language*

For students with limited formal schooling, this adapted activity develops their visual memory for the written word using the technique of simultaneous oral written language (SOWL).

1. Select four visually presented words from the text, such as *fountain, mountain, bridge,* and *garden*.

2. Write these four words in a grid on the board. Together, say and point to each of the words on the grid. As needed, refer to the illustrations in the book.

Example:

fountain	mountain
bridge	garden

3. Make a word card for each.

4. One by one, have students place each word card on the matching word in the grid.

5. After students master the four grid words, one by one, hold each of the cards so that it is visually distant to the grid. For example, hold a card in front of yourself. Ask the students to recognize the word on the card by pointing to it on the grid.

6. Slowly increase the distance between the grid and each card. For example, put the cards on a desk that is across the room so that the student must hold the written word in their memory as they walk back to check the grid.

7. The final step is to dispense with the grid altogether and allow students to read the words in random order.

8. Review the cards the next day.

9. If students have diffculty with this technique, then make the grid and the cards with the illustrations and repeat the steps as before.

10. Repeat this sequence with another four words.

IV

Creating Process Analysis Infographics From Learners' Life Experiences

Tamara Mae Roose

Levels	Intermediate to advanced
Ages Suitable for Activity	Adult
Aims	Discover process analysis
	Develop critical thinking and creativity
	Build bridges between out-of-school knowledge and language development
	Develop cultural and social awareness
Class Time	20–45 minutes
Preparation Time	10 minutes
Resources	Activity ideas (Appendix A)
	Sample infographics (Appendix B)
	Paper and colored pencils/crayons/markers, or access to the internet on laptops or tablets

Infographics are visual representations of information that communicate ideas in a clear and simple way (Lankow et al., 2012; Smicklas, 2012). This can enhance communication, comprehension, learning, and motivation in the language learning classroom (Bicen & Beheshti, 2022; Rezaei & Sayadian, 2015). In this activity, learners practice process analysis by creating infographics to explain how something is done. In the process, they must draw upon their diverse funds of knowledge from their lives outside of school (González et al., 2005). This activity promotes critical thinking and creativity and helps learners develop cultural and social awareness.

PROCEDURE

1. Ask students to think about something specific they know how to do well. Encourage them to be creative and consider all the things they know how to do from their hobbies, jobs, experiences, and language and cultural backgrounds. Invite learners to share their ideas aloud as a whole class, in partners, or in small groups.

   a. Be prepared with some of your own examples (e.g., cook a particular dish, do a style of dance). See Appendix A for more suggestions.

   b. Alternatively, transform this warm-up into a writing and brainstorming activity by modeling mind mapping on the board and then instructing learners to do this on their own sheets of paper.

2. Elicit what makes this skill different from other similar skills (e.g., if they chose planting a vegetable garden, what makes this different from planting flowers? Or if they chose doing judo, what makes this different from doing karate?).

3. Discuss the importance of instructions when learning how to do something new (e.g., follow a recipe, construct a bookshelf) and how frustrating it can be if the instructions are unclear.

4. Ask learners to think about how they would explain to someone how to do the skill they have chosen. Tell them to write down all the specific steps involved in the process.

5. Ask learners to create an infographic to illustrate the steps of the process in the order they typically occur.

   a. Be prepared to share examples of infographics (Appendix B) and emphasize that the steps should be in chronological order and include specific details.

   b. Provide students with art supplies and blank paper, or, if technology is available, share suggested websites for creating infographics, such as Canva (canva.com).

6. Invite learners to share their infographics in small groups and to give each other feedback. Then give learners time to revise their infographics. They can add more details based on the comments and questions they receive.

7. If time permits, have a few learners come to the front of the class and present their infographics.

CAVEATS AND OPTIONS

- Extend the activity by asking learners the common mistakes people make when they first start learning their chosen skill; have learners include cautions and tips at the bottom of their infographics.

- Adapt this activity for a younger age or lower level by providing cue cards with different common daily tasks written and/or displayed as images (e.g., brush your teeth, ride a bike, make a cup of tea) and sentence starters (e.g., *First, you should…*, *Next, you need to…*, *Finally, don't forget to…*).

- Make this a speaking activity by asking learners to act out their infographics and have the class guess or name the steps involved. This may also help learners discover missing steps they have forgotten along the way and then add more details to their infographics.

- Put learners in pairs or small groups to work together. This increases the communication needed to cocreate their infographics.

- Use this as an in-class activity or take-home assignment and have learners come back to class and share.

- Instruct learners to create their infographics by hand or use online templates to increase digital literacy skills.

IV

REFERENCES AND FURTHER READING

Bicen, H., & Beheshti, M. (2022). Assessing perceptions and evaluating achievements of ESL learners with the usage of infographics in a flipped classroom learning environment. *Interactive Learning Environments, 30*(3), 498–526. https://doi.org/10.1080/10494820.2019.1666285

González, N., Moll, L., & Amanti, C. (Eds). (2005). *Funds of knowledge: Theorizing practices in households, communities and classrooms.* Erlbaum.

Lankow, J., Ritchie, J., & Crooks, R. (2012). *Infographics: The power of visual storytelling.* John Wiley & Sons.

Rezaei, N., & Sayadian, S. (2015). The impact of infographics on Iranian EFL learners' grammar learning. *Journal of Applied Linguistics and Language Research, 2*(1), 78–85.

Smiciklas, M. (2012). *The power of infographics: Using pictures to communicate and connect with your audiences.* Que Publishing.

APPENDIX A: *Sample Activity Ideas*

Prompts to Promote Cultural Awareness

How to make your favorite holiday food

How to greet someone older than yourself in your culture/community

How to give a good housewarming gift

How to travel around your hometown

How to prepare for a wedding in your culture/community

Prompts to Promote Daily Life Skills

How to make a doctor's appointment

How to get a driver's license

How to buy a car

How to prepare for a job interview

How to return something to a store

Prompts to Promote Social Skills

How to be a good listener

How to talk about your grades with your teacher

How to be a good neighbor

How to apologize when you hurt someone

How to be a good family member

APPENDIX B: *Infographic Templates*

Samples of infographic templates shared with learners available through Canva (www.canva.com)

Decoding a Total Physical Response

Lisa Horvath

Levels	All
Ages Suitable for Activity	Any
Aims	Develop observation and inference skills
	Practice listening and speaking
	Develop self- and social awareness
Class Time	5–45 minutes
Preparation Time	10
Resources	Prompts (see Appendix)

nterpersonal relationships are influenced by the ability to read and interpret facial expressions and body language. Paying attention to and interpreting visual cues in other people is a key social skill. In this activity, learners practice reading and interpreting facial expressions and body language. In pairs, learners physically respond to a spoken prompt and verbally respond to the physical response. This activity promotes creativity and helps learners develop self- and social awareness.

PROCEDURE

1. Divide the class into pairs. One person from each pair will be the actor and the other person will be the interpreter.
2. Instruct actors to close their eyes and use their imaginations.
3. Provide a spoken prompt, such as the following:

    It's early morning. The sun is slowly rising and beginning to shine in through your window. You wake up, stretch your arms, rub your eyes, pull back the curtain, and look outside. There is a large tree just outside the window. You see it every day. But today there's something different. Today, you see something coming out from behind the tree's trunk. What is it? Get a clear image in your mind of what's coming out from behind the tree. React to it and freeze your reaction!

4. Actors open their eyes.
5. Instruct interpreters to look at the actor and interpret their physical reaction. The interpreter describes three things:
    a. what the actor imagined they saw
    b. the emotional reaction
    c. the reason for the reaction

    For example, a higher level student may say:

    [Partner's name] saw a giant squirrel with a napkin tied around its neck, a knife in one hand, and a fork in the other. It looks very hungry. [Partner's name] is terrified because they think the squirrel wants to eat them. But the squirrel only wants to eat the giant walnut that is under the window.

6. Monitor conversations between pairs. If interpreters are having a hard time, ask guiding questions, such as "Was [actor's name] happy? What makes *you* feel happy? (Marshmallows.) So maybe [actor's name] saw a delicious marshmallow?"

7. Actors then tell interpreters how accurate their interpretation was and what they really "saw" in their imaginations.

8. Invite a few pairs to come to the front of the class. The actor shows their physical response, the interpreter tells their interpretation, and then the actor tells the class what they really saw.

9. Notice how the tone of your voice affects the reactions the actors have. If you provide the prompt with a happy, excited tone of voice, your learners are more likely to respond with a happy response. If you provide the prompt with a fearful voice, responses will tend to be that of fear.

CAVEATS AND OPTIONS

- Adapt this activity for any age and level by changing the context and language level of the prompt.

- Use this activity as a 5-minute warm-up or extend it to a full-length class with several prompts and/or extension activities.

- Extend the learning by having actors draw what they saw and interpreters draw their interpretations. Then, actors and interpreters write a description of what was seen.

- Have pairs work together to write a story (including background details and resolution) based on a combination of their response and interpretation.

REFERENCES AND FURTHER READING

Asher, J. J. (2009). *Learning another language through actions*. Sky Oaks Productions.

Heathfield, D. (2014). *Storytelling with our learners*. Delta Publishing.

APPENDIX: *Prompts*

You walk down the street. It's cold and rainy. You pull out your umbrella, but when you open it, out pops a...

You are riding the bus. A clown gets on the bus, reaches into their pocket, and pulls out a...

You are sitting at your desk taking a test. Suddenly, the lines on the paper start to shift and move, then slide off the paper forming a...

You are a sloth climbing a tree. You hear a low rumbling sound and feel a vibration in the tree. After a few minutes, you see...

You are sleeping when an unfamiliar sound wakes you up. You grab a flashlight, shine it under your bed, and see...

You are at the top of a tall skyscraper. The wind picks up and starts to swirl around you. Looking into the whirlwind, you see...

You are diving in the Mediterranean Sea looking at a school of tiny colorful fish. All at once, they turn in the same direction and swim away. A dark shadow appears. You look back and see…

You are digging in the dirt when your shovel hits something hard. You reach down, brush away the dirt, and see…

You are taking selfies with your friends. When you take a closer look at the picture, you see someone was behind you. It was…

You are walking through a desert. It's hot and the sun is beating down on your neck. You look into the distance and see…

You are an eagle flying high over an open field. Looking down, you see…

You are stranded on an island. You've been there, alone, for three years. One day, you are sitting on the beach. Suddenly, something comes ashore. It's…

You are sitting in class. Two people in front of you are looking at their phones and laughing. You look over their shoulders and see…

You are a stealthy cat, stalking a bird in a tree. Suddenly you hear a noise. You turn and see…

You are drinking your favorite drink. Looking into the glass, you see…

IV

Designing and Describing Your Ideal Creative Workspace

Sheena Moleta

Level	Intermediate
Ages Suitable for Activity	Secondary to university
Aims	Build descriptive vocabulary related to creative workspaces
	Correctly use adjectives, prepositional phrases, and complex sentences
	Develop visualization and creative thinking skills
	Design and describe their ideal workspace
Class Time	1 hour
Preparation Time	30 minutes
Resources	Handout (Appendix B)
	Access to the internet on laptops or tablets
	Laptop and projector
	Optional: Art materials and magazine clippings

This activity is designed to help students practice descriptive writing and grammar while encouraging creative thinking. By exploring the concept of creative workspaces through mood boards, students will improve their abilities to visually organize their thoughts and emotions, explore relationships between images, and express ideas nonverbally.

PROCEDURE

1. *Reading:* Distribute the reading on elements of a creative workspace (Appendix A). Have students read carefully, paying special attention to descriptive language, particularly vocabulary related to design and creativity. Instruct students to consider how these elements might influence their own ideal workspace.

2. *Mood Board Creation:* Encourage students to create a mood board for their ideal creative workspace.

   a. Begin by discussing what a mood board is and how creatives use them. Explain that a mood board is like a collage of ideas—it brings together images, colors, and textures to capture a specific theme or feeling. Tell students that designers use mood boards to gather inspiration and refine their vision before they start creating. Show examples of mood board templates (Appendix B).

   a. Instruct students to create a visual representation of their ideal creative workspace using at least seven images that reflect the atmosphere, tools, and design elements they envision.

   a. Have students create their mood boards digitally, using Padlet (padlet.com), Canva (canva.com), or another platform. Alternatively, provide art supplies and have students create physical mood boards. Direct them to select images of patterns, colors, and textures that align with their vision of a workspace that fosters creativity.

3. *Descriptive Paragraph:* Have students write a 200- to 250-word descriptive paragraph about their ideal creative workspace.

   a. Instruct students to incorporate specific vocabulary from the reading. They should include at least five adjectives to describe the characteristics of the space (e.g., *spacious, bright, calm*).

   b. Require students to use prepositional phrases to describe the location of objects within the workspace (e.g., "The desk is by the window to maximize sunlight.").

   c. Ensure that students include complex sentences to show relationships between ideas (e.g., "Because I find it easier to concentrate in a quiet environment, I would choose a room that is away from busy areas.").

   d. Depending on the learners' proficiency level, share the sample sentences in Appendix C for scaffolding and support.

4. *In-Class Presentation:* Have students orally present their mood boards and descriptive paragraphs in class. Instruct them to explain the key elements of their ideal workspace, describing how the images and design elements on their mood board would support their creative work.

CAVEATS AND OPTIONS

- For students who may not be familiar with creating digital mood boards, provide the option to create a physical board using magazine clippings or printed images. Alternatively, take the time to provide a demonstration of a tool like Padlet and model mood board creation before Step 2c.

- Although this activity focuses on designing a creative workspace, mood boards can be used for many other purposes. Adapt the activity by allowing students to choose a different theme that resonates with them (see Appendix D). Also, encourage students to think beyond these suggestions and explore themes that are personally meaningful or relevant to their interests.

APPENDIX A: *Reading for Vocabulary*

Lighting: Natural light is ideal for creativity, as it boosts mood and energy. If natural light isn't available, use warm artificial lighting to create a cozy and inviting atmosphere.

Colors: The color of your workspace can affect your creativity. Bright colors like yellow and orange can stimulate the mind, whereas softer tones like blue and green can have a calming effect.

Furniture: Comfortable and ergonomic furniture is essential for long hours of work. A spacious desk and a comfortable chair are key elements, and so are storage solutions to keep the space organized.

Personal Touches: Adding personal elements like artwork, plants, or inspirational quotes can make the space feel more welcoming and reflective of your personality.

Minimalism: A clutter-free environment can help reduce distractions and improve focus. Keeping your workspace tidy and organized is crucial to maintaining a productive environment.

Tools and Technology: Having the right tools and technology at hand is essential. Whether you need filming equipment, art supplies, or design software, make sure your workspace is equipped with everything you need.

APPENDIX B: *Sample Mood Board Template*

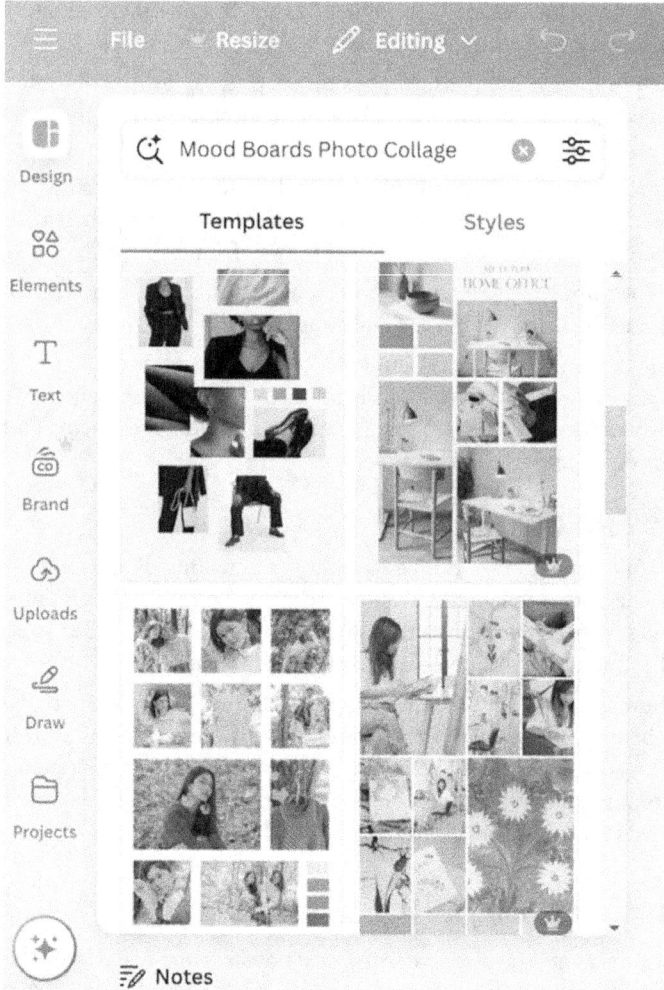

Example Mood Board Templates from Canva.com

APPENDIX C: *Example Sentences*

Adjectives: Use adjectives to describe the characteristics of your space. Include at least five adjectives from the reading. Here are some examples:

- I want a *spacious* room with *natural* light.
- My workspace would have *comfortable* seating and a *minimalist* design to reduce distractions.
- I prefer a *bright* room with *warm* lighting to create a *welcoming* atmosphere.

Prepositional Phrases: Use prepositional phrases to indicate where things are located. Here are some examples:

- The desk is *by the window* to maximize sunlight.
- I would place my easel *near the window* so I can work with natural light.
- Shelves *on the wall* would hold all my art supplies.

Complex Sentences: Combine ideas and show relationships between them using complex sentences. Here are some examples:

- Because I find it easier to concentrate in a quiet environment, I would choose a room that is away from busy areas.
- I would like a large desk where I can spread out my materials so that I can work on multiple projects at once.
- If I had more space, I would include a reading corner where I could relax and find inspiration.

APPENDIX D: *Potential Themes for Your Mood Board*

Wedding Planning: Plan your dream wedding with sections for themes, color schemes, venue decorations, and floral arrangements.

Outfit Inspirations: Focus on fashion, categorizing outfits by season or occasion.

Garden and Landscaping: Include plants, garden layouts, and outdoor accessories that reflect your ideal outdoor space.

Personal Branding: Create a mood board for your personal or professional brand with logos, fonts, and color palettes.

Travel and Adventure: Visualize your dream travel destinations, including landscapes, cultural experiences, and iconic landmarks.

Art and Craft Projects: Compile do-it-yourself project ideas, materials, and techniques for future creative endeavors.

Home Renovation Projects: Create a visual plan for home improvement projects, such as kitchen or bathroom remodels.

Seasonal Decorations: Collect images of and ideas for decorations for important traditional holidays in your culture (e.g., Holi, Lunar New Year, Christmas, Ramadan).

IV

Expressing Emotions Through Visual Art

Elena Taylor

Levels	High beginner to intermediate
Ages Suitable for Activity	Any
Aims	Encourage self-expression and emotional awareness
	Develop descriptive language and vocabulary related to emotions, colors, and art techniques
	Practice reflective writing and speaking about personal creative work
Class Time	60 minutes
Preparation Time	15 minutes
Resources	Art supplies (colored pencils, markers, crayons, paper, etc.)
	Writing materials (paper and pens)
	Sample image of abstract art

V isual art can be a powerful medium for exploring and expressing emotions, which makes it an excellent tool in the classroom to help students articulate and reflect on their feelings in English (Yenawine, 2013). This creative activity encourages students to develop visual literacy and vocabulary related to emotions, colors, and art techniques.

PROCEDURE

1. Introduce the idea of using art to express emotions or concepts. Show students an example of simple abstract art (e.g., a combination of colors or shapes) and explain how different colors or shapes can represent various emotions. For instance, blue might symbolize calmness or sadness, while jagged lines could represent anger or uneasiness (see Caveats and Options, at the end of the activity, for more insights).

2. Introduce vocabulary related to emotions (e.g., *sad, nostalgic, surprised*), colors (e.g., *bold, warm, vibrant*), and art techniques (e.g., *soft, intricate, realistic*). You can find additional adjectives in Appendix A.

3. Ask students to think of one emotion (e.g., anger, sadness, happiness) or concept (e.g., love, family, loneliness) that they could represent visually, through art. Distribute art supplies. Give students 15–20 minutes to create their piece of art. Encourage students to think about how they can use particular shapes and/or colors to represent that emotion or concept.

4. After students finish their artwork, ask them to write a short reflection (five to seven sentences) describing their piece. In their reflections, students should briefly explain why they chose particular colors and/or shapes. Provide sentence starters for lower level students (see Appendix B for ideas).

5. Display the students' artwork around the room (i.e., on the tables or the walls). Have students walk around and look at each other's artwork, writing down questions/comments for each piece.

6. After students have viewed each other's work, put them in small groups and ask them to discuss it: Each student needs to ask one or two questions about their classmate's art. For example, they could ask, "Why did you choose this color? What emotion/concept were you trying to express?" Encourage students to use their written reflections to help them answer their classmates' questions.

7. Bring the class back together and invite a few volunteers to share their artwork with the class, explaining the emotion and/or concept behind their art as well as their creative choices.

CAVEATS AND OPTIONS

- Be mindful of cultural differences related to the interpretation of colors. Ask students to share how different emotions are associated with colors in their home cultures.

- If students are uncomfortable with drawing, allow them to create simple abstract art (i.e., simple shapes).

- For more advanced students, extend the written reflection by asking them to analyze how their home culture or personal background influenced their artwork.

REFERENCES AND FURTHER READING

Yenawine, P. (2013). *Visual thinking strategies: Using art to deepen learning across school disciplines.* Harvard.

APPENDIX A: *Vocabulary Lists*

Adjectives for Emotions	Adjectives for Colors	Adjectives for Art Styles
angry	bold	abstract
confident	cool	chaotic
excited	dull	eclectic
fearful	earthy	fluid
happy	faded	geometric
hopeful	monochromatic	jagged
sad	pastel	intricate
nostalgic	warm	minimalist
peaceful	vibrant	realistic
surprised	vivid	soft

APPENDIX B: *Sample Sentence Starters*

- In my artwork, I used [color] because it represents [concept/emotion].
- I drew [object] because...
- I chose [shape/line] to show [concept/emotion] because it looks [description].
- My artwork is about [concept/emotion] because...
- The [object/shape] in my drawing represents [concept/emotion] because...
- I used [color/shapes] to express [concept/emotion] because...

A Floral Garland

Amy Bohman Blanco and Khemendra Kumar

Levels	Beginner
Ages Suitable for Activity	Early childhood to elementary
Aims	Learn to weave a floral garland
	Practice listening and speaking
	Foster cultural and social awareness
	Understand what a garland means and represents
Class Time	1 hour
Preparation Time	15 minutes
Resources	Flowers
	String
	Needles
	Measuring tape
	Scissors
	Handout (Appendix)

This activity aims to develop valuable social and communication skills as students listen to and interpret visual cues while creating a traditional welcome gift. Students in groups share their thoughts by responding to questions that center on the construction of a traditional floral garland. As there are many similarities that transcend across cultures, this activity provides an opportunity for discussions through engagement. This activity promotes ingenuity and individual learners' growth in cultural and social awareness.

PROCEDURE

1. Activate prior knowledge by asking learners what they know about floral garlands. If learners are unfamiliar with floral garlands, explain that they are sometimes displayed decoratively, representing beauty, love, peace, and purity. Let learners know that they also are often given symbolically to recognize achievement or to honor and respect a special person, elder, or leader.

2. Display pictures of types of floral garlands. Search the internet for the following: *lei* (Hawaiian), *salusalu* (Fijian), or *mala* (Indian) to offer reference points.

3. Invite someone from the community to share their experience making a garland and demonstrate the basics of putting one together. If no one from the community is available, explain the process of making a garland to the class:

   a. Flower preparation: Trim off the stems of each flower.

   b. String preparation: Measure 1 meter of string and tie a knot at one end. Attach the other end to a needle.

    c. Stringing flowers: Weave the stems of each flower in a uniform pattern using the needle. All flowers should face outwards. String until you reach the needle end. Remove the needle and tie both ends together.

4. Divide the class into groups. Provide each group with the required resources: flowers, string, needle, scissors, and measuring tape.

5. Select group leaders who may have weaved a garland or feel confident leading the group.

6. Tell students to decide on the type of garland they wish to weave and ask them what flowers they plan to use, the size, the pattern, and ways to secure the piece.

7. Have students work in groups to weave garlands with the support of group leaders, or an elder and/or volunteer from the community (if possible).

8. Circulate and facilitate small-group discussions while monitoring groups as they are weaving their garlands (see Appendix A). Be sure to emphasize the symbolism of the garland.

9. Invite each group to show their finished garland to the class and explain why they chose to make it in a particular style, who the garland is for, and what it represents.

CAVEATS AND OPTIONS

- Select shells, seeds, leaves, or beads if flowers are unavailable.
- Additional preparation time might be needed to collect flowers (as a class) or other items for the garlands.
- Invite someone (or several people) from the school or community who students can present the garlands to, if possible.
  — Discuss why these people were chosen and what the garlands represent for each person.
  — Before the special guest arrives, choose one representative from each group who will be responsible for placing the garland on the neck of the visitor. Have the representative practice before the guest arrives.
  — If an elder or volunteer from the community participates, have the students show their appreciation.

REFERENCES AND FURTHER READING

Bais, M. (2017, December 1). Mala: The floral garlands of India. *Garland Magazine.* https://garlandmag.com/article/mala-the-floral-garlands-of-india/

Hawaii Flower Lei. (2021). *The Hawaiian lei tradition.* https://hawaiiflowerlei.com/lei-history/

Vundilo, T. (2017, December 6). Na noqu salusalu: Garlands in Fiji. *Garland Magazine.* https://garlandmag.com/article/na-noqu-salusalu

Warschauer, M. (1997). A sociocultural approach to literacy and its significance for CALL. In K. Murphy-Judy & R. Sanders (Eds.), *Nexus: The convergence of research & teaching through new information technologies* (pp. 88–97). University of North Carolina.

IV

APPENDIX: *Discussion Questions*

Who is the garland for?

What does your garland represent?

Where would you see this garland worn?

When would you wear a garland?

Why would you wear a garland?

How are you making the garland?

Inspiring Speech Through Visual Arts

Sohani Gandhioke and Chanchal Singh

Level	All
Ages Suitable for Activity	Any
Aims	Practice speaking skills through storytelling
	Develop self-confidence
	Improve skills for collaborative learning
Class Time	5–55 minutes
Preparation Time	5 minutes
Resources	Blank A4-size paper or chart/poster paper

rt is the language of a deeper cognizance. Creative expression blossoms in a collaborative learning environment where learners are encouraged to practice the skills of verbally and visually expressing themselves through the medium of art. Furthermore, as stated by Anderson (2017), "arts support conventional literacy skills—reading, writing, speaking, and listening."

PROCEDURE

1. Divide the class into groups of four, six, or eight learners.
2. Give each group a large blank piece of paper (size A4 or larger). Fold the paper into four, six, or eight squares, depending on how many students are in the group.
3. Tell learners that they will illustrate a story and tell it as they draw it, taking turns as follows:

   a. The first learner draws a picture in the first square. As they draw, they speak aloud, describing their picture and what their art conveys.

   b. Tell learners to pass the paper to the next learner in their group. The next learner adds to the story by drawing another picture in the next square, building upon the story and artwork of the first learner. As they add their drawing to the story, they speak aloud in the target language, explaining their work of art, thereby weaving a story connecting every stroke of the artwork on the paper.

   c. The paper should keep moving until each member of the group has added their artwork and spoken their contribution to the story. It is essential that learners listen attentively to the peers before them to interpret the previous artwork, get inspired, plan their input, and construct their drawing.

   d. Move among the learners during the task, closely observing and guiding them in case of artist's block. Provide support to keep learners focused. Most importantly, assist them when they need help with pronunciation or grammatical errors.

4. Instruct students to exchange their completed artwork with another group. Have each group look at another group's artwork and write their own interpretation of the images. Tell learners to imagine and write a story based on what they see, without knowing the intended story of the original group.

5. Invite groups to present the story they wrote about another group's artwork to the whole class. Then the original group (i.e., the creators) tells their original story.

6. Discuss the differences between the two stories. Ask the interpretation group to explain why they wrote the story the way they did. What visual cues in the artwork influenced their choices in interpretation?

CAVEATS AND OPTIONS

- Allow creativity to flow and chatter to flourish, unrestrained and boundless, within the groups. Remember, the purpose of this task is language production and peer collaboration through creative visualizations.

- The outcome of this activity may vary depending on learners' proficiency levels, learner motivation, and skills for peer collaboration—all of which are integral to the success of this task.

- Depending on your goals, use this activity as a 5-minute warm-up or extend it for an entire class time, adding several stages (i.e., more complex stories or a jigsaw activity) to augment the learning outcomes.

- Or, use this activity to fill extra time left at the end of a class. This ensures students leave the class completely animated and excited to have had an enriching English language learning experience, and they will look forward to the next class.

- Add variety and review prior learning by instructing the learners to use vocabulary that was previously taught in class when speaking and writing.

- Adapt this activity for a lower level with the following variation: Instead of instructing learners to draw, have them examine a picture. Ask learners to look at the picture, speak about what they see in the picture, and take turns to develop a story, connecting to what their peers have already said before them. To scaffold the activity, model the task as an example for the students before they begin.

REFERENCES AND FURTHER READING

Anderson, A. (2017). How and why the arts support language learning and cognition: A picture is worth a thousand words. *Psychology Today*. https://www.psychologytoday.com/us/blog/arts-all-children/201709/how-and-why-the-arts-support-language-learning-and-cognition

Brown, H. D. (2007). *Principles of language learning and teaching* (5th ed.). Pearson Longman.

Celce-Murcia, M. (2001). *Teaching English as a second language or foreign language* (3rd ed.). Heinle & Heinle.

Layers of the Earth

Amy Bohman Blanco and Runaaz Sharma

Level	Beginner
Ages Suitable for Activity	Early childhood to early secondary
Aims	Learn about the layers of the earth
	Create a visual representation
	Practice listening and speaking
	Foster cooperative learning in groups
Class Time	1 hour
Preparation Time	15 minutes
Resources	Projector or equipment to watch video/s online
	Handouts (Appendixes A–D) as needed
	Art supplies

This project-based activity is centered on communication through planning and creating a visual representation of the layers of the earth. Students will be introduced to the necessary vocabulary and scientific knowledge related to each of the earth's layers and be provided with opportunities to use the newly acquired scientific language. Through reading, planning, and negotiating ideas, learners develop visual literacies in both interpreting and producing visual content.

PROCEDURE

1. Activate prior knowledge by asking learners what they know about the layers of the Earth.

2. Discuss what they see every day on the layer of the Earth on which they live, the crust. Examples that learners could suggest might include streets, buildings, and houses. Help them also think of natural features such as lakes, rivers, mountains, trees, plants, rocks, etc. Then, explain that we live on the earth's crust, and that there are other layers beneath the crust.

3. Introduce vocabulary for the layers of the Earth: *crust, mantel, outer core, inner core* (see Appendix A).

4. Distribute or project the information about the layers of the earth in Appendix B.

5. Tell students to close their eyes and imagine what they think each layer of the Earth looks like.

6. Have students create a visual representation of the layers of the Earth. Encourage them to use their imaginations and be as creative as possible. See Appendix C for project suggestions. Allow students to work individually or in pairs and complete a project plan (see Appendix D). Students can complete their projects in class or for homework.

CAVEATS AND OPTIONS

- This activity could be integrated with another discipline, like art or science.
- Additional time may need to be added to prepare and gather materials to build the projects.
- To extend learning, find a YouTube video to share about the layers of the Earth.
- Provide worksheets to reinforce learning. Free worksheets can be found at: www.sciencefacts.net/worksheets/layers-of-the-earth-worksheet and www.teaching-expertise.com/classroom-ideas/earth-layers-activity.
- Selection of handouts and project ideas can be adjusted for age, ability, and focus.
- Invite a geologist to share their knowledge of the Earth's layers.

REFERENCES AND FURTHER READING

Stocking, N. (2010). *Conceptual understanding and retention of vocabulary for visual learners.* Education Masters (Paper 104). https://fisherpub.sjf.edu/cgi/viewcontent.cgi?article=1103&context=education_ETD_masters

APPENDIX A: *Layers of the Earth Vocabulary*

1. Crust – the layer of rock that forms Earth's outer surface
2. Mantle – the layer of hot, solid material between Earth's crust & core
3. Outer core – a layer of molten iron and nickel that surrounds the inner core of the Earth
4. Inner core – a dense sphere of solid iron and nickel at the center of the Earth

APPENDIX B: *Composition of the Earth*

Each layer of the earth is made from something different.

Crust

- The crust is the thin outer layer of the Earth where we live.
- It is between 5 km (under the ocean) and 70 km (on land) thick.
- The crust is made of rocks.

Mantle

- The mantle is the layer under the crust.
- It is about 3,000 km thick.
- The mantel is also made of rocks.

Outer Core

- The outer core is very hot (4,500 degrees Celsius)!
- It is liquid because it's so hot.
- The outer core makes a magnetic field that protects the Earth from the sun.

Inner Core
- The inner core is also very hot (5,000 degrees Celsius), almost as hot as the sun!
- Even though it is very hot, it is not liquid because it is under so much pressure.
- The inner core is the hottest part of the Earth,

APPENDIX C: *Project Ideas*

Directions: Choose a creative way to demonstrate your understanding of the layers of the Earth.
- Create layers of the Earth from colored clay.
- Draw or paint a picture.
- Make a picture by gluing different materials (sand, beans, pasta, cloth) for each layer.
- Make a 3D model with various materials.
- Bake a layered cake.
- Make a layered jar of different materials that represent the layers of the Earth.
- Create a flipbook making each page differently to reveal layers of the Earth.

IV

APPENDIX D: *Project Planning Sheet*

Project Planning Sheet

Name/s:	
Topic/Idea:	**Date to be completed:**

Description of Activity:

Action Plan:

Steps:	**Materials:**
1.	▪
2.	▪
3.	▪
4.	▪
5.	▪
6.	▪
7.	▪
8.	▪

Museum of Us: Self-Expression Through Art Exploration

Mandy Gearhart

Levels	All
Ages Suitable for Activity	Any
Aims	Learn and use vocabulary associated with sculptures and dioramas Answer questions related to important objects Sculpt and/or make a diorama
Class Time	90 minutes
Preparation Time	60 minutes (plus time to secure art supplies for activity)
Resources	Plastic tablecloths Modeling clay in multiple colors Air-dry clay Construction paper Liquid glue and glue sticks Drawing paper and pens, markers, or paints Shoeboxes Laptop and projector

This activity develops learners' visual literacy and language skills by exploring sculpture and diorama creation. Students express personal identity and cultural values through hands-on art making while practicing relevant vocabulary and descriptive language.

PROCEDURE

1. *Introduce Themes and Vocabulary (20 minutes):* Create a digital presentation or use the board to introduce the concepts of sculpture and dioramas and teach associated vocabulary.

   a. Introduce vocabulary that students will need in order to complete the art-making task: *make, sculpt, shape, arrange, design, object, clay, miniature, sculpture, diorama, representation.*

   b. Introduce vocabulary that students will need in order to complete the group questions and writing task: *thing, love, important, hobby, free time, favorite.*

   c. Show one or more videos about sculpting and/or diorama making as inspiration (see Appendix A).

2. *Guiding Questions in Groups (10 minutes):* Divide students into small groups. Tell students, "Today we're going to be thinking about important things in our lives. We will talk together and use some different tools to help us make representations of these important things." Hand out or project the following group discussion questions:

a. What are some things you use every day? What is the most important thing you own?

b. What was your favorite toy or object (i.e., thing) when you were a child? Why? In your home country/culture, are there special things you give someone on important occasions, such as when they move into a new house or have a baby?

c. What is your favorite hobby (i.e., thing to do for fun)? What things do you need to do this hobby (e.g., for playing football/soccer, you need a ball to kick)?

d. If I were to make a doll, avatar, or action figure of you, what are five accessories it would have (e.g., striped shirt, glasses, cookbook, pet, smartphone)? Why?

3. *Making a Sculpture/Diorama (45 minutes):* Guide students through the following steps to create their sculpture or diorama of a meaningful thing or object:

a. Ask students to identify an object that represents themselves or is meaningful to them.

b. Guide students to make one of the following artworks:

Option 1 – Create a 3D sculpture of their object in clay or papier-mâché using provided materials.

Option 2 – Create a 2D representation with paper and pens, pencils, paint, etc.

Option 3 – Create a 3D diorama that highlights their object using provided materials (e.g., clay, papier-mâché, markers or paints, shoebox).

c. When time is up, instruct students to clean up their art materials.

4. *Descriptive Writing (15 minutes):* Have students create exhibit labels for their art, including giving the object a title, describing what it is, and sharing why it is important to them. Have students share their completed labels and art pieces in groups or as a whole class.

CAVEATS AND OPTIONS

- Adjust your choices of guiding questions and example videos based on your location and student population. For example, you might adapt this activity to be about important people instead of important objects.

- To reduce the cost of supplies, origami could be substituted for clay, or other art mediums can be incorporated.

- Reduce the time of the activity for lower level learners, or extend the activity over multiple days to give higher level students more time and opportunity to create.

REFERENCES AND FURTHER READING

Myakota, A. (2023, July 5). *Why arts education is vital in supporting multilingual learners.* Participate Learning. https://www.participatelearning.com/blog/arts-education-for-multilingual-learners/

APPENDIX A: *Videos for Inspiration*

"Learn Sculpting - Activity 1 - Clay Modeling" (Learn Sculpting, 2011; www.youtube.com/watch?v=AFKnG-vENUw)

"Clay Rose Making Easy" (Clay Crafts, 2020; www.youtube.com/watch?v=TLSa-UrQ8n8)

"Easy Way to Make Clay Pot Without Wheel" (Creative Ideas by Shefu, 2020; www.youtube.com/watch?v=0z2cE8VOhfg)

"Rainforest Diorama school project [how to]" (StormAdventures, 2020; www.youtube.com/watch?v=c3ZrwtlJHmw)

"DIY Diorama for Kids" (Tensy StyLe, 2020; www.youtube.com/watch?v=i-W4f02S7AA)

APPENDIX B: *Example of a Student Sculpture and Description*

The tea cup is important to me because we drink a lot of tea in my home country, Kyrgyzstan. My mother has a beautiful tea cup and teapot. It makes me think of her. I miss her very much.

Image credit: Paul Thomas, Trellus. Used with permission.

IV

The Path Forward: A Visual Road Map

Sheena Moleta

Level	Intermediate to Advanced
Ages Suitable for Activity	Secondary to university
Aims	Visualize future goals in a structured and meaningful way
	Develop digital design skills
	Foster self-reflection and personal goal setting through creative expression
	Develop the ability to present ideas visually without relying on text
Class Time	1 hour and 30 minutes
Preparation Time	30 minutes
Resources	Access to the internet on laptops or tablets

In this activity, students will create an image-only presentation to represent what they envision for their future. Using visual road mapping, students will reflect on their personal and professional goals, visualizing key milestones. This activity encourages students to creatively express their future aspirations through visuals. It also develops students' digital literacy skills as they use online design platforms to create their presentations.

PROCEDURE

1. *Introduction to Visualization and Goal Setting:* Begin by discussing how visualization can help with setting goals. Explain that visualizing goals helps people stay motivated and on track, making the future feel more tangible and within reach.

2. Ask students to discuss the following questions in small groups:

   a. How can visualizing your future help you stay focused on your goals?

   b. How do small milestones contribute to long-term success?

   c. What symbols or images could represent your future aspirations?

3. Introduce road maps as a way to represent progress over time. Show example images of how visual road maps can help people organize ideas, track progress, and set achievable goals (see Appendix A for an example).

4. *Designing a Road Map for the Future:* Guide students through the following steps to create their own road maps:

   a. Ask students to log into the free version of Canva (canva.com) or any other online design tool that provides templates for timelines. Provide a brief tutorial if needed.

   b. Tell students to create a road map of their future goals. This should be a visual timeline that includes personal and professional goals and milestones, including the following:

  v. Short-term goals (e.g., upcoming educational achievements, new skill developments)

  vi. Long-term goals (e.g., career aspirations, major life milestones, personal growth)

 c. Encourage students to use symbols, icons, arrows, and images to depict milestones and progression from present to future. Tell students to include only minimal or no text—the visuals should tell the story.

5. *Presenting the Visuals:* Have each student present their visual road map to the class. They should explain their goals and how they plan to achieve them, relying on visuals and oral explanations. Encourage classmates to ask questions, engage with the visuals, and provide positive feedback on how well the visuals communicate the student's vision.

6. *Reflection & Discussion:* After all presentations are finished, hold a group reflection session where students discuss:

 a. what they learned about themselves and their aspirations through this process,

 b. how visualization helped them clarify their goals and see their path more clearly, and

 c. how breaking down their future goals into small, visual steps made them feel more achievable and realistic.

CAVEATS AND OPTIONS

- For students who are less familiar with Canva or your chosen digital tool, offer a brief tutorial or provide step-by-step resources to guide them through basic design functions.

- Adapt this activity by assigning it as group work, where students collaborate on shared goals and visions.

- For a low-tech version, have students draw and illustrate their road maps on paper instead of digitally.

APPENDIX: *Visual Road Map*

MY FUTURE, MY GOALS

Created using Canva.com template and images.

Reducing Xenophobia and Creating Connections Through Food Dishes

Andrea Lypka and Christy Williams

Levels	Intermediate to advanced
Ages Suitable for Activity	Adult
Class Time	3 (75-minute) sessions
Preparation Time	2 hours
Resources	Selected reading material (see Appendix A)
	Access to the internet on laptops or tablets
	Laptop and projector

Drawing on readings about food, culture, and prejudice, students explore how culinary traditions can counter stereotypes and foster intercultural understanding. In this project-based activity, students learn about key elements of infographics, including layout, design principles, and data visualization techniques, and apply their knowledge to create infographics tailored to newcomers' needs. By highlighting culturally significant dishes from their own background, students create infographics that not only inform, but also build empathy, reduce xenophobia, and support social inclusion. The project integrates language development with visual literacy and promotes the respectful exchange of cultural knowledge.

PROCEDURE

Part 1: Introduction to Reading, Infographics, and Understanding the Target Audience

1. *Reading and Vocabulary (20 minutes):* Have students read the selected text (see Appendix A) on their mobile devices, or by distributing hard copies. Define any unknown vocabulary, then ask students to discuss the following prompts:

    a. How can food connect people?

    b. How can food fight stereotypes and racism?

    c. What are some traditions related to food and guests in your countries?

2. *Introduction to Infographics (10 minutes):* Explain what an infographic is and its purpose. Introduce the elements of infographic design (see Appendix B). Provide and analyze examples of effective infographics with the whole class (see Appendix C for examples; also see www.freepik.com/free-photos-vectors/food-infographic and www.canva.com/templates/?query=food-infographics).

3. *Identifying the Target Audience (10 minutes):* Discuss newcomers' characteristics and needs. Brainstorm challenges and useful information for newcomers. Emphasize tailoring infographics to these needs.

4. *Brainstorming and Sketching (15 minutes):* Divide students into small groups. Brainstorm and sketch infographic ideas that highlight the cultural significance of food and how sharing traditional dishes can build understanding, challenge stereotypes, and foster connections across cultures. Encourage creativity and collaboration.

Part 2: Design Principles and Data Visualization Techniques

5. *Design Principles (15 minutes):* Introduce balance, contrast, color schemes, typography, and alignment (see Appendix D). Show examples and check understanding.

6. *Selecting Visuals and Icons (15 minutes):* Explain the importance of relevant visuals and icons to compose an infographic that communicates meaning effectively. Demonstrate how to search for and select appropriate visuals.

7. *Data Visualization Techniques (15 minutes):* Discuss and show examples of different types of data visualizations. Explain when and how to use each type effectively. Provide tips for simplifying complex data.

   Software Demonstration (20 minutes): Demonstrate using Canva (canva.com) to create infographics (see Appendix E for support). If students do not have access to Canva, show how to use Microsoft PowerPoint or Google Slides to create infographics (see Appendix F for a list of more free digital tools).

8. Give project directions and explain the assessment rubric (Appendix G).

Part 3: Designing Infographics for Newcomers

9. *Review (10 minutes):* Recap key design principles learned in the previous session. Remind students to consider the target audience for their infographics.

10. *Design Time (40 minutes):* Students work individually or in pairs using chosen software to design their infographics. Provide guidance and feedback. Encourage experimentation with design elements.

11. *Feedback and Circulation (Up to 25 minutes):* Pair students to provide peer feedback using the provided rubric (Appendix G).

CAVEATS AND OPTIONS

- In low-technology contexts, have students create infographics on paper.
- Discuss how students will share their finished projects.
- Create a series of events to celebrate other cultures and invite community members.
- Teach students how to talk about cultural differences respectfully and knowledgeably.

APPENDIX A: *Suggested Readings*

Alexis, A. C. (2021, June 14). *What are food deserts? All you need to know.* Healthline. https://www.healthline.com/nutrition/food-deserts

Barnhill, A., Ramírez, A. S., Ashe, M., Berhaupt-Glickstein, A., Freudenberg, N., Grier, S. A., Watson, K. E., & Kumanyika, S. (2022). The racialized marketing of unhealthy foods and beverages: Perspectives and potential remedies. *Journal of Law, Medicine & Ethics, 50*(1), 52–59. https://doi.org/10.1017/jme.2022.8

Cheung, H. (2019, April 13). Cultural appropriation: Why is food appropriation such a sensitive subject? *BBC News.* https://www.bbc.com/news/world-us-canada-47892747

Mukhopadhyay, A. (2021, September 20). Culinary ignorance can breed racism. *Deutsche Welle.* https://www.dw.com/en/opinion-culinary-ignorance-can-breed-racism/a-59215768

IV

APPENDIX B: *Elements of Infographics*

Infographics are powerful tools for visual communication. They combine data, visuals, and text to present complex information in a digestible and engaging format.

Following are the key elements of infographics:

1. **Title and Subtitle**
   a. *Title:* The main headline that captures the essence of the infographic. It should be clear, concise, and engaging to draw the audience's attention.
   b. *Subtitle:* Provides additional context or elaboration on the main title, offering a more detailed description of what the infographic is about.

2. **Visual Elements**
   a. *Icons:* Small, simple images that represent ideas or concepts. They help in reducing text and making the information more visually appealing.
   b. *Images:* High-quality photos or illustrations that support the narrative of the infographic. They should be relevant and add value to the content.
   c. *Illustrations:* Custom drawings that can convey unique messages or themes, often adding a creative touch to the infographic.

3. **Data Visualizations**
   a. *Charts and Graphs:* Various types of data visualizations, such as bar charts, pie charts, line graphs, and scatter plots, which represent numerical data.
   b. *Maps:* Geographic representations that show data related to locations, such as population density, climate patterns, or election results.
   c. *Timelines:* Linear representations of events over time, highlighting chronological data and trends.

4. **Typography**
   a. *Font Choice:* Selection of fonts that enhance readability and align with the overall design theme. Consistency in font styles and sizes is crucial for maintaining a professional look.
   b. *Hierarchy:* Use of different font sizes, weights, and colors to establish a visual hierarchy, guiding the reader's eye through the information in a logical order.
   c. *Legibility:* Ensuring that text is clear and easy to read, avoiding overly decorative fonts or poor color contrasts.

5. **Color Scheme**
   a. *Color Palette:* A carefully selected range of colors that complement each other and enhance the visual appeal. Colors should align with the theme and purpose of the infographic.
   b. *Contrast:* Use of contrasting colors to highlight key information and ensure readability. High contrast can draw attention to important elements.
   c. *Consistency:* Maintaining a consistent color scheme throughout the infographic to create a cohesive and professional appearance.

6. **Layout and Structure**
   a. *Grid System:* A structured layout that organizes content into columns and rows, ensuring alignment and balance across the infographic.
   b. *White Space:* Strategic use of empty space to avoid clutter and improve readability. White space helps to separate different sections and makes the infographic more visually appealing.

   c. *Flow:* Logical arrangement of information that guides the viewer from one section to the next, creating a seamless narrative.

7. **Text and Labels**

   a. *Headings and Subheadings:* Clear and concise headings that introduce different sections and break up the content into manageable parts.

   b. *Body Text:* Brief, informative text that provides context and explanations without overwhelming the reader with too much information.

   c. *Labels:* Descriptive text for charts, graphs, and icons that provides necessary details and enhances understanding of the visuals.

8. **Sources and Citations**

   a. *Source Attribution:* Citing the sources of data and information used in the infographic to establish credibility and allow readers to verify the information.

   b. *Footnotes:* Additional notes or explanations that provide context or clarification for specific data points or statements.

APPENDIX C: *Infographics Examples*

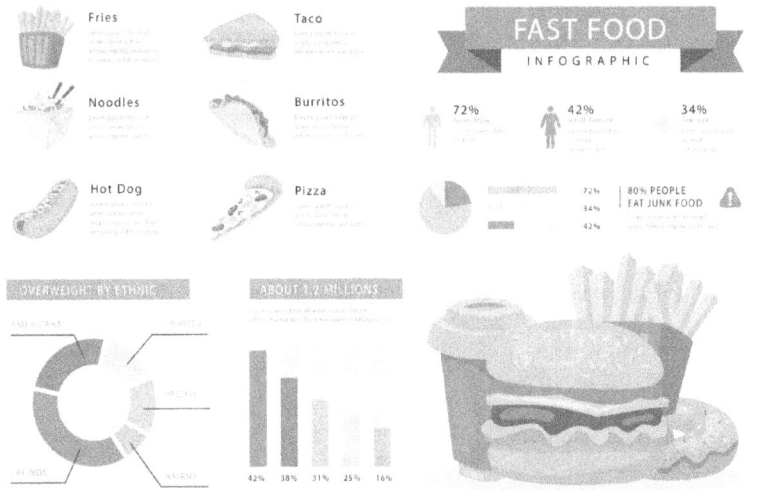

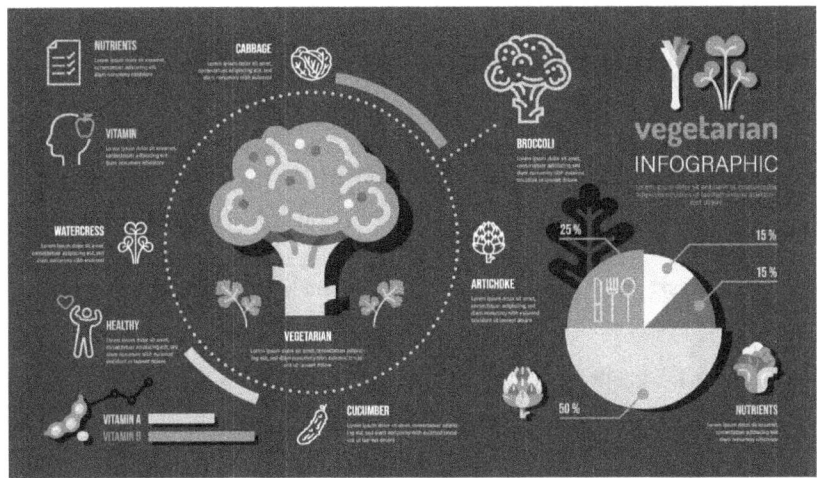

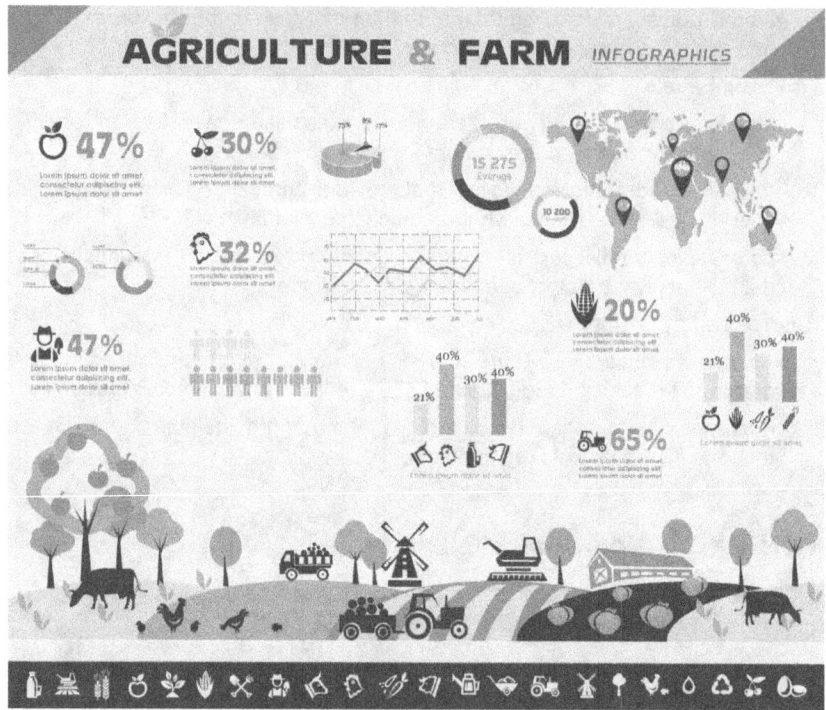

APPENDIX D: *Design Principles for Infographics*

Balance
Explain the concept of visual balance, including symmetrical and asymmetrical balance. Discuss how balancing elements can create a harmonious look and prevent one side from feeling too heavy.

Contrast
Describe how contrast can draw attention to key areas of the infographic. Use examples of contrasting colors, shapes, and sizes to illustrate this point.

Color Scheme
Introduce basic color theory, including complementary, analogous, and triadic color schemes. Discuss how color schemes can evoke emotions and maintain visual coherence.

Typography
Highlight the importance of choosing readable fonts and maintaining consistency in font style and size. Discuss the impact of typography on the overall tone and readability.

Alignment
Explain the role of alignment in creating a clean, organized look. Show how grid systems and alignment of text and images can guide the viewer's eye through the infographic.

APPENDIX E: *Steps for Software Demonstration*

1. Briefly introduce the software (e.g., Canva, Piktochart), highlighting its features and benefits for creating infographics.

2. Walk through the main interface, pointing out key areas such as the toolbar, template library, and workspace.

3. Show how to start a new infographic project by selecting the appropriate template size or creating a custom size.

4. Navigate to the template library and select a template that suits the infographic topic. Discuss criteria for choosing a template, such as layout and theme.

5. Demonstrate how to edit the text in the template, including changing fonts, sizes, and colors. Show how to add new text boxes if needed.

6. Explain how to replace existing images with new ones from the built-in image library or by uploading custom images. Show how to add icons and adjust their size and color.

7. Illustrate how to move elements around the template, align objects, and ensure balance and readability.

8. Show how to insert various types of charts (e.g., bar, pie, line) and input data. Demonstrate customization options for colors and labels.

9. If applicable, demonstrate how to add maps and customize them to display geographical data.

10. Demonstrate how to apply a cohesive color scheme to the entire infographic, ensuring consistency.

11. Explain the importance of reviewing the infographic for errors and consistency. Finally, demonstrate how to export the infographic in different formats (.PNG, .PDF, etc.).

APPENDIX F: *Free Infographic Creator Websites*

- **Canva** (canva.com) is a versatile design tool that offers a wide range of templates and design elements for creating infographics, presentations, social media graphics, and more.

- **Piktochart** (piktochart.com/) specializes in creating infographics, reports, and presentations, offering an intuitive editor and numerous templates to help visualize data and information.

- **Vista Create** (create.vista.com) provides a variety of design templates, including infographics, that can be customized with text, images, and icons.

- **DesignCap** (www.designcap.com) offers easy-to-use tools for creating infographics, presentations, and other visual content, with many customizable templates.

- **Snappa** (snappa.com) is a graphic design tool that simplifies the creation of infographics and other visuals with drag-and-drop functionality and a library of pre-made templates.

- **Easil** (about.easil.com) provides templates for infographics, social media graphics, and other visual content, along with customization tools to personalize your designs.

- **DesignBold** (designbold.com) offers a range of templates for infographics, posters, and other graphic design projects, with a user-friendly interface for customization.

- **Digifloat** (digifloat.io/graphic-design-services/) provides graphic design services, including tools for creating infographics tailored to various needs and preferences.

- **Desygner** (desygner.com/) allows users to create infographics, banners, and other visual content using a wide range of templates and design elements.

IV

APPENDIX G: *Project Directions and Grading Rubric*

Instructions

1. Select one or two unique dishes or delicacies from your culture that you would like to share with your classmates.

2. Get into pairs and describe the chosen foods with each other as a warm-up and brainstorming activity. Discuss ingredients, preparation methods, cultural significance, and any interesting anecdotes related to the dishes.

3. Create an infographic that not only informs people about the dishes but also provides cultural context. Highlight how these foods are a part of your cultural heritage.

4. Use both images and text in your infographic. Describe the dishes in a way that would be easily understood by someone who has just moved to your country. Include ingredients, preparation methods, and any cultural significance.

5. Incorporate at least three vocabulary words from the reading introduced in Part 1 into your infographic. Ensure these words are used correctly and help convey the message clearly.

6. Use Canva (canva.com) to design your infographic. Choose appropriate templates and customize them with your images, text, and design elements.

Grading Rubric

Criteria	Points
Design an infographic for newcomers	2
Use text and images to describe 1–2 culturally important dishes	2
Use at least three vocabulary words correctly from the reading	3
Use grammar and punctuation correctly	3
Total Points Possible	10

Story in Tableau: A Collaborative Physical Image Creation Activity

Richard Silberg

Levels	All
Ages Suitable for Activity	Any
Aims	Identify an image that highlights the basic conflict or a pivotal moment in a story
	Activate imagination through physical expression
	Work collaboratively with a small group
	Use the body to create images that communicate meaning
Class Time	2 (45-minute) sessions or 1 (90-minute) session; extensions are possible
Preparation Time	10 minutes
Resources	A shared story (either oral or written) that the class is familiar with

aking strong, mental images is a skill that helps readers understand a text. Being able to develop mental images of a story in a collaborative, physical representation is a form of visual literacy that builds on important imaginative and cooperative skills.

PROCEDURE

1. Introduce the term *tableau*. This is a theatrical technique in which actors freeze in poses that create a picture of a significant moment in a story. *Tableaux* (pronounced the same) refers to the plural.

2. Create a tableau for your students:

   a. Say, "I will create a tableau (a frozen picture) of a person doing something. See if you can guess what I'm doing."

   b. Give yourself the following cue: "1, 2, 3, picture!"

   c. Make a tableau of a basketball player shooting a ball. (Use any image that is relatable to your students in their context).

   d. Have students identify what they see. Ask students, "What is the body doing? What is the face saying?"

3. Ask students to practice making a tableau. Have them create their version of a basketball player shooting a basket. Give them the cue: "1, 2, 3, picture!" Demonstrate being specific with your gestures and facial expression, and have students adjust their tableaux. Explain, "We will continue with making other tableaux. Try to be as specific and still as you can."

4. Have students make a few more tableaux. Between each tableau, have students go back to a neutral position. Say, "On the count of three, make a picture of someone reading a book; 1, 2, 3, picture! Relax and back to neutral. Now, make a picture

of someone reading a scary book..." Continue to give your own cues for further group practice. See Appendix A for suggestions.

5. Next, establish the concept of relating in a picture. Have students create a five-person tableau to demonstrate in front of the class.

   a. Say, "Make a picture of winning the lottery, but this time try to show that you are one family winning the lottery; 1, 2, 3, picture! Notice how people are relating—literally looking, touching, or showing relationship in some way."

   b. Note other qualities of a good tableau (e.g., posing at different vertical levels, having an expressive body and face, offering visual information about the cue). If needed, act as a director and adjust the group members so that these qualities are present.

6. Create groups of four to five students. Distribute the groups around the room. Instruct groups to create their tableaux simultaneously with as little discussion as possible.

   a. Assign each group an imaginary location that is the backdrop for their group's tableau. At the count of three, groups create a tableau of what people might be doing at that location.

   b. Remind students to relate to each other in their tableau.

   c. Say, "Ready? 1, 2, 3, picture." Encourage students to scan the room, while remaining frozen, to see what other groups created. Alternatively, you can spotlight one group at a time.

   d. Practice with other backdrop locations that are appropriate for your context. See Appendix B for suggestions.

7. Increase the challenge by asking students to create group tableaux with conflict.

   a. Give groups 2 minutes to plan, create, and practice a tableau that includes a conflict, obstacle, or problem.

   b. The teacher can either give everyone the same location, or have groups select a location.

   c. It is important to tell students that the conflict, obstacle, or problem must be something other than a physical fight or argument. The goal is for the groups to create an exciting, dynamic image filled with energy, yet frozen. See Appendix C for suggestions.

   d. Encourage students to scan the room, while remaining frozen, to see what other groups created. Alternatively, you can spotlight one group at a time.

8. Now, apply tableau creation to a story. This can be a shared story that the class has read or been told, or an original story that was created by the students. Tell the story again, or elicit the main ideas of the story from the whole class.

9. In the same or new groups, give students 2 minutes to plan, create, and practice a tableau that highlights a moment of conflict or a pivotal moment in the story. Remind students of the attributes of a good tableau (e.g., relationship between actors, dynamic images, posing at different levels).

10. Say, "Ready? 1, 2, 3, picture." Encourage students to scan the room. Alternatively, you can spotlight one group at a time, so students can see each other's images.

11. Discuss the different tableaux. Did groups use the same or different moments from the story? Were the same moments shared differently? What visual elements made each tableau effective? What can be done to make a tableau more effective?

CAVEATS AND OPTIONS

- Remind groups that some students can play inanimate objects in a scene (e.g., a piece of furniture, a tree).
- Vary group size.
- For ideas to extend the activity, see Appendix C.

REFERENCES AND FURTHER READING

Flynn, R. M. (2017). *Tableau classroom drama activities: Active learning via silent, still images*. Create Space Independent Publishing Platform.

Kelin, D. A. (2009). *In their own words: Drama with young English language learners*. New Play Books.

Rohd, M. (1998). *Theatre for community conflict and dialogue: The hope is vital training manual*. Heinemann.

Sillberg, R. (n.d.). *English language teaching through drama and storytelling*. https://www.richardsilberg.com

APPENDIX A: *Ideas for Individual Tableaux*

- Watching a scary movie
- Eating a hot slice of pizza
- Drinking a very hot beverage
- Walking a big dog that pulls
- Looking for a lost dog, child, or item
- Watching a spaceship land in the distance
- Seeing your favorite celebrity walk down the street

APPENDIX B: *Ideas for Group Tableau Locations*

- The market or grocery store
- A birthday party
- A wedding
- The schoolyard
- The hospital
- A restaurant
- A cemetery at midnight
- A train or bus station
- A concert
- A soccer game, tennis match, or other sporting event

APPENDIX C: *Extension Activities*

1. *Thought and Dialogue Bubbles:* While students are in a tableau, you can point to one character and ask the class: "What do you think this character is thinking?" "What is this character feeling?" "What do you think this character might be saying?" This can be repeated for each character. To keep the actors from having to maintain a pose for long periods of time, take a photo of the tableau and project it on an LCD projector. Students can also write and perform monologues for the character they are representing in the tableau.

2. *The Moment Before and the Moment After:* After students make a tableau, ask, "What do you think happened the moment before? What do you think will happen the moment after?" Having students brainstorm and establish a story sequence can provoke a fruitful conversation in your class.

3. *Human Slide Show:* Have students create several frozen pictures in chronological order as a variation on the story tableau creation activity.

    a. Say: "I want you to recreate the story in a series of four to five tableaux. Imagine you are an artist hired to illustrate a book based on this story. For this activity, you will make illustrations using your bodies. What "events" would you choose to illustrate?"

    b. Challenge students to make the transitions between their tableaux as smooth and as theatrical as possible.

    c. Putting the resulting "slide show" to music is another great variation.

Using a Picture Book and Crayons to Celebrate Uniqueness

Heidi Haavan Grosch

Levels	All
Ages Suitable for Activity	Any
Aims	Explore the meaning of diversity
	Develop an understanding that all have something to contribute
	Practice oral language skills
Class Time	15–30 minutes
Resources	Different colored cloth pieces
	Pieces of paper or Post-it notes
	Mixed crayons in a bag or box

Talking about difficult subjects, like racism, bullying, or inequality, can be challenging. This activity is inspired by the picture book *The Crayon Box That Talked* (DeRolf, 1997), a story about a box of crayons that do not get along. Only by working together do they discover that every color is important. Add a few pieces of colored fabric and a simple role-play, and you have an easily differentiated activity that enables students to recognize that to paint a beautiful picture, all colors of the rainbow are important.

IV

PROCEDURE

1. Have students select one crayon randomly from a bag. It is important they do not see what they select. Then, have students form groups with others who picked the same color crayon. Preselect the number of colors depending on the number of students, so in the end there will be five to seven different color groups.

2. On a Post-it note or small piece of paper, have each student draw an object that is the color of the crayon they have. Hang all the drawings on the wall. Discuss how each of the different images was drawn in a single color.

3. Give each student a piece of fabric (or paper; see Caveats and Options) that is the same color as their crayon. Each person should wear their color in some way by tying or pinning it to some part of their body. The students need to wear their color to facilitate the role-play and the final group image compiled by the artist.

4. Position the color groups around the edges of the room. They will change position as you give them directions.

5. Choose one student to be the artist and remove this student from their group. The artist will have a role to play in Steps 10–11. You may want to take this student aside and verbally coach them on their role or provide a written set of instructions before continuing with the activity.

6. Start with two color groups, such as red and yellow. (Leave the colors that cannot be skin colors, such as green, purple, or blue, until the end of Step 7.) Call

these two groups to meet in the center of the room, give each other high fives, and say, "Hi, Yellow!" The other group replies, "Hi Red!" Then, have the two groups move together to one side of the room and sit down.

7. Have the next color group enter (e.g., pink) and say, "Hi, Red! Hi, Yellow!" Have the first two groups respond, "Hi, Pink!" Then, pink goes to the middle and sits on the floor. Continue this way until only one color group and the artist are left.

8. Have the last color group enter the middle of the room (e.g., purple). They greet each color group by name, but this time, tell each color group to respond, "We don't like [purple]." Tell the last group to show how they feel sadder and sadder because no other color accepts them.

9. After all the groups reject this color group, tell the artist to speak up and play their role. The artist says, "Wait! I have an idea!" Have the artist position all the students, each wearing their preassigned color, in an imaginary scene (e.g., blue becomes the sky, brown the earth). Let the artist choose what picture to create, although you may need to guide them. Ensure that the last group to be placed into the picture is the last color (e.g., purple becomes a flower).

10. Guide the color groups to notice each other in a new way: "Hey, I like purple! Blue is perfect for the sky." You may need to prompt or guide the students in what to say.

11. Have the artist conclude the activity by saying, "Look, every color of the rainbow is important." All the colors respond, "We need every color to make a beautiful picture." Allow for improvisation of lines.

CAVEATS AND OPTIONS

- To find pieces of fabric for Step 4 in an affordable and sustainable way, use scraps of fabric students bring from home, or cut small pieces from old clothes, towels, or curtains from home or a second-hand store. You can also use colorful construction paper or even strips of white paper colored by the students; if you do this, cut the paper into strips and make into rings so students can wear them on the head, around the neck or as a bracelet.

- As the selection of crayons is random, some groups will be larger than others. In addition, because this is not preplanned, students may find themselves working with classmates they normally do not work with, which reinforces the message of the activity.

- For younger learners, model the sentence for each step and prompt students to state only their group's color: "I am blue," "I am yellow," "I\we don't like purple."

- For older learners, have them improvise the dialogue themselves after receiving initial direction from the teacher.

- If you have more time, direct the scene first and then run the scene a second time with the participants directing themselves.

- Conduct a read-aloud with the picture book *The Crayon Box That Talked* (DeRolf, 1997) as a follow-up activity. This is a good way to initiate conversations about diversity. There are also many versions available on YouTube if you search for that title.

- Take a picture of the class after Step 9 and show it to the students. Use that as inspiration for students to draw individual versions on paper of what the artist has created.

REFERENCES AND FURTHER READING

DeRolf, S. (1997). *The crayon box that talked*. Random House Books for Young Readers.

IV

Using Comics as a Summary of a Written Text

Heidi Haavan Grosch

Levels	All
Ages Suitable for Activity	Any
Aims	Extract key ideas from a text
	Summarize ideas
	Create a multimodal text using both visual and digital literacy skills
Class Time	20–60 minutes
Preparation Time	Varies, depending on whether the reading of the original text is included in the timing of this task. If so, add the time needed to read or work with the original text.
Resources	Copies of text(s) to be summarized
	Paper and pens or pencils, if creating the comic by hand
	Access to the internet on laptops or tablets, if creating the comic digitally

Processing text can sometimes be a challenge. Providing students with the opportunity to create a three-panel comic helps them process what they have read and put it into their own words and pictures. This intertwining of words and pictures, either drawn by hand or created with an online comic generator, helps students learn how words and pictures support each other as they complete an activity that increases motivation and builds self-confidence.

PROCEDURE

1. Distribute copies of the text to be summarized. See Caveats and Options for ideas.

2. Ask learners to read the text alone, as a pair, or in small groups. The text can be read silently or aloud.

3. Elicit key words or themes from the text, or ask students to summarize what the text is about in one or two sentences. If the chosen text is a novel or story, have the students select a key scene to summarize.

4. Choose the format of the comic: digital or hand drawn. (See makebeliefscomix. com and www.storyboardthat.com for free digital comic generators). The entire class can use the same format, or individual learners can choose the format that they prefer. Giving students the choice is a good way to differentiate the task and allow for learners to have control over their own learning.

5. As individuals, pairs, or in small groups, have students create a three-panel comic that illustrates with words and pictures one of the following:

   a. key words or themes

   b. a summary of the text

   c. a scene from the text

6. Circulate to monitor and provide support. Give students a time frame for completing their comics.

7. When time is up, gave the individuals, pairs, or small groups share their comics with each other by presenting to the class or in a gallery walk.

CAVEATS AND OPTIONS

- For Steps 1–2, have the class read the same text, different texts on the same theme, or self-chosen texts. However, all the learners in one pair or group should read the same text. Determine if you will ask students to summarize the entire text, the main parts of the text, or a certain section of the text.

- If this is the first time learners are using a digital comic generator, have them play with the format in an earlier activity.

- Easily differentiate the task by varying the difficulty of the original text. This activity also works well for those with a variety of language skills as the amount of text is limited and the images and text support each other.

- To integrate translanguaging, work with a text in another subject, in a language that is not English, and have students create their comics in English.

- Instead of creating a comic about a text they have read, have learners create a three-panel comic with key points based on course material, such as a classmate's oral presentation or a video or film they have watched. They can also summarize the theme of (or one thing they remember from) a video game, a song, or a podcast they have listened to. Letting the learners have freedom to decide can be a rich learning experience for the teacher as well.

IV

Part V

Semiotics

Introduction: Semiotics as Part of Visual Literacy Competency

The growing need for a focus on visual literacy in English language teaching is increasingly informed by developments in semiotics, the study of signs and meaning-making processes. As language learners engage with multimodal texts—those that combine words, images, symbols, and other visual or auditory cues—teachers must equip learners with the skills to interpret, critique, and create such materials. The activities in this section introduce innovative classroom practices centered on semiotic and visual analysis to enhance English language development and global awareness. The activities explore how signs—literal, symbolic, and cultural—function as complex communicative acts by drawing attention to both their visual form and contextual significance (Cook, 2022; Kress, 2003).

For example, Priya M. Dabak's activity, "Interpreting Multimodal Street Signs," exemplifies how semiotic awareness can be cultivated through everyday visual texts. Through guided analysis of street signage, including conventional warnings and visually ironic variants, learners are invited to apply observational, interpretive, and critical thinking skills. Using a variety of cognitive skills, learners explore how humor and surprise can emerge from incongruities between images and texts, reflecting principles of multimodal irony (Burgers et al., 2013). The activity raises questions about the cultural familiarity required to decode symbols effectively and encourages learners to reflect on why certain messages are more memorable when conveyed humorously or unexpectedly.

Similarly, in "Symbols of Identity and Resistance: Palestinian Keffiyeh," Fatima Aldajani demonstrates how cultural symbols function as potent tools for social communication and historical expression. Focusing on the keffiyeh, a traditional Palestinian scarf rich with political and aesthetic meanings, this activity enables learners to interpret visual cues and associate them with concepts such as solidarity, identity, and resistance. The activity blends visual analysis with personal reflection, prompting learners to connect global symbols to cultural emblems from their own backgrounds and to articulate the sociopolitical meanings behind patterns, colors, and contexts. Through multimedia resources and creative output, learners develop vocabulary and narrative fluency around topics of culture and symbolism (Said, 1994; Zulaihah, 2023).

Taken together, these activities and the others in this section emphasize that visual literacy is not only about recognizing what one sees, but also about engaging with what images signify and how they function within a broader communicative ecosystem. As learners interpret signs or cultural icons, they participate in meaning-making processes shaped by context, perspective, and power. Such activities align closely with and complement communicative language teaching and culturally sustaining pedagogies, thereby supporting learners as they develop interpretive competence alongside linguistic proficiency.

REFERENCES AND FURTHER READING

Burgers, C., Van Mulken, M., & Schellens, P. J. (2013). On verbal irony, images and creativity: A corpus-analytic approach. In T. Veale, K. Feyaerts, & C. Forceville (Eds.), *Creativity and the agile mind: A multi-disciplinary study of a multi-faceted phenomenon* (pp. 293–312). De Gruyter. https://doi.org/10.1515/9783110295290.293

Cook, V. (2022). *The language of the English street sign*. Multilingual Matters. https://doi.org/10.21832/9781800414570

Kress, G. (2003). *Literacy in the new media age*. Routledge. https://doi.org/10.4324/9780203299234

Said, E. W. (1994). *Culture and imperialism*. Knopf.

Zulaihah, S. (2023). Keffiyeh trend on social media as a form of solidarity for Palestine. *Digital Theory, Culture & Society, 1*(2), 135–144. https://doi.org/10.61126/dtcs.v1i2.27

Communicating With Emojis in Written Text

Nadia M. Mohamed and Mariana Alvayero Ricklefs

Levels	Beginner to intermediate
Ages Suitable for Activity	Early secondary
Aims	Develop observation and inferencing skills
	Apply creative thinking with visual literacy
	Identify and explain the meaning of select emojis
	Create new emojis
Class Time	45 minutes–1 hour
Preparation Time	5–10 minutes
Resources	Chart of emojis (Appendix)
	Paper and coloring materials, or access to the internet on laptops or tablets

Incorporating visual literacy, as well as digital literacy, in English language classrooms creates opportunities for multilingual learners of English to discover, analyze, and critique meaning embedded in the interplay of visual and various other modalities (Ricklefs et al., 2022; Rowsell et al., 2012). In this activity, learners practice analyzing emojis for the emotional messages they convey, then design their own emojis as multimodal texts. As writers (creators) and readers (interpreters) of emojis, students are encouraged to use emojis to enrich their written discourse in English.

PROCEDURE

1. Ask students what emojis are. Do they have any favorite emojis or ones they use when communicating with friends?

2. Ask students what emojis do. What is an emoji's purpose? How do they help us communicate our ideas or feelings? How do they help us, as readers, understand the writer's message or feelings? (Accept all answers.)

3. Show students the chart of emojis (see Appendix). Lead students through a think, pair, share activity on the following questions:

    a. Choose three emojis from the chart.

    b. What do they mean?

    c. What do they convey to you as a reader?

    d. How would you use them if you were texting a friend?

4. Ask students to share their responses with the whole class. Accept all answers and point out how individuals may interpret the emojis differently if students provide differing responses. Ask why we might understand the emojis differently to elicit the idea that we interpret and explain what we see through our own experiences.

5. Explain that students will be adding to the emoji chart. Provide students with drawing materials and instruct them to design their own emoji. Alternatively, if students have access to the internet on mobile devices, direct students to one of the following digital drawing websites:

   a. Labeley (labeley.com/emojis)

   b. Angel Emoji Maker (emoji-maker.com/designer)

6. Tell students they should be prepared to explain what their emoji represents. They should be able to answer the following questions: What feelings does this convey? When would someone use this emoji? What does the emoji tell your readers?

7. Allow students time to work individually to create their emoji. They may work in pairs to brainstorm ideas if preferred.

8. Put students into small groups and tell students to share their emojis. They should answer the following questions: What is the emoji you made? What does it mean? What feeling or idea does it show?

9. Ask students to write a short text message to the teacher or a friend and include the emoji in the text. They can write the text message below their drawing, or if working online, students can post their text message and emoji to a Google Doc that you share with the class.

10. As a class, view each student's text messages with their emojis. First, ask the class to guess what each emoji means. Then, allow the emoji author to tell the class what they intended the emoji to mean.

11. Discuss as a class how the meaning of the new emojis aligned with or did not align with the author's text and intended meaning. Challenge students to consider why they may have understood the emojis differently in a brief discussion.

CAVEATS AND OPTIONS

- Some students may not be very familiar with emojis. Ask students when and where they have seen emojis (e.g., texting, social media platforms, art). You may also provide a diverse set of emojis and ask students to indicate which emojis they are familiar with, because these symbols may vary across cultures.

- Adapt this activity for higher levels by asking learners to compile a dictionary of emojis, including pictures and student-friendly definitions.

- Assign students to fill out the Frayer model for their created emojis, requiring students to provide more specific descriptions and examples in context.

- Add a tactile component to this activity by having students build their own creative emojis in modeling clay, paper collage, or other physical media.

REFERENCES AND FURTHER READING

Baker, L. (2015). How many words is a picture worth? Integrating visual literacy in language learning with photographs. *English Teaching Forum, 53*(4), 2–13.

Ricklefs, M. A., Slobodianiuk, H., & Werderich, D. (2022). Digital literacy in Ukraine and the United States. *Kappa Delta Pi Record, 58*(1), 21–26. https://doi.org/10.10 80/00228958.2022.2124208

Rowsell, J., McLean, C., & Hamilton, M. (2012). Visual literacy as a classroom approach. *Journal of Adolescent and Adult Literacy, 55*(5), 444–447

APPENDIX: *Chart of Emojis*

Image from Pixabay (pixabay.com/vectors/emojis-emoji-hipster-funny-4518355/)

Exploring 19th-Century Zodiac Signs of Jaipur, India

Tannistha Dasgupta

Levels	High intermediate to advanced
Ages Suitable for Activity	Secondary to adult
Aims	Identify and describe the cultural and artistic elements present in the artifact
	Interpret the symbolism in the artifact and acknowledge its multiple meanings
	Develop the ability to interpret an artifact critically and creatively
	Understand the significance of creative and critical analysis in the appreciation of cultural artifacts
Class Time	90 minutes
Preparation Time	20–30 minutes
Resources	Image (Appendix A)
	Laptop and projector, or printed color copies of the image

In this activity, learners delve into the rich cultural and artistic history of 19th-century Jaipur, India, as they analyze an image showing the 12 zodiac signs. Through creative and critical analysis, students will develop their observational skills, increase their cultural understanding, and improve their ability to interpret symbolism. The activity is also designed to foster a deeper appreciation for art and historical artifacts.

PROCEDURE

1. *Introduction (10 minutes)*: Begin the activity by introducing the concept of zodiac signs and their significance in different cultures (see Appendix B). The term *astrology* comes from the Greek words *astron* [star] and *logos* [study of]. Therefore, astrology can be translated as the study of the stars.

2. Show the image of 19th-century Jaipur zodiac signs (Appendix A) and discuss it as a whole class. Elicit the observable similarities and differences between the zodiac signs. Ask students specific questions about what they notice and what they think the image represents. The following questions are based on three dimensions of viewing (i.e., affective, compositional, and critical; Callow, 2005).

    a. How does the image make you feel? Why? (affective question)

    b. What elements can you see in the background? (compositional question)

    c. What message does the image transmit? (critical question)

3. *Background Knowledge (10 minutes)*: Provide students with brief historical context about Jaipur, India in the 19th century, focusing on the cultural and artistic aspects of the region as well as the importance of zodiac signs in Indian culture (see Appendix C).

4. *Creative Observation (15 minutes)*: Instruct students to take a few minutes to closely observe the image individually. Encourage them to pay attention to details, patterns, and symbols. Ask students to jot down their observations, and ask them the following questions to develop the ability to look beyond an image's literal meaning:

   a. What other images come to mind when you see it? (affective question)

   b. How is the image framed or composed? From what angle or point of view has the image been taken? (compositional question)

   c. Who is the intended audience for the image? (critical question)

5. *Small-Group Discussion (20 minutes)*: Divide the class into small groups of three to four students each. Instruct the group members to share their individual observations and interpretations. Encourage students to discuss any similarities or differences in their observations and interpretations.

6. *Guided Analysis (20 minutes)*: Bring the class back together and facilitate a guided analysis of the image as a whole class. Ask students to share their group's most interesting findings. Lead a discussion that delves deeper into the symbolism, cultural elements, and artistic choices evident in the image. Prompt students to think critically about the possible meanings behind the placement, colors, and representations of the zodiac signs in the context of 19th-century Jaipur. Ask them the following questions to guide the discussion:

   a. What do you think lies beyond the frame? (compositional question)

   b. In what ways do you think the colors and representations in the image may reflect the religious, cultural, and societal values of that time and place? (critical question)

   c. Are any of the images stereotypical, idealized, or nonrepresentative? (critical question)

7. *Individual Reflection (10 minutes)*: Instruct students to individually write a short reflection on their personal understanding and interpretation of the image. Ask them the following questions for reflection:

   a. What does the image remind you of? (affective question)

   b. Do you think the image is positive or negative? Or, do you feel indifferent toward it? Why? (affective question)

   c. Can you think of the potential messages or ideas that could be conveyed through the choices of colors and depictions used in the image? (critical question)

8. *Conclusion (5 minutes)*: Wrap up the activity by encouraging a few students to share their reflections with the class, fostering further discussion. Emphasize the importance of creative and critical analysis in understanding and appreciating art and cultural artifacts.

CAVEATS AND OPTIONS

- Consider the students' prior knowledge of zodiac signs, art history, and cultural context.

- Take into account the language proficiency of the students. Adapt the activity materials and instructions to suit their level, providing vocabulary support or simplifying complex concepts if needed.

- Ensure that the image and materials used in the activity are accessible to all students, including those with visual impairments or other accessibility needs. For instance, for visually impaired students, the teacher can ask peers to orally describe each zodiac sign depicted in the image.
- Adjust the duration of each step to fit within the available class time, considering the need for thorough observation, group discussion, and individual reflection.
- The activity can be adapted for different levels by adjusting the complexity of the analysis questions and expectations. For younger students, focus on basic observations and simple interpretations. For adult learners, incorporate additional research or expand the discussion to broader cultural and historical contexts.
- Encourage an inclusive and respectful environment where diverse perspectives are acknowledged and valued.

REFERENCES AND FURTHER READING

Callow, J. (2005). Literacy and the visual: Broadening our vision. *English teaching: Practice and critique, 4*(1), 6–19.

Goldstein, B. (2016). *Visual literacy in English language teaching: Part of the Cambridge papers in ELT series.* Cambridge. https://www.cambridge.org/us/files/7015/7488/7845/CambridgePapersInELT_VisualLiteracy_2016_ONLINE.pdf

The Heritage Lab. (n.d.) *You searched for Jaipur.* https://www.theheritagelab.in/?s=jaipur

World Heritage Convention. (n.d.). *Jaipur City, Rajasthan.* UNESCO. https://whc.unesco.org/en/list/1605/

APPENDIX A: *Twelve Zodiac Signs, 19th Century, Jaipur, India*

बारह राशियों के चिन्ह, 19वीं शती जयपुर
Twelve Zodiac Signs, 19th Century, Jaipur

Image source: Albert Hall Museum, Jaipur, India
Image credit: Tannistha Dasgupta

APPENDIX B: *Introduction to the Concept of Zodiac Signs*

Zodiac signs are a part of astrology, an ancient practice that assigns symbolic meanings to the positions and movements of celestial bodies. Different cultures, such as the Indian, Chinese, and Western traditions, have developed unique zodiac systems that play significant roles in their folklore, mythology, and personal identity concepts.

Indian astrology, also referred to as Vedic astrology or *Jyothishasthra,* is one of the oldest systems of astrology. It draws its principles from the Vedas, the ancient texts of Hinduism. In India, many people believe that celestial bodies, including planets, significantly affect human life. In Hindu astrology, the 12 Rashis represent the zodiac signs. These signs, deeply embedded in Vedic tradition, carry significant astrological meaning. They are

- Mesha (Aries)
- Vrishabha (Taurus)
- Mithuna (Gemini)
- Karka (Cancer)
- Simha (Leo)
- Kanya (Virgo)
- Tula (Libra)
- Vrishchika (Scorpio)
- Dhanu (Sagittarius)
- Makara (Capricorn)
- Kumbha (Aquarius), and
- Meena (Pisces).

Each Rashi plays a distinct role in astrological interpretations, shaping individual characteristics and guiding predictions.

The Chinese zodiac, comprising 12 animal signs, is deeply rooted in Chinese culture, with each sign representing specific personality traits and characteristics based on the year of one's birth.

This is similar to the Western zodiac system, which has 12 astrological signs determined by the sun's position at birth. These signs impact individual personalities and life trajectories.

REFERENCES AND FURTHER READING

Bhatt, V. (2023, June 9) Understanding the twelve zodiac signs in Vedic astrology: Ruling planets, elements, and traits. https://vinayakbhatt.com/twelve-zodiac-signs-in-vedic-astrology/

Stockstill, E., & Simón, Y. (2023, November 7). *The 12 Chinese zodiac animals.* HowStuffWorks. https://entertainment.howstuffworks.com/horoscopes-astrology/what-s-your-sign-understanding-the-chinese-zodiac.htm

TOI Astrology. (2024, July 6). The twelve zodiac signs in Indian astrology: Characteristics and traits. *The Times of India.* https://timesofindia.indiatimes.com/astrology/zodiacs-astrology/the-twelve-zodiac-signs-in-indian-astrology-characteristics-and-traits/articleshow/111537506.cms

V

APPENDIX C: *Historical Context of Jaipur, India*

In the 19th century, Jaipur, India was a vibrant center of cultural and artistic activity, known for its rich traditions in architecture and crafts. It was ruled by Maharaja Sawai Madho Singh II (1880–1922 A.D.) who made Jaipur as a planned city. Founded in the 18th century and also known as the Pink City, Jaipur boasts a rich history reflected in its majestic forts and palaces. The city's cultural vibrancy thrives on a blend of Rajput and Mughal influences, evident in its colorful festivals, traditional crafts, and vibrant art forms, such as miniature paintings, dazzling textiles, and exquisite jewelry.

Jaipur, like much of India, has a deep-rooted tradition of astrology. Zodiac signs have historically influenced personal decisions and cultural practices. This influence extends to various aspects of life, such as getting married, starting a new business, or moving into a new home. In Hindu culture, newborns are traditionally named based on their astrological birth chart, or *kundali*, and even now marriages are often arranged by families according to the compatibility of the couple's kundalis.

Exploring Emotions Through Emojis: Enhancing Social Awareness With Visual Literacy

Huili Hong and Amber Warren

Levels	Beginner to intermediate
Ages Suitable for Activity	Primary
Aims	Facilitate empathetic understanding of emotions through emojis
	Provide equitable and enjoyable learning experiences that enhance social awareness
	Develop visual literacy
	Promote critical thinking about cultural and emotional connotations of emojis
Class Time	50 minutes
Preparation Time	10–30 minutes
Resources	Cards with sample emojis and their meanings
	Writer's notebook or vocabulary book
	Option 1: Printed copies of emojis for students to cut out, color, and use in reading and writing activities
	Option 2: Access to the internet on laptops or tablets
	An emotionally rich picture book (in print or online; see References)

This set of activities is designed to enhance students' literacy and social-emotional learning through the creative and multipurpose use of emojis. By integrating emojis into literacy activities, including read-alouds, teachers can promote equitable participatory learning opportunities that help students understand and explore emotions in themselves and in others. Completing both activities in sequence develops students' visual literacy and fosters a deeper understanding of social awareness and empathy.

PROCEDURE

Warm-up to Introduce Emojis (5 minutes)

1. Ask students if they have ever used emojis in their daily lives.

2. Write the word *emoji* on the board and elicit a few examples. Ask students to share their thoughts and experiences with these symbols.

3. Explain that in the next class, we will explore how emojis can be used to express feelings and convey meaning in reading and writing.

Activity 1: Morning Circle Using Emojis to Express and Communicate (10 minutes)

1. Begin the next class by sharing how you are feeling today and using an emoji card to illustrate your feelings. Write down the corresponding word on a chart paper or board.

2. Then, distribute a set of emoji cards (with emojis on one side and their meanings in big font letters on the other) and ask students how they are feeling today.

3. Give the students options to participate: They can 1) simply hold up an emoji card that represents their feelings and emotions or 2) choose an emoji or a few emojis and talk about their feelings and emotions.

4. During the sharing time, record the students' description words for their feelings on the chart paper or board (as a word bank).

Activity 2: Use Emoji to Develop Vocabulary and Reading Comprehension (30 minutes)

1. Choose an emotionally rich anchor text for an interactive read-aloud, such as *A Bad Case of Stripes* (Shannon, 1998) or *You Are Loved* (O'Hair & Sanchez, 2023). The book should include feelings that can help students navigate their and/or others' emotional worlds.

2. Before reading, do a quick picture walk. During your picture walk, flip through the pages of the book and focus on the images without reading the text. Ask students to observe characters' feelings in the illustrations and then communicate the characters' feelings with chosen emojis. Encourage students to describe the characters' feelings and make connections to their personal lives.

3. Read the book aloud. During your reading, ask students to identify and write down words related to feelings in their writer's notebook or vocabulary book.

4. After the read-aloud, have students work in pairs or small groups to choose emojis that represent the emotion-related words they write in their notebooks and draw the emojis beside these words. Give students the emoji cards from the Activity 1 as a reference.

5. Then, invite a couple of students to share their chosen words and explain how they describe the characters or events in this story.

6. Lastly, summarize and review the most common emotion words and emojis identified by the students and encourage them to think about whether they remember similar feelings from their real-life experiences.

7. Ask students to reflect on how emotion words and emojis are used to express similar or different emotions. Discuss any cultural nuances that you observed in their emoji uses and promote an understanding of diverse emotional expressions.

CAVEATS AND OPTIONS

- If students are unfamiliar with emojis, provide support during the warm-up by sharing a concise overview of the most frequently used emojis and their meanings.
- Modify this activity for various proficiency levels by altering the difficulty and the length of the read-aloud text.
- Encourage students to respect cultural differences and avoid using emojis that may be offensive or inappropriate in certain situations.

REFERENCES AND FURTHER READING

Boyd, C. (2018, February 15). *Nine ways to use emojis in the English classroom.* British Council. https://www.britishcouncil.org/voices-magazine/emojis-english-language-classroom

Burns, M. (2022, January 5). *How to use emojis in teaching: The fun little characters can add visual cues to student assignments and help you manage classroom routines.* Edutopia. https://www.edutopia.org/article/how-use-emojis-teaching

Harvey, S., & Goudvis, A. (2017). *Strategies that work: Teaching comprehension for understanding, engagement, and building knowledge, Grades K–8.* Stenhouse.

O'Hair, M., & Sanchez, S. (2023). *You are loved.* Scholastic.

Sexton, W., & Beegle, R. (2020). Academic language in an emoji world. *English in Texas, 50*(2), 6–10. https://files.eric.ed.gov/fulltext/EJ1304544.pdf

Shannon, D. (1998). *A Bad Case of Stripes.* Blue Sky.

V

Follow the Signs: A Library Exploration Floor Plan

Sheena Moleta

Level	Intermediate
Ages Suitable for Activity	Secondary to university
Aims	Learn to navigate a library
	Interpret signs, symbols, and layout to identify key resources and services
	Create a visual map that demonstrates comprehension
Class Time	1 hour 30 minutes
Preparation Time	30 minutes
Resources	Examples of maps and symbols found on maps
	Blank paper and drawing materials
	Access to a library (physical or virtual tour)

This library exploration activity is designed to help students become more comfortable navigating the library environment. Students will develop visual literacy skills by interpreting signs, symbols, and color cues to navigate and label real-world spaces. Through exploration, analysis, and map creation, students will discover various library resources and services. In addition, the activity will promote collaboration and communication, reinforcing practical language skills, including describing locations and giving directions.

PROCEDURE

1. Begin by initiating a class discussion:
    a. Have you ever used a map before?
    b. How do maps help us find information?
    c. What visual elements make a map easy or difficult to read?
2. Show some examples of different types of maps (e.g., subway, city, amusement park) and ask students:
    a. What do you notice about these maps?
    b. How do symbols, colors, and labels help us understand information?
3. Before beginning the activity, teach or review important library-related vocabulary (e.g., help desk, circulation desk, floor directories, study area, computer stations, multimedia). This will help students connect the words to the visuals they will encounter during the activity. For examples of common library visuals and symbols, see the Appendix.
4. Go to your library. Divide students into small groups of three to four to encourage teamwork and communication. Instruct students to explore the library and, while doing so, complete the following tasks:

a. Sketch a basic floor plan of the library, focusing on the general layout rather than precision.

b. Label the locations of key resources.

c. Draw quick sketches of the signs, colors, and symbols that helped them find each location.

    Remind students before starting that the library is a shared academic space; they should walk calmly and avoid loud disruptions during the activity.

5. Once the scavenger hunt is complete, invite a librarian to give a brief tour of the library. The librarian can provide further insights into available resources and services. Be sure to ask the librarian to point out the signs, symbols, and colors that could have helped them find the locations and understand the services offered.

6. After the tour, gather students back in the classroom. Ask each group to present their floor plans and discuss the resources they located during the scavenger hunt. Encourage them to use the library terms they practiced earlier to explain their findings. This reflection will help reinforce what they've learned and allow them to share any challenges or interesting discoveries.

CAVEATS AND OPTIONS

- If physical library access is limited, consider using virtual library tours.
- To extend the activity, consider including additional questions such as the following:
    — Locate the computer stations. How many are there? What services do they offer (e.g., printing, scanning)?
    — Locate the group study area. How many group study rooms are there?
    — Find a quiet study area. What floor is it located on?
    — Locate the circulation desk. What services can the staff at this desk help you with?
    — Where do you go to request a multimedia item (e.g., DVD, CD) in the library?

APPENDIX: *Types of Visuals Found in a Library*

Type	Examples	Visual Features
Directional signs	Arrows to sections, floor directories, elevator/stair signs	Arrows, directional text, floor numbers
Section labels	Fiction, nonfiction, reference, periodicals, multimedia areas	Large text signs, color-coded areas, icons
Service points	Circulation desk, help desk, printing/scanning stations, computers	Book icons, question mark symbols, printer icons
Call number systems	Dewey decimal signs, Library of Congress codes (e.g., "P–Language")	Number ranges, alphabetical codes
Accessibility symbols	Wheelchair symbols, braille signage, assistive listening device icons	Universal accessibility symbols

(continued)

Type	Examples	Visual Features
Study space markers	Quiet zones, group study areas, silent study rooms	Shushing icons, reserved signs, calendar icons
Behavior & policy signs	No food/drink, turn off phones, library hours	Crossed-out icons, schedules
Emergency signs	Exit signs, fire alarms, first aid stations	Exit arrows, fire icons, medical crosses, red or green
Promotional displays	Event posters, new arrivals, staff picks	Posters, banners, featured book displays

Interpreting Laughter in Text

Beatrix Burghardt

Levels	High intermediate to advanced
Ages Suitable for Activity	Secondary to adult
Aims	Compare emojis used to encode typed laughter
	Characterize laughter as a sequence of negotiable actions
	Evaluate one's laughter practice and its impact on interaction
Class Time	50 minutes
Preparation Time	20 minutes
Resources	Sample text message exchanges (Appendix)
	Student's screenshot of a text message with a laughing emoji
	One copy per group of the following graphs:
	• McKay, 2020, Figures 3, 5, 6
	• Petitjean & Morel, 2017, pp. 16–17

Conversational laughter is orderly; its meaning arises in discourse and can be negotiated (Glenn, 2003; Jefferson, 1979). In online interactions between friends, individual emoji choice may require negotiation to ensure that the meaning is interpreted as intended across texting platforms (McKay, 2020; Petitjean & Morel, 2017; Takahashi et al., 2017). In this activity, learners explore the pragmatics of laughter in text messages and how laughter is managed to support interaction. The activity promotes self-awareness of interactional practices and an understanding of cross-cultural differences.

PROCEDURE

1. Ask students: "What are five emojis or other ways you use to show laughing when texting?"

2. Show the symbol used to indicate laughter from your sample text message (see Appendix). Ask students: "What does this symbol mean to you?"

3. Show your complete sample text message (Appendix, Sample 1). Guide students to infer the conversational situation by asking them questions like the following:

   a. "Who are the participants and what is their relationship? How do you know?"

   b. "What is the topic of this conversation? How do you know?"

   c. "What is the purpose of this conversation? How do you know?"

4. Put students into pairs. Tell them they are going to perform the text message in a role-play, with various possible interpretations of the symbol in context. They should give attention to accurate delivery (e.g., duration [number of symbols], intensity, tone).

5. Depending on the context, explain the choice of symbols in the message: "I chose this as the symbol for laughing because..." or "I heard my friend's symbol as laughter because...", or "I also added an emoji because...."

6. Guide students to understand how the laughter interpretation arises, while also emphasizing the process of turn taking.

   a. Start showing the turn preceding the laugh and reveal message content line-by-line, mimicking how interaction unfolds in real life.

   b. Identify the spot where something laughable can be found by asking students, "What or who could be 'laughed at' here? Why?"

   c. Ask, "What type of laughter is most appropriate here? Why?"

   d. Ask, "Which text symbol would you type to indicate the laugh? Why?"

   e. Show the laughter symbol used in the sample text message. Explain the meaning of that symbol.

   f. Ask, "What and how would you respond? Why?" Explore possible responses, whether in words or with another emoji or symbol for laughing.

   g. Show the next turn (i.e., the response to the laughter). Explain what it meant in the context and why that response was (or was not) appropriate.

7. Students work in pairs to analyze the second pair of sample text messages by answering the questions in Step 6. Monitor analysis.

8. Ask, "How would the meaning of the message change if this laugh symbol were placed somewhere else?"

9. Show the edited version.

10. Identify possible consequences of the interaction (e.g., fewer shorter exchanges, closing) and its impact on preserving the friendship.

11. Hand out the graphs from McKay (2020, Figures 3, 5, 6) and Petitjean & Morel (2017, pp. 16–17). Students work in groups to answer the question "How does your use of symbols compare to the research?"

CAVEATS AND OPTIONS

- Instruct students on appropriate content for sharing text messages.

- Many answers will vary, and that is one of the goals. A particularly rich conversation ensues from comparing interactions between multilingual speakers.

- Students enjoy learning that researchers count syllables of laughter and that they use the symbol @ when transcribing it (Chafe, 2001).

- Extend the activity by having students swap messages for analysis. This prompts negotiation of meaning and exposure to foreign characters used to indicate laughter.

- Extend learning by adding a value activity: Learners carry out a mini-research project. Warn students that this activity requires risk taking, so offer yourself to act as the friend.

  — Have learners initiate a funny text message with a friend in real life, (or with you, if you are acting as the friend).

  — During texting, they should unexpectedly insert a symbol for laughing. Alternatively, they refrain from reacting when someone inserts a symbol for laughing; they watch and see how the exchange unfolds.

  — Have students share their findings about laughter as risk.

REFERENCES AND FURTHER READING

Chafe, W. (2003). Laughing while talking. In D. Tannen & J. E. Alatis (Eds.), *Georgetown University round table on languages and linguistics (GURT) 2001: Linguistics, language, and the real world discourse and beyond* (pp. 36–49). Georgetown.

Glenn, P. (2003). *Laughter in interaction: Studies in interactional sociolinguistics.* Cambridge.

Jefferson, G. (1979). A technique for inviting laughter and its subsequent acceptance/declination. In G. Psathas (Ed.), *Everyday language: Studies in ethnomethodology* (pp. 79–96). Irvington.

McKay, I. (2020). Some distributional patterns in the use of typed laughter-derived expressions on Twitter. *Journal of Pragmatics, 166,* 97–113.

Petitjean, C., & Morel, E. (2017). "Hahaha": Laughter as a resource to manage WhatsApp conversations. *Journal of Pragmatics, 110,* 1–19.

Takahashi, K., Oishi, T., & Shimada, M. (2017). Is 😊 smiling? Cross-cultural study on recognition of emoticon's emotion. *Journal of Cross-Cultural Psychology, 48,* 1578–1586.

APPENDIX: *Sample Text Messages*

The following screenshots provide examples of conversations between friends using different types of laugh symbols (top) and the redacted versions of the message (bottom). Additional messages can be found in McKay (2020, p.9) and in Petitjian & Morel (2017).

Sample 1   **Sample 2**

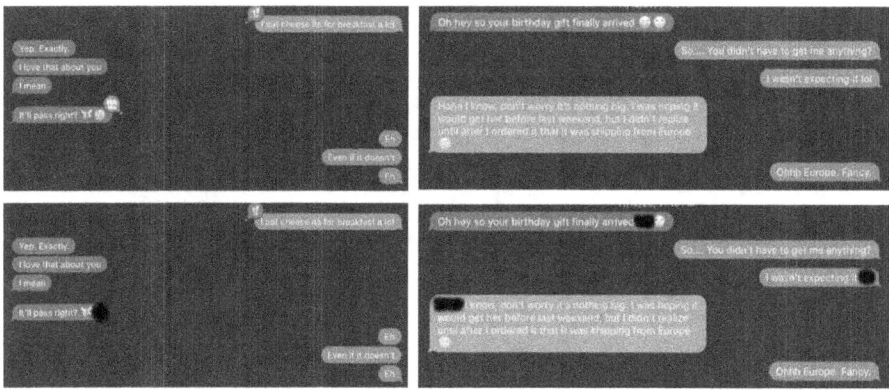

Sample text message between two friends with laugh reactions (top) and redacted (bottom)

Sample text message with nervous laughter emoji, *lol,* and *haha* (top) and redacted (bottom)

Interpreting Multimodal Street Signs

Priya M. Dabak

Levels	Intermediate to advanced
Ages Suitable for Activity	Secondary to adult
Aims	Observe and describe multimodal elements on street signs
	Interpret how multimodal elements work together to make meaning
	Explore the role of humor and surprise in communication
Class Time	1 (90-minute) session or 2 (45-minute) sessions
Preparation Time	10 minutes
Resources	Images (Appendixes A and B)
	Sticky notes or a big sheet of paper

Multimodality refers to the use of multiple modes or channels to convey meaning (e.g., text, images, sound, gestures). We assume that words are the primary vehicle of meaning, whereas visuals simply support or enrich the message. In reality, words and images can work together to convey meaning—sometimes in unexpected ways that create room for humor and irony. In this activity, decoding multimodal information challenges learners to engage a range of interpretive and pragmatic skills.

PROCEDURE

1. Display a conventional "No Feeding Wildlife" street sign (Appendix A). Give students 2–3 minutes to independently reflect on the sign using this scaffolding:

   Observe: What do you see?
   (Describe the image, text, color, upper/lowercase, ...)

   Decode: How do the elements interact?
   (Placement of the text and image, size, ...)

   Interpret: What does it mean?
   (Message, purpose, location, intended response, ...)

   Analyze: What is the effect?
   (Do you find it effective, useful, funny,...?)

2. Invite students to share their guesses about 1) the purpose of the street sign, 2) where it might be located, and 3) how they reached this conclusion.

3. Define *multimodality* as our ability to make sense of different modes of information, such as written and spoken words; visual symbols (e.g., images, icons, graphs); and sounds, movements, and gestures.

4. Ask students, "What is more important in conveying the message on this street sign: the text or the images?" Ask students to answer with gestures:

   a. Have them raise their *left* hand if they think only text is enough.

....

b. Have them raise their *right* hand if they think only an image is sufficient.

c. Have them stand with *both* hands raised if they believe both are needed.

5. Now show students one of the unconventional "Don't Feed Wildlife" signs (Appendix B). Use the same scaffolding and interpret it in a whole-group discussion. Students can speak and you can make notes, or they can put up sticky notes under each heading.

Observe:	What do you see? (Describe the image, text, color, upper/lowercase, ...)
Decode:	How do the elements interact? (Placement of the text and image, size, ...)
Interpret:	What does it mean? (Message, purpose, location, intended response, ...)
Analyze:	What is the effect? (Do you find it effective, useful, funny,...?)

6. Lead the class to reflect on how the mismatch between the text and the image in this unconventional sign creates humor and conveys a sharper message.

7. Now share the other two unconventional signs. Have students work in pairs to understand the signs. They may use the same scaffolding or present their analysis in their own way.

CAVEATS AND OPTIONS

- Vary group size according to your class size and student proficiency level.
- Adapt the activity for lower levels by providing less complex scaffolding (e.g., see, think, wonder) and doing more teacher modelling.
- Extend the activity by asking students to create their own novel, unexpected signs.
- Try this extended discussion prompt: Why does humor help us pay attention to warnings or messages we might otherwise ignore?
- Try this extended reflection prompt: What is the cultural knowledge needed to analyze and interpret these signs? For example, the bear or alligator signs may not work in all contexts.

REFERENCES AND FURTHER READING

Burgers, C., Van Mulken, M., & Schellens, P. J. (2013). On verbal irony, images and creativity: A corpus-analytic approach. In T. Veale, K. Feyaerts, & C. Forceville (Eds.), *Creativity and the agile mind: A multi-disciplinary study of a multi-faceted phenomenon* (pp. 293–312). De Gruyter. https://doi.org/10.1515/9783110295290.293

Cook, V. (2022). *The language of the English street sign*. Multilingual Matters. https://doi.org/10.21832/9781800414570

Kress, G. (2003). *Literacy in the new media age*. Routledge. https://doi.org/10.4324/9780203299234

APPENDIX A: *Conventional Street Sign*

APPENDIX B: *Signs Using Multimodal Irony or Visual Puns*

Symbols of Identity and Resistance: Palestinian Keffiyeh

Fatima Aldajani

Levels	Low intermediate to high intermediate
Ages Suitable for Activity	Secondary to adult
Aims	Explore the cultural and political relevance of the Palestinian keffiyeh
	Analyze the keffiyeh as a symbol using visual culture skills
	Discuss how visual symbols can represent identity, resistance, and solidarity
	Improve vocabulary and understanding through contextual discussions
	Encourage critical thinking about the use of symbols in social movements
Class Time	60 minutes
Preparation Time	15 minutes
Resources	Image and description of the Palestinian keffiyeh (Appendix)
	Additional images of the keffiyeh from an internet search
	Laptop and projector
	Whiteboard and markers
	Video: "Keffiyeh: How It Became a Symbol of the Palestinian People" (CBC News, 2023; youtu.be/JMB2od3at-o)

This activity introduces the Palestinian keffiyeh, also spelled *kufiya*, a traditional scarf that has remarkable cultural, political, and historical value. Students explore the symbolism behind the keffiyeh, using visual analysis to develop skills in interpreting visual culture while enhancing their awareness of global social issues.

PROCEDURE

1. *Warm-up (5 minutes):* Introduce the concept of symbols in culture and politics.

    a. Explain that symbols express shared meanings, values, and identities. They can unite communities, express power, and influence social and political movements.

    b. Then, ask students if they are aware of any cultural symbols from their countries and what they represent (see Kircadi, 2024).

        i. For example, national flags, religious symbols, and historical emblems often carry deep cultural and political significance.

        ii. According to Kircadi (2024), the olive branch is widely recognized as a symbol of peace, whereas the raised fist has historically represented solidarity and resistance in social movements.

    c. Ask students to share their ideas.

2. *Video Viewing (5 minutes):* Show the video "Keffiyeh: How It Became a Symbol of the Palestinian People." Ask students to share one thing they learned from the video.

3. *Vocabulary Development (10 minutes):* Introduce key vocabulary related to the keffiyeh and its cultural significance (e.g., *solidarity, resistance, identity, symbolism, nationalism*). Have students match the vocabulary words with definitions or images from the activity.

4. *Visual Analysis (15 minutes):* Display different images of the keffiyeh, including the image in the Appendix. (Search the internet and select photos of the keffiyeh worn by political figures; during protests; or as seen in art, daily life, and fashion.) Ask students to observe and describe what they see, focusing on the colors, patterns, and settings of the images:

   a. What do the different patterns and colors of the keffiyeh represent?

   b. Where do they see the keffiyeh being worn, and by whom?

   c. How does the setting affect the meaning of the keffiyeh?

5. *Discussion (15 minutes):* Show the video again. Then, put students in groups and give them the following list of discussion questions to guide their exploration of the keffiyeh as a symbol:

   a. What is the meaning of the keffiyeh in Palestinian culture?

   b. How is the keffiyeh used?

   c. What does wearing the keffiyeh represent?

   d. Can you think of other items in your own culture that symbolize resistance or identity?

   Encourage students to share personal reflections and connections to their own cultural symbols.

6. *Reflection and Creative Activity (10 minutes):* Ask students to create visual representations of identity or resistance using symbols from their culture. They can sketch, design, draw, or write about their chosen symbols. Have students present their work to the class and explain its meaning, encouraging them to use new vocabulary (e.g., from Step 3) and complete sentences.

CAVEATS AND OPTIONS

- The activity includes discussions sensitive topics, including political symbols and colonization. Ensure that students are respectful when sharing their perspectives.

- Modify the activity for lower levels by simplifying vocabulary and focusing more on the visual analysis of the images rather than the discussion.

REFERENCES AND FURTHER READING

CBC News. (2023, December 15). *Keffiyeh: How it became a symbol of the Palestinian people* [Video]. YouTube. https://youtu.be/JMB2od3at-o

Kiricard. (2024, August 7). *20+ cultural symbols and their meanings.* https://kiricard.com/20-cultural-symbols-and-their-meanings/

Kufiya.org. (2023, August 9). *What does the Palestinian keffiyeh symbolize?* https://kufiya.org/what-does-the-palestinian-keffiyeh-symbolize/

Said, E. W. (1994). *Culture and imperialism.* Knopf.

Zulaihah, S. (2023). Keffiyeh trend on social media as a form of solidarity for Palestine. *Digital Theory, Culture & Society, 1*(2), 135–144. https://doi.org/10.61126/dtcs.v1i2.27

APPENDIX: *About the Palestinian Keffiyeh*

Image description: A loom at work making a traditional Palestinian keffiyeh in the Hirbawi factory, Hebron, Palestine.

Retrieved from: commons.wikimedia.org/wiki/File:Palestinian_keffiyeh_loom.jpg.

This photograph is from the last and only factory still weaving fabric for keffiyeh in Palestine. It was founded in 1961 by Yasser Hirbawi, who witnessed the closure of other factories across Palestine and faced restrictions in his trade due to the blockades and checkpoints imposed by Israel, as well as the competition from cheaper fabrics produced globally and facilitated by the open market (Kufiya.org, 2023).

The patterns woven into the keffiyeh hold deep symbolism. The fishnet represents the relationship that Palestinians have with the sea. The olive leaves represent the central place olive trees hold in Palestinian agriculture and economy, and a strong connection to the land through the trees' deep roots. Finally, the bold lines represent historical trade routes (Kufiya.org, 2023).

Part VI

Multimodalities

Introduction: Developing Multimodal Visual Literacy Competencies

The development of multimodal communication skills is an essential component of visual literacy and communicative competence in the 21st-century language classroom. As Kress (2003) and others have noted, communication increasingly takes place across multiple modes—linguistic, visual, spatial, gestural, and digital—requiring learners to interpret, evaluate, and produce meaning through the integrated use of diverse inputs. The activities in this section provide multilingual learners of English with opportunities to explore and experiment with multiple modes of communication, equipping them with the skills to successfully navigate today's multimodal and media-rich landscape.

The multimodal activities presented here foster critical thinking, creativity, and intercultural awareness by engaging learners in the analysis and production of materials that combine text, image, sound, and design. Through a variety of tasks, such as exploring linguistic landscapes, analyzing movie posters, engaging with advertisements, designing posters, participating in digital museum tours, and investigating cultural narratives, students experience firsthand how meaning is constructed through the interaction of different communicative elements. These activities draw attention to the ways that visual, linguistic, and spatial resources work together to convey complex messages.

Pedagogically, these activities are grounded in research that emphasizes the value of applying classroom learning to real-world contexts (Mavridi & Xerri, 2020). Learners are encouraged to become active participants in and producers of multimodal texts, expanding their abilities to use language in flexible and dynamic ways. In addition, these activities promote critical visual literacy as students learn to analyze persuasive techniques and cultural narratives embedded in visual media.

The activities in this section draw on a variety of approaches designed to integrate multimodal practices into language learning. Activities emphasize transferable skills that support both language development and multimodal competence. Teachers will find that these approaches foster engagement, collaboration, and autonomy.

By incorporating multimodalities into English language teaching, educators help students develop essential skills needed to understand and contribute meaningfully to the diverse environments they encounter every day. These activities prepare learners to engage with and shape the visual-verbal synergy that defines communication in our increasingly complex and interconnected world.

REFERENCES AND FURTHER READING

Kress, G. (2003). *Literacy in the new media age*. Routledge.

Mavridi, S., & Xerri, D. (2020). *English for 21st century skills*. Express Publishing.

VI

Analyzing Movie Posters Across Cultures

Sarah Warfield

Levels	Intermediate to advanced
Ages Suitable for Activity	Secondary to adult
Aims	Develop learners' visual literacy skills
	Develop learners' persuasive writing skills
	Raise awareness of rhetorical strategies
	Apply concepts from rhetoric to analyze and interpret visual texts
	Consider how cultural differences might affect the meaning and interpretation of images
Class Time	60 minutes
Preparation Time	10–20 minutes
Resources	Printed copies of movie posters from different countries
	Projector and laptop, or printed copy of Appendix A
	Handouts (Appendixes B–D)

ultimodal pedagogies are crucial in second language writing classrooms as they enable students to engage with a range of communication modes beyond print text (Hocks, 2003). Visual literacy is also essential in our modern society where we are constantly exposed to visual information (Bolter, 2001). Movie posters are one such visual medium, holding significant power in shaping the public's perception of a film. In this activity, students analyze movie posters from diverse cultures using logos (appeal to logic), ethos (appeal to credibility or authority), and pathos (appeal to emotions) to interpret their messages. Through practicing visual literacy, students will develop skills to understand and engage with multimodal communication.

PROCEDURE

1. Before the activity, collect images of movie posters from around the world. Find images by searching Wikimedia (commons.wikimedia.org), Openverse (openverse.org), and other online platforms. Find and print the following sets of posters:

    a. *Set A:* Four movie posters of the same film from at least two different countries

    b. *Set B:* Four movie posters of a different film, also from at least two different countries

2. Begin the activity by introducing the concept of visual literacy. Explain the importance of analyzing images as a way to understand different cultural perspectives and messages. Display a movie poster for a well-known movie as an example (e.g., Appendix A).

3. Introduce the concept of rhetorical analysis and the three rhetorical appeals: logos, ethos, and pathos. Explain how these appeals are used in persuasive communication and how they can be applied to analyze visual texts.

    a. Use the worksheet Understanding Ethos, Logos, and Pathos (Appendix B) to introduce the topic to the class.

4. Use the worksheet Rhetorical Analysis: Connecting Logos, Ethos, and Pathos (Appendix C) to lead a discussion on the relationship between rhetorical appeals and rhetorical analysis.

5. Divide the class into pairs. Give each pair one movie poster from Set A or Set B and a copy of the worksheet Practicing Rhetorical Analysis (Appendix D). Each pair should analyze their movie poster using the rhetorical analysis framework and the appeals of logos, ethos, and pathos.

6. After a few minutes, the pairs who have the posters from the same set come together in groups of four to share their observations and discuss what they think the posters are trying to communicate.

7. Form new groups of four with one pair who analyzed posters from Set A and one pair who analyzed posters from Set B. Ask them to share what they noticed about the movie posters for their assigned movie and to discuss the similarities and differences in the rhetorical strategies used in the movie posters for the two movies.

8. As a class, discuss the similarities and differences in the rhetorical strategies used in the movie posters for the two movies. Ask groups to share their results.

9. Facilitate a class discussion to share insights about how different posters use logos, ethos, and pathos to appeal to different audiences and cultural contexts. Encourage the students to draw on their own cultural knowledge and experiences as they analyze the posters, considering how cultural differences might affect the meaning and interpretation of the images.

10. After the students have completed their analysis, have them outline an essay arguing whether or not the movie is worth seeing based on the poster they analyzed. Remind them to use evidence from the poster and from rhetorical analysis to support their argument.

CAVEATS AND OPTIONS

- Consider your students' cultural backgrounds when choosing posters, as some images may be more or less familiar or relatable to different groups of students.

- If your students all share the same home language, choose posters from familiar or culturally relevant movies, rather than from multiple countries, to encourage deeper analysis.

- Encourage students to draw on their own cultural knowledge and experiences while avoiding reliance on stereotypes.

- Provide additional scaffolding and support, such as discussion and/or practice, for students who are not accustomed to analyzing visual texts or who are unfamiliar with rhetorical appeals.

- Choose posters that are age- and maturity-appropriate for the students.

- Provide context or background information about the movies or cultures represented in the posters if needed.

VI

REFERENCES AND FURTHER READING

Bolter, J. D. (2001). *Writing space: Computers, hypertext, and the remediation of print.* Routledge.

Ferris, D. R., & Hedgcock, J. S. (2023). *Teaching L2 composition: Purpose, process, and practice.* Routledge.

Fletcher, J. (2015). *Teaching arguments: Rhetorical comprehension, critique, and response.* Stenhouse.

Hocks, M. E. (2003). Understanding visual rhetoric in digital writing environments. *College Composition and Communication, 54*(4), 629–656.

APPENDIX A: *Example Movie Posters*

Image source: Bhedenberg, CC BY-SA 4.0, commons.wikimedia.org/w/index.php?curid=112422805

Image source: Brian Hedenberg, CC BY-SA 4.0, commons.wikimedia.org/w/index.php?curid=112927562

VI

APPENDIX B: *Understanding Ethos, Logos, and Pathos*

Logos (Logic and Reason): Logos is using facts, data, and logic to make an argument. It's about convincing with evidence. Think about how the following examples use evidence to make an argument. How does each type of evidence improve the argument?

- Showing statistics to support an argument.
- Using logical reasoning to explain a concept.
- Presenting research findings to prove a point.

Now, write down your own example of a logos appeal:

Example: _____

Ethos (Credibility and Authority): Ethos is about trust and credibility. It's when someone or something is seen as trustworthy or knowledgeable. Think about what makes these examples trustworthy. Why do they appeal to your sense of what is credible?

- A doctor in a white coat endorsing a medicine.
- A history professor explaining a historical event.
- An expert scientist discussing climate change.

Now, write down your own example of an ethos appeal:

Example: _____

Pathos (Emotions): Pathos appeals to your emotions. It's about making you feel a certain way to persuade you. Think about what makes these examples persuasive. Why do they make you feel the way you do?

- A sad commercial with music to raise empathy.
- A campaign poster showing images of happy children.
- Using words that create fear to sell security products.

Now, write down your own example of a pathos appeal:

Example: _____

APPENDIX C: *Rhetorical Analysis: Connecting Logos, Ethos, and Pathos*

Key Elements of Rhetorical Analysis

Purpose: Why is the message being conveyed? What's the goal?

Audience: Who is the message intended for? Consider their beliefs and interests.

Context: What is the surrounding historical and cultural background?

Tone: What emotions or attitude does the message convey?

Message: What's the main idea or argument presented?

Connecting Rhetorical Strategies to Appeals

Ethos (Credibility and Authority)

Purpose: Establish trust by using expertise, qualifications, or reliable sources.

Example: Citing renowned experts.

Audience: Align with the audience's values and beliefs to build trust.

Example: Appealing to shared cultural values.

Logos (Logic and Reason)
Purpose: Use logic, evidence, and reasoning to support the argument.
Example: Presenting data and statistics.
Audience: Make sure the logical argument makes sense to the audience.
Example: Addressing the audience's rationality.

Pathos (Emotions)
Purpose: Evoke specific emotions in the audience.
Example: Using emotionally charged language.
Audience: Ensure the emotional appeal resonates with the audience's feelings and values.
Example: Connecting with the audience's sensibilities.

APPENDIX D: *Practicing Rhetorical Analysis*

1. What is the main message or theme conveyed by the images in the poster? How do you know?

2. Identify the rhetorical appeals used in the poster:

Logos (appeal to logic) e.g., *statistics, facts, logical arguments*	
Ethos (appeal to credibility or authority) e.g., *celebrity endorsements, historical or cultural significance*	
Pathos (appeal to emotions) e.g., *emotionally-loaded language, use of colors and images*	

3. How does the poster use these appeals to persuade its audience?

4. Consider the cultural context of the poster. Are there any symbols or references that are specific to a particular culture or community? How might this affect the poster's reception by different audiences?

5. What is your personal reaction to the poster? Do you find it effective or persuasive? Why or why not?

VI

Building Voice and Identity Through Multimodal Practices

Qianyu Yang and Huixin Wang

Levels	Low advanced to high advanced
Ages Suitable for Activity	Adult
Aims	Develop understanding of visual literacy and how various modes convey meaning, while enhancing their ability to express their voice and identity through multimodal resources like photographs, art, and symbols
	Enhance speaking and communication skills, socio-emotional, creative, and critical thinking abilities, interpreting and sharing personal stories through visual and symbolic storytelling
Class Time	90 minutes
Preparation Time	30 minutes
Resources	Examples of symbolic images (Appendix A)
	Flora's story in images and text (Appendixes B–D)
	Handout (Appendix E)
	Laptop and projector
	Access to the internet on laptops or tablets, or paper and art supplies

This activity helps students explore visual literacy through multimodalities, including creative art and symbols. Students use multimodal semiotic resources to tell their personal stories, explore embedded cultural and social meanings, and express their voices and identities. This process builds a deeper understanding of how meaning is expressed through both visual and linguistic elements and supports social-emotional learning by fostering self-awareness, self-management, social awareness, and relationship skills (Zins et al., 2004).

PROCEDURE

1. *Warm-up (20 minutes):* Start by showing a few examples (Appendix A) of images or symbols (e.g., a national flag, a personal object, a piece of clothing) and ask students what these images or symbols mean to them and what they may represent. Then, invite students to discuss in groups how images, symbols, and signs convey meaning. Ask them to think about how they can express aspects of their identity with images. Encourage each student to think of an image of something that represents themselves (e.g., family, culture, hobbies) and exchange ideas with their group members.

2. *Introducing Flora's Story (10 minutes):* Introduce the story of Flora, a former international student who used photography, symbols, and creative artwork to tell her story of studying abroad and express her emotions, voice and identity. Display the images in Appendixes B and C sequentially, and facilitate a class discussion about what each image may represent. Use Appendix D as a guide to highlight the symbolism of various aspects in the images as they relate to Flora's story.

3. *Group Discussion (20 minutes):* Put students into small groups. Give each group a copy of the reflective prompts in Appendix E (or project the questions on the board). Invite students to reflect on how Flora employed different modes—such as imagery, symbols, and signs—to create meaning and express her voices and emotions. More importantly, encourage students to discuss how multimodal and multisemiotic elements contributed to the depth of her narrative by focusing on the changes of these three stages. Circulate to monitor and support discussions.

4. *Creative Multimodal Project (20 minutes):* Have students create their own multimodal and multisemiotic narrative projects to express their voices and identities. They can use photographs, symbols, text, and creative visuals to tell their personal stories, just like Flora's example. Allow students to either work digitally (with laptops or tablets) or physically (with art supplies). Encourage them to think critically about how they combine different modes and signs to convey deeper meaning and reflect their identities.

5. *Sharing and Reflection (20 minutes):* Ask students to share their creations with the class and explain the choices behind their multimodal compositions. Encourage reflection on how their identities and voices are expressed through the combination of visuals, text, and symbols.

6. *Closing Discussion (10 minutes):* Lead a discussion on how multimodal visual literacy enables new ways of expressing oneself and communicating complex emotions and experiences. Use the following prompts to guide reflection:

   a. Consider how a single symbol or image can be interpreted in different ways depending on context. How could the same symbol evoke different emotions or ideas for different people or cultures?

   b. Think about an image or object you have seen in a photograph or artwork (as shown in Appendixes B and C). How might someone else interpret it differently than you?

   c. Are there symbols in your own culture that have one meaning, but may carry a completely different meaning in another culture or setting?

CAVEATS AND OPTIONS

- Be mindful of cultural differences in interpreting visual elements, symbols, and gestures.
- Students may interpret images in different ways due to their personal experiences, cultural background, or emotional state. Ensure that no single interpretation is seen as the correct one.

REFERENCES AND FURTHER READING

Bezemer, J., & Kress, G. (2015). *Multimodality, learning and communication: A social semiotic frame.* Routledge.

Kress, G. (2010). *Multimodality: A Social Semiotic Approach to Contemporary Communication.* Routledge.

Wei, L. (2018). Translanguaging as a practical theory of language. *Applied linguistics, 39*(1), 9–30.

Zins, J., Weissberg, R., Wang, M., & Walberg, H. J. (Eds.). (2004). *Building academic success on social emotional learning: What does the research say?* Teachers College.

VI

APPENDIX A: *Symbols*

Images credit: Unsplash.

Flags

Objects

Clothing

APPENDIX B: *Flora's Journey Through Photographs*

Images credit: Flora. Used with permission.

Stage 1: Embarking on Study Abroad

Figure 1. A sense of freedom from living alone, away from family.

Figure 2. A sense of happiness and enjoyment of the freshness brought by a new environment.

Figure 3. A sense of desire to be or do something different and to feel unique.

Figure 4. A sense of desire to make friends and build relationships with others.

Figure 5. A desire to climb to a high point; the goal of attaining higher grades.

Stage 2. The Adaptation of Studying Abroad

Figure 6. Joining local activities, making local friends, and getting involved in local culture.

Figure 7. Making good friends, having fun, and facing challenges.

Figure 8. Going on excursions with friends and exploring nature with excitement and happiness.

Stage 3. The Achievement of Studying Abroad

Figure 9. A sense of enjoyment in the study abroad life after 1 year, having found her own way of life.

Figure 10. A sense of achievement and peacefulness, feeling proud of personal growth.

Figure 11. A sense of strong friendships and success that comes from them.

VI

Figure 12. A sense of belonging to the university and its communities; a feeling of connection to the study abroad experience.

APPENDIX C: *Flora's Journey Through Art*

Stage 1. The Embarkation of Studying Abroad

Figure 1. Sense of exclusion and inability to adapt to the study abroad life.

Stage 2. The Adaptation of Studying Abroad

Figure 2. Start to make friends and integrate into the study abroad life.

Stage 3. The Achievement of Studying Abroad

Figure 3. A sense of belonging to the community and happiness from integrating into diverse cultures, with a welcoming atmosphere symbolized by hand-holding gestures.

APPENDIX D: *Flora's Story*

Flora is an international student who expresses her experiences of studying abroad through photography and visual artwork. Her creative outputs serve as a reflective medium, capturing moments of personal transformation and emotional depth as she navigates life in a new cultural environment.

Appendix B includes examples of Flora's photographs, and Appendix C presents a sample of her creative artwork. These visual pieces offer insight into her inner world and the challenges and triumphs of her international journey.

Figure 1 in Appendix B, for instance, shows Flora standing in the center of the frame with arms outstretched and one leg lifted. This pose evokes a sense of joy, freedom, and self-expression. The natural lighting, with a bright sky and soft shadows, enhances the uplifting atmosphere of the image. Symbolically, the open posture conveys confidence and a release from constraints.

In her creative artwork, themes of isolation and adaptation emerge. Figure 1 in Appendix C depicts a solitary figure standing apart from a group. The spatial separation between the individual and the crowd visually represents the emotional and social distance often felt in unfamiliar surroundings. The shadows and faceless group figures further emphasize feelings of marginalization and invisibility within a new cultural context.

APPENDIX E: *Question Prompts*

Questions for Analyzing the Photographs

1. How do gestures and symbols add meaning to photographs or creative artworks?
2. What cultural meanings are conveyed through these images?
3. How do the emotions expressed in the photos deepen your understanding of the subjects' experiences?
4. In what ways do the photos reflect self-awareness or personal growth?
5. What changes are evident across the three stages of Flora's story, as portrayed through modes, gestures, or symbols in the photos?

VI

6. How can our bodies express feelings, emotions, and thoughts through symbols? Can you find examples in your own photo albums that tell your story?

7. How does analyzing these photos help you reflect on your emotional and social awareness in relation to your own life?

Questions for Analyzing the Artworks

1. What cultural meanings are conveyed through these artworks?

2. How do the emotions expressed in the artworks help you understand the subjects' experiences?

3. In what ways do the artworks reflect self-awareness or personal growth?

4. How does the combination of different modes or mediums affect your understanding?

5. Can you identify any social dynamics or relationships depicted in the artwork? How are these portrayed through visual or symbolic elements?

6. What changes can you observe across the three stages of Flora's story, as reflected through different modes, gestures, or symbols in these artworks?

7. How can we use different elements to express feelings, emotions, and thoughts in artworks? Can you think of any ideas or examples for creating such artworks?

Cultural Narratives Through Multimodal Visual Media Analysis

Ali Caszadeh Mataki

Levels	High intermediate
Ages Suitable for Activity	Adult
Aims	Use knowledge from analyzing multimodal visual media to identify narrative components, cultural symbols, and visual techniques
	Participate in engaging discussions that analyze various cultural narratives with critical thinking skills that showcase comparison and contrasting abilities
	Create interesting cross-cultural narratives using personal experiences and cultural symbols that are inspired by visuals
Class Time	90 minutes
Preparation Time	20 minutes
Resources	Multimodal visual media expressing cultural narratives (see Appendix A for suggestions)
	Handout (Appendix B)
	Laptop and projector
	Whiteboard or flipchart
	Art supplies (e.g., markers, colored pencils)

In this activity, students experience an immersive exploration of visual storytelling across cultural boundaries. Learning various techniques for analyzing multimodal visual media will improve learners' cognitive abilities and deepen their cross-cultural understanding while building linguistic fluency.

PROCEDURE

1. *Engaging Introduction (5 min):* Spark student interest by showing three or four ultra-short "hook" visuals (10–15 seconds each) that show different cultural backgrounds. See Appendix A for suggestions. Encourage feedback about their initial impressions. Stress the importance of visual media in understanding a variety of perspectives. Visual media is not just about entertainment; it's a powerful tool for cultural exploration. By analyzing and interpreting what we see, we can gain insights into the beliefs, values, and traditions of different societies.

2. *Introducing Multimodal Visual Media (15 min):* Show one core exemplar, a 2- to 3-minute excerpt from Chimamanda Ngozi Adichie's TED talk, "The Danger of a Single Story." (Play from 00:00 to 02:35, for example.) Guide students through the following sequence:

   a. Preteach the six narrative terms: *characters, setting, action, cultural symbol, visual technique, emotion.* Write the six words on the board and have students copy them into a chart, as in Appendix B.

b. Play the TED Talk excerpt straight through once with no pauses. Ask: "What story do you see or hear?" (Accept one-sentence answers.)

c. Replay the excerpt, pausing at two planned moments (e.g., 01:10 and 01:55). After each pause, ask one targeted question, such as "Who is the character here?" or "What cultural symbol appears?" Students write notes in their charts (Appendix B).

d. Organize students in pairs for think, pair, share. Have pairs compare notes and add one detail they missed.

3. *Group Analysis and Discussion (20 min):* Divide the class into pairs or small groups and assign each team a different visual media example to analyze.

a. Instruct groups to identify narrative components in their example media, along with any potential interpretations from a cultural element perspective. They should also study the example's overall symbolism within their assigned form of graphic imagery.

b. Distribute copies or project the chart in Appendix B to help guide discussions.

c. After 15 minutes, gather the whole class and ask groups to share their insights. Take notes on key points from the group discussions, either via whiteboard or flipchart. Highlight unique perspectives resulting from different analyses of visuals in various cultures. Focus on diverse narratives created through unique perceptual filters across societies worldwide.

4. *Collaborative Narrative Creation (25 min):* Create new groups or keep the groups from Step 3. Tell learners to work together to create a multimedia narrative inspired by one or more of your provided visual aids. Groups follow this mini-process:

- Plan (5 min): agree on a message, choose three panels, list at least two cultural symbols.

- Draft (15 min): create visuals (poster or digital) and write short English captions.

- Rehearse (2 min): decide who explains each panel in the presentation.

They should incorporate personal experiences and cultural symbolism into their works. (For lower level classes, support their success by providing vocabulary lists, sentence frames, or other scaffolds.)

5. *Cultural Narrative Presentations (20 min):* Ask each group to present their cultural narrative (via gallery-walk stations or 2-minute lightning talks). Encourage peer review and reflection to increase learners' understanding of different perspectives and cultures.

6. *Reflection and Closure (5 min):* Lead a whole-class discussion about the importance of diversity and varied narratives worldwide. Ask learners to reflect on their own learning by sharing their insights from creating cultural narratives.

CAVEATS AND OPTIONS

- To accommodate learners at lower language proficiency levels, consider simplifying the materials you choose for Steps 1 and 2. It's vital to choose materials that match the class's language abilities.

- For younger learners, concentrate on age-appropriate visuals and content. Offer extra vocabulary support as necessary.
- Inspire learners to include their individual experiences and cultural symbols while creating their narratives. This will promote inclusivity and foster personal expression.

REFERENCES AND FURTHER READING

TED. (2009, October 7). *Chimamanda Ngozi Adichie: The danger of a single story* [Video]. https://www.youtube.com/watch?v=D9Ihs241zeg

APPENDIX A: *Suggested Multimodal Visual Media*

- Vibrant street market scene photograph
- Short documentary video on traditional dance performances
- Instagram posts by influential figures promoting inclusivity
- Iconic landmark photograph symbolizing cultural heritage
- Animated short film with diverse characters and cultural references
- Collection of social media posts discussing global events from different cultural perspectives
- Photograph collage of cultural symbols and artifacts
- Travel vlog showcasing a multicultural city and its neighborhoods
- TikTok video capturing a cultural celebration or festival
- Art piece representing cultural fusion and exchange

Note: Provide links to the sources when sharing these images or video resources with students.

APPENDIX B: *Discussion Guide*

Narrative Elements	
Characters (who is depicted)	
Settings (where and when)	
Actions (what is happening)	
Cultural symbols (symbols and objects representing a particular culture)	
Visual techniques (use of color, framing, perspective)	
Emotions (in narration, images, sound)	

VI

Engaging With Advertisements in the Educational Landscape

Leigh Yohei Bennett

Levels	Intermediate to advanced
Ages Suitable for Activity	Secondary to university
Aims	Develop learners critical thinking skills by reevaluating the visual information available in their school campus
	Provide opportunities for learners to use English to express their feelings
	Talk about the salient features of the advertisements using pre-taught vocabulary
Class Time	40–50 minutes
Preparation Time	5–10 minutes
Resources	Photos of posters and advertisements found in the community
	Devices for taking photographs (e.g., tablets or smartphones)

Linguistic landscapes refer to the languages that are visible all around us–in our neighborhoods, town and city centers, and schools. Linguistic landscaping is a "powerful tool for education" (Shohamy & Waksman, 2009, p. 326) and there is a growing need for students to be aware of and notice the multiple layers of meanings displayed in public spaces.

Drawing on the affective (feelings and attitudes), structural, and critical lenses, this activity invites learners to view advertisements and 1) express their immediate sensual response, 2) identify the salient structural elements, and 3) examine the image beyond its literal meaning. The activity promotes learners' critical and analytical dispositions toward everyday advertisements found in their educational communities.

PROCEDURE

1. Show learners a series of advertisements taken from the local community, school campus, or familiar websites. Ask students if they recognize any of the advertisements.

2. Elicit an affective (emotional) response from learners. Possible questions include:

    a. How does the image make you feel?

    b. Why does it make you feel this way?

    c. Do you identify with or relate to any of the advertisements? If so, how?

3. Focus on one of the advertisements introduced in Step 1. Briefly elicit the purpose/aim of the advertisement followed by eliciting any information from this advertisement that supports or explains its purpose/aim. Write the purpose/aim of the advertisement on the board.

4. Create small groups. Ask learners to work together to brainstorm a list of features of the advertisement that explain or support this purpose/aim. Elicit and write answers from each group on the board.

5. Referring to the advertisement for examples, preteach vocabulary about the structural elements of the image (e.g., background, captions, font, foreground, frame, slogan, text, viewpoint). Write the terms on the board and elicit or give their definitions.

6. Explain to learners that in their groups they will have 10 minutes to walk around their school campus (or search online; see Caveats and Options) and take three different photos of advertisements with text and imagery.

7. Once learners have returned to the classroom, allow them time to discuss their findings with their groups. Have students select one advertisement to share with the class. They should prepare to use the vocabulary and categories introduced in Step 7 to describe their chosen advertisement and explain its purpose/aim.

8. Have groups make their presentations. After each group has finished, invite the rest of the class to identify and discuss alternative interpretations of the chosen advertisement. Possible guiding questions include:

   a. Who/what is represented in this advertisement? How are they represented?

   b. Who is the target audience for this advertisement? (Elicit specific responses considering age, gender, nationality, race, etc.)

   c. In what other ways could the advertisement be interpreted?

   d. Are the advertisements stereotypical, idealized, or nonrepresentative of the people or culture they portray?

9. Elicit a response from the presenting group. Continue in this way until all groups have presented and explained their advertisements.

CAVEATS AND OPTIONS

- If it is not feasible for students to go outside and search for advertisements in the surrounding area, they can search online using their laptops or tablets. Provide guidance on where to search, such as suggested websites or keywords.

- For Step 8, depending on the size of the class, the instructor may want to extend the amount of time or preassign the task so that all groups are able to present.

- Extend the activity to focus on students' critical thinking and observation skills by questioning the presence of English or other languages on signs and posters on campus. For example, ask questions that encourage students to

  — appreciate the language diversity or lack thereof on campus,

  — reflect on which groups are being included or excluded and what is being valued or devalued, and

  — imagine how they would redesign the visual elements of an advertisement to create a more diverse and inclusive representation.

- For a follow-up activity, ask students to categorize the advertisements that their peers gathered based on their perceptions of the ad's purpose (i.e., to persuade, inform, entertain, or provoke) as conveyed through language and imagery.

VI

This analysis of communicative intentions can be followed by a whole-class mingling activity, where students search for ads that share similar goals or emotional effects as their own.

REFERENCES AND FURTHER READING

Shohamy, E., & Waksman, S. (2009). Linguistic landscape as an ecological arena: Modalities, meanings, negotiations, education. In E. Shohamy & D. Gorter (Eds.), *Linguistic landscape: Expanding the scenery* (pp. 313–331). Routledge. https://doi.org/10.4324/9780203930960

Solmaz, O., & Przymus, S. D. (n.d.). *LL in ELT: A pedagogical guidebook.* LL in ELT Project.

Exploring the Unusual in Your Campus or Neighborhood

Jacqueline Jacob

Levels	Intermediate to advanced
Ages Suitable for Activity	Secondary to adult
Aims	Engage with real-world visual images and create multimodal messages
	Develop effective multimodal communication skills
Class Time	15 minutes of a class prior to the weekend and a 90-minute activity.
Preparation Time	15 minutes
Resources	3-slide PowerPoint or Google Slides presentation (see Appendix for sample)
	Laptop and projector
	Devices for taking photographs (e.g., tablets or smartphones)
	Access to the internet on laptops or tablets

The transfer of learning or application of in-class learning to other contexts is an essential goal in English language teaching (James, 2006). Furthermore, communicating multimodally is an essential 21st-century skill that students must develop to thrive in the digital age (Mavridi & Xerri, 2020). Inspired by the see, think, wonder routine from Harvard's Project Zero (2019), this activity allows students to develop their multimodal communication abilities and apply those skills to their real-world digital communications.

PROCEDURE

Session 1: Introducing See, Think, Wonder (15 minutes)

1. Begin the activity by asking students if they've ever come across an unusual object or thing on campus. Elicit responses.

2. Demonstrate the see, think, wonder routine using your slides (see Appendix):

   a. *See*: Show students Slide 1 (image of an unusual find on campus). Tell students that you noticed this object on a desk in a campus building. Ask students, "What do you see?" Elicit student responses before revealing what the image actually is.

   b. *Think*: Ask students, "What are your thoughts and ideas about this photo?" Tell students to write a two-sentence response. Elicit student responses, then reveal Slide 2.

   c. *Wonder*: Ask students how they could visually express what the image makes them wonder about? Elicit student responses, then reveal Slide 3.

VI

3. Ask students to explore their university campus (or their neighborhood) before the next class session and take some photos of new, unusual, unique, strange, weird, or mysterious objects that intrigue, fascinate, or stand out to them. Provide students the following options on where to locate their unusual objects/things:

   a. Academic spaces (e.g., libraries, laboratories, lecture theaters, seminar rooms, auditoriums)

   b. A gym, swimming pool, or basketball court

   c. A historical building

   d. A place with beautiful views

   e. Your favorite coffee shop

   f. Your usual grocery store

   g. Your special study spot

   h. Your favorite garden or a lovely old tree

4. Ask students to select one favorite photo from their explorations of unusual things. Instruct students to design a presentation using Google Slides, Microsoft PowerPoint, or another digital presentation platform. Each presentation must contain the following:

   a. *Slide 1, See:* Insert your photo only.

   b. *Slide 2, Think:* Write 50-60 words expressing your thoughts on the photo.

   c. *Slide 3, Wonder:* Express what the unusual thing makes you wonder 'visually' using ONE of the following options: an illustration, a sketch, an infographic, a doodle, a painting, an AI-generated image, a video, or a photo. Prepare a 50- to 60-word spoken description of your visual.

Session 2: Student Presentations (90 minutes)

5. Invite each presenter to demonstrate the see, think, wonder routine using their slides. Allow each student a maximum of 5 minutes to present, including question time at the end.

6. Have the presenter introduce their first slide saying "I came across this at [location]." The presenter then elicits responses from peers on what they *see* in the photo. Finally, the presenter shares a brief description of what their chosen unusual item is.

7. Next, the presenter elicits their peers' ideas on what they *think* about the photo on Slide 1. Then, the presenter reveals Slide 2 with the student's personal thoughts on what the unusual find made them think about.

8. Finally, the presenter reveals Slide 3 with their chosen visual medium to express what the unusual item made them *wonder*. The presenter gives a brief spoken description. Allow the class the opportunity to ask the presenter one or two questions.

9. Invite students to optionally post their unusual finds or the visual they created to express wonder, plus a brief caption or description, on their preferred social media platforms (e.g., Facebook, Instagram, YouTube, Little Red Book (Xiaohongshu), WeChat) and to comment on each other's posts.

CAVEATS AND OPTIONS

- Have students add a slide with a photo of the location.
- Adapt the activity to suit other contexts by asking students to find new or unusual objects near their language school or in their city.

REFERENCES AND FURTHER READING

James, M. A. (2006). Teaching for transfer in ELT. *ELT Journal, 60*(2), 151–159. https://doi.org/10.1093/elt/cci102

Mavridi, S., & Xerri, D. (2020). *English for 21st century skills.* Express Publishing.

Project Zero. (2019). *See, think, wonder.* Harvard Graduate School of Education. https://pz.harvard.edu/sites/default/files/See%20Think%20Wonder_2.pdf

APPENDIX: *See, Think, Wonder Presentation Slides*

Instructions to Teacher

Ideally, create a digital presentation following the model in this Appendix but with content drawn from your teaching environment. You will need three slides, titled *See*, *Think*, and *Wonder*. Optionally, you can include a fourth slide titled *Where?* with a photo of your object's location.

Slide 1: SEE

The engravings on this desk date back to the years of World War I.

Image credit: Celuci on Wikimedia Commons; https://commons.m.wikimedia.org/wiki/File:Choir_desk_graffiti,_Hospital_of_St_Cross,_August_2018.jpg

Slide 2: THINK

"For me, these engravings on a desk in the John Woolley Building evoke a sense of history as they preserve the memory of students from a time long gone by. I see the students in the 1900s were not that different from us after all. They, too, relieved

VI

boredom and stress with graffiti on their desks. A-ha!"

Slide 3: WONDER

Image credit: Dominic Robinson on Wikimedia Commons (https://commons.wikimedia.org/wiki/File:Banksy_Girl_and_Heart_Balloon_(2840632113).jpg)

"The engravings on the desk made me wonder about similarities to Banksy's street art graffiti. Students often draw and doodle on desks as a means to express their individuality, mark their presence or rebel against formal structures. This is much like street artists like Banksy use graffiti as a form of artistic expression to transform walls and urban spaces."

Multimodal Poster Discussion

Alexandra Krasova

Levels	All
Ages Suitable for Activity	Any
Aims	Encourage critical thinking
	Analyze visual elements of a poster
	Identify various modes of communication
	Create a positive environment among students
Class Time	45–50 minutes
Preparation Time	5–10 minutes
Resources	Example of a multimodal poster (see Appendix)
	Laptop and projector
	Access to the internet on laptops or tablets

According to Zerin and Khan (2013), a poster is a "visual aid to present any specific information in a concise way in an academic environment" (p. 129). While working with posters, learners use nonlinguistic resources together with linguistic resources, promoting the use of different modes for successful communication (Lim & Polio, 2020). It is crucial for multilingual learners of English to effectively use various modes (e.g., linguistic, visual, spatial) to make meaning. This activity promotes creativity, develops multimodal skills, and encourages critical thinking.

PROCEDURE

1. Ask students where they can typically see posters and what posters are used for.

2. Show students an example of a multimodal poster using the projector (see Appendix). You can use the sample provided, create your own poster with Canva (canva.com), or find an example online by entering *multimodal poster* in your search bar.

3. Put learners in pairs or groups to discuss the visual elements they can see in the poster (e.g., colors, images, use of space). Ask them to be as descriptive as possible.

4. Facilitate a whole-class discussion about the elements of the poster, such as text, images, logos, size of fonts, colors, etc.

    a. Based on their analysis of the visual elements, ask students to make predictions about the message of the text.

    b. Ask learners to explain the relationship between the visuals and the text of the poster.

    c. Elicit the topic of the poster, its purpose, and message.

    d. Continue the discussion until no new information about the poster can be elicited.

VI

e. Elicit what students think about the poster. Is it thought provoking? What kind of emotions does it evoke?

5. Put students in groups. Tell groups to find another example of a multimodal poster by searching online and then analyze it in the same way they analyzed the sample poster.

   a. Groups should discuss the visual elements of the poster, the text, the use of space, and the relationship of images to the text.

   b. Based on their findings, they should identify its topic, purpose, and message.

6. Have each group present their chosen poster to the class. Help students think about the relationship of images to text and the messages they communicate by asking students: "What do the visual elements communicate that the text does not communicate? What message in the text do the visual elements support or contradict?" Elicit answers from the groups.

7. Ask each group to create and ask different questions about other groups' chosen posters. Use these questions for a whole-class discussion.

8. Ask the class to vote for their favorite poster based on its visual elements and the message it conveys. Discuss the reasons for their favorite poster choice.

CAVEATS AND OPTIONS

- Adapt this activity for younger learners by replacing the provided sample poster and choosing a more age-appropriate topic.

- Adapt this activity for a lower level by doing the activity as a class and providing the definition of a poster in the beginning.

- Adapt this activity for a higher level by using multiple posters with various topics for different groups during the initial discussion activity.

- Extend the activity by asking students to create multimodal posters in pairs, groups, or individually after the discussion.

- Extend the learning by having students bring the posters they create to the next class. Discuss their created posters and provide feedback to each group.

REFERENCES AND FURTHER READING

Lim, J., & Polio, C. (2020). Multimodal assignments in higher education: Implications for multimodal writing tasks for L2 writers. *Journal of Second Language Writing, 47,* Article 100713. https://doi.org/10.1016/j.jslw.2020.100713

Zerin, S., & Khan, S. A. (2013). Poster–A visual stimulus for active learning. *GSTF International Journal of Law and Social Sciences, 3*(1), 129–134.

APPENDIX: *Multimodal Poster Example*

Image credit: Alexandra Krasova

Teaching Sense Verbs for Description Through Media

Irene Rahmaniar

Level	Low intermediate
Ages Suitable for Activity	Secondary
Aims	Use the five senses to connect visual media to prior knowledge
	Use sense verbs and adjectives in developing descriptions
Class Time	45 minutes
Preparation Time	5 minutes
Resources	Videos and images that show food, pets, and weather
	A projector and screen for displaying videos and images

This ctivity activates the five senses for describing visual media. By making connections between sensory input and visual media, understanding is expanded and descriptions can be enhanced.

PROCEDURE

1. Ask students if they can name their five senses: sight, smell, hearing, touch, taste.

2. Provide sentence structures appropriate to your students' level. For example:
   a. I see / smell / hear / feel / taste [noun].
   b. There is a [adj] [noun].
   c. The [noun] looks / smells / sounds / feels like / tastes like [adj].

3. Display a video or image (that shows food, pets, or weather) and ask students what they would see, smell, hear, feel, or taste if they were present where the video or image was taken. Help students use the sentence structure provided in the previous step to discuss the video or image.

4. Display another video or image and have students write three sentences about the video or image using three different sense verbs.

5. Ask students to share their sentences in small groups. Each group will choose one sentence to share with the whole class.

6. Repeat with a new video or image.

7. Tell students you will show them one more video or image and that this time they will compete to see which group can write the greatest number of descriptive sentences. Show the video or image. Give each group time to write as many sentences as they can. Call time and have each group count how many sentences they wrote. The team with the most sentences wins.

8. Have the winning group read all of their sentences aloud to the class. Check for accuracy.

CAVEATS AND OPTIONS

- If technology is not available, take the class for a walk outside or around the classroom/school and use the senses to talk about what can be seen, heard, smelled, tasted, and felt.
- Have students pick their favorite video or image and write a descriptive paragraph about it.

VI

Using Digital Museum Tours to Teach Narration

Gargi Sarkar

Levels	Intermediate to advanced
Ages Suitable for Activity	Secondary to adult
Aims	Develop writing and public speaking skills
	Encourage higher order thinking skills
	Use collaboration and research skills
	Develop cross-cultural awareness
Class Time	5 (60-minute) sessions
Preparation Time	80 minutes
Resources	Access to the internet on laptops or tablets
	Headphones and microphones for recording (if not using live narration)
	Grading rubric (Appendix A)
	Worksheet for narration (Appendix B)
	Optional: Cardboard and art supplies

igital museum tours are an engaging and interactive resource for improving learners' language proficiency through narrative expression. Integrating technology in the classroom allows teachers to connect with 21st-century learners and to design authentic and entertaining language learning opportunities.

PROCEDURE

1. *Introduction to Online Museum Tours (20 minutes):* Discuss the importance of museum tours. Explain the objective and steps of the activity. Students may not be familiar with digital museum tours, so before moving on, present examples of existing digital museum tours, such as Smithsonian Open Access (www.si.edu/openaccess).

2. *Exploring Artwork (40 minutes):* Assign students to explore an online museum or pick artwork to spark their interest. Encourage and help students choose artwork that is relevant to their personal interest. Ask questions, such as "What do you see? What is the [object]? Can you tell how old the art is? Who is the exhibit intended for?"

3. *Developing Narration Skills (60 minutes):* Dedicate a class to teach skills for effective spoken narration.

   a. Teach voice modulation and clarity.

   b. Teach the structure of narration (i.e., introduction, description, analysis) and the use of adjectives and storytelling techniques.

4. *Creating Virtual Galleries (60 minutes):* Dedicate the next class session time for students to create their virtual museums.

    a. Introduce a tool for creating digital galleries, such as Virtual Art Gallery (virtualartgallery.com).

    b. Divide the class into small groups of four to five students and guide them in creating an online exhibition from selected artwork.

    c. Encourage students to collaborate and ask them to discuss and decide on word choices.

    d. Instruct students to write a title and description for each artwork. Help students see that the writing and the artwork fit together.

5. *Recording Narrations (60 minutes):* Tell groups to prepare an oral narrative to accompany their digital museum tour. Hand out the Worksheet for Narration (Appendix B). Students can choose to present their narrations live while the virtual tour is being shown to the class or to prerecord their narrations using screencasting software. Provide technical support.

6. *Presentation and Feedback (60 minutes):* Have groups present their virtual museum tours to the class or, for online classes, upload screencasts. Ask peers to give feedback and suggest revisions, including corrections to the language. This is a collective effort and everybody participates.

CAVEATS AND OPTIONS

- When choosing artwork and subjects, keep cultural sensitivity in mind.
- Ensure that every student has access to suitable equipment and internet connectivity.
- For students in low-resource environments or interested in hands-on activities, provide materials for creating a physical gallery, like cardboard boxes and art supplies. Have students design and construct a miniature museum or gallery.
- If necessary, provide additional language support, such as preteaching museum vocabulary.
- Run this activity as a short-term project, incorporated into the syllabus of a communicative course.

REFERENCES AND FURTHER READING

Falk, J., & Dierking, L. (2000). *Learning from museums: Visitor experiences and the making of meaning.* Bloomsbury Academic.

VI

APPENDIX A: *Grading Rubric*

Grading rubric	
Criteria	**Points**
Appropriate content was used	
Ideas were organized logically	
The narration used appropriate vocabulary	
Students demonstrated teamwork	
Additional comments:	

APPENDIX B: *Worksheet for Narration*

Hook:
Introduction to the Tour Theme:
Artwork 1:
Artwork Title and Artist:
Brief Description:
Context:
Connection to Tour Theme:
Artwork 2:
Artwork Title and Artist:
Brief Description:
Context:
Connection to Tour Theme:
Artwork 3:
Artwork Title and Artist:
Brief Description:
Context:
Connection to Tour Theme:
Artwork 4:
Artwork Title and Artist:
Brief Description:
Context:
Connection to Tour Theme:
Conclusion:
Closing Statement:
Acknowledgements (List all students' names and their task descriptions):

Part VII

Visualization

Introduction: Deepening Understanding Through Visualization

Visualization is central to visual literacy. It supports learners in analyzing and interpreting visual, textual, auditory, and experiential input and making meaning out of it in a way that is personally relevant and meaningful. The skill of visualization enables learners to create mental images that bridge abstract concepts with concrete understanding, a process that enhances active engagement, comprehension, and retention (Paivio, 2007; Suggate & Lenard, 2022).

The ability to visualize data, concepts, and relationships is a critical 21st-century skill that enhances comprehension, communication, and creative thinking across all disciplines. The activities in this section provide opportunities for learners to explore and apply visualization strategies to support and deepen their understanding of the world around them.

These activities cover a wide range of approaches to visualization, including

- interpreting graphs, charts, diagrams, and photographic representations;
- using graphic organizers and templates to scaffold complex concepts;
- practicing image-based annotation to enhance reading comprehension; and
- employing photography and collage to foster identity exploration and reflective practice.

Through visualizing grammar concepts, creating identity maps, investigating global linguistic patterns, and crafting vision boards, learners actively develop their capacity to interpret, process, visually organize, and deepen their understanding of various forms of information.

Integrating visualization into language learning enhances cognitive engagement and promotes critical thinking by encouraging students to examine details, identify patterns, and draw connections between abstract ideas and real-world experiences (Zhou & Meng, 2020). In doing so, learners build transferable skills that serve not only their language learning needs but also their ability to navigate and contribute to an increasingly data-driven and visually oriented global society.

REFERENCES AND FURTHER READING

Paivio, A. (2007). *Mind and its evolution: A dual coding theoretical approach* (1st ed.). Psychology Press. https://doi.org/10.4324/9781315785233

Suggate, S., & Lenhard, W. (2022). Mental imagery skill predicts adults' reading performance. *Learning and Instruction, 80*(2). https://doi.org/10.1016/j.learninstruc.2022.101633

Zhou, Y., & Meng, X. (2020). *Multimodal approaches to language learning: Theories and applications*. Routledge.

VII

A Backwards Approach to Teaching Graph Literacy

Mina Gavell

Levels	All
Ages Suitable for Activity	Elementary to university
Aims	Develop awareness about pie and bar graphs
	Practice listening and speaking
	Represent data in a graphic form
	Accurately describe the graph (in oral or written form)
Class Time	45–90 minutes
Preparation Time	5 minutes
Resources	Paper, markers, crayons, pens/pencils

Graph literacy, the ability to read and extract information from graphs and charts, is an important aspect of basic literacy—and an integral skill in many other fields, particularly those related to STEM. Repeated and explicit instruction and practice with reading graphs can easily become dull before yielding positive results. Instead, this activity takes a backwards approach and asks students to create their own graphs. Students work in groups to create and conduct surveys and then use their results to create graphs.

PROCEDURE

1. Warm up the class with some survey-style questions, such as the following. Record results on the board:

   a. What is your favorite season?

   b. What is your favorite animal?

   c. What is the name of a close family member?

   For the third question, begin to record results on the board; however, it will soon become clear that the answers are too varied.

2. Use the survey results to demonstrate by drawing on the board how the answers to Question A might best be represented in a pie graph, the answers to Question B might be most clear in a bar chart, and the answers to Question C are not suitable to be represented in a graph or bar chart.

3. Divide the class into groups of three. Ask groups to brainstorm a survey question they would like to ask their classmates. After brainstorming, they should choose the best one (based on interest and suitability as a survey question).

4. Regroup students by having them count off in their groups (1, 2, 3). Students with the same number form a new group. Each student then conducts their survey within this group and records the information. (In the case of a small class of 12

or fewer, limiting this step to two groups may be preferable, as this will increase the sample size).

5. Have students return to their original group in order to compile and analyze their data.

6. Ask groups to decide whether a pie or bar graph best represents the information, and work together to create their graph.

7. Have groups practice describing the graph to one another. Then, invite groups to present to the class.

8. Wrap up the activity with a discussion of why graphs are important, how they communicate information, and in what other contexts they might prove useful. Students can also reflect on challenges and successes in the activity.

CAVEATS AND OPTIONS

- Students may try to use line graphs; explicitly remove those as an option as they are a reflection of change over time. They might be suitable for a subsequent activity.

- Adapt this activity for younger ages and lower levels by having a set survey question for students to answer; compile and analyze the data as a whole class. For early beginners, provide explicit instruction on creating the graphs.

- Adapt this activity for older ages and higher levels in one or more of the following ways:
  — Have students create a survey comprised of several related questions.
  — Have students conduct their surveys outside of class or in the form of a questionnaire.
  — Incorporate technology that collects, organizes, and graphically displays data (e.g., Google Forms, Microsoft Excel).
  — Instruct students to write a summary of the graph (or compare two graphs) as practice for the IELTS Writing Task 1.
  — For Step 7, instead of presenting their own graphs, have students analyze and present each other's—or create quiz-style questions related to their graphs.

REFERENCES AND FURTHER READING

Kagnarith, C., Theara, C., & Klein, A. (2007). A questionnaire project: Integrating the four macro skills with critical thinking. *English Teaching Forum, 45*(1), 2–8.

Zucker, A., Staudt, C., & Tinker, R. (2015). Teaching graph literacy across the curriculum. *Science Scope, 38*(6), 20–24.

Connecting Patterns and Written Descriptions

Monique Evans

Levels	All
Age Suitable for Activity	Secondary
Aims	Describe growing patterns
	Connect parts of a written description to growth
	Compare and critique descriptions of a single pattern
Class Time	30 minutes
Preparation Time	10 minutes
Resources	1 set of sequence cards (Appendix A)
	1 copy per student of Descriptions 1 and 2 (Appendixes B–C).

This activity supports the development of visual literacy through asking students to recognize and describe growing patterns, then read and write descriptions of them. Students weave their observations into increasingly precise and concise descriptions. As students' descriptions grow more sophisticated, they attend to sequential elements and part–whole relationships. By reading and critiquing different descriptions of the same pattern, students expand their own capacity to describe. In this activity, students sequence terms of a pattern and analyze descriptions collaboratively. The activity enables students to gradually extend their skills by interpreting more complex patterns.

PROCEDURE

Part 1

1. Organize a fishbowl discussion activity: Select four students and have them form an inner circle around a desk or table. The rest of the class observes as the outer circle. Give each student in the inner circle a card from Appendix A, showing a term in the sequence. Leave the fifth card face down.

2. Each student in the fishbowl describes their term (i.e., card) in detail without showing it to the inner circle, while those behind them in the outer circle can peek.

3. The inner circle discusses and determines the order of the terms, placing cards face down.

4. The inner circle collaboratively describes their expectations for the face-down fifth card.

5. Students reveal the ordered cards for all to see and check.

Part 2

1. Seat students in groups of four. Distribute Description 1 (Appendix B) to each student. Each student selects a portion of the text to read according to the font style: plain, bold, underlined, or italic.

2. Each student reads their portion aloud. First, they read for flow. On the second reading, students annotate the card sequence pictured on the handout by drawing arrows, circling, numbering, grouping, or making other markings to connect the description to the images (see Figures 1 and 2).

3. Repeat Steps 1–2 for Description 2 (Appendix C).

4. Have groups discuss which description better characterizes how the pattern grows and how to make predictions (e.g., what the 10th term in the sequence would look like). Prompt students to be specific about why their selected description is better.

5. In a whole-class discussion, ask groups to share which description they selected and why. Facilitate a discussion to compare reasoning.

CAVEATS AND OPTIONS

- Have students annotate a single shared image, so that they will need to come to an agreement. Alternatively, allow individual annotations but require structured discussion to agree on the clearest way to represent understanding.

- In later activities, provide students with other patterns of growth, such as from Visual Patterns (www.visualpatterns.org), to stretch their understanding of more complex patterns.

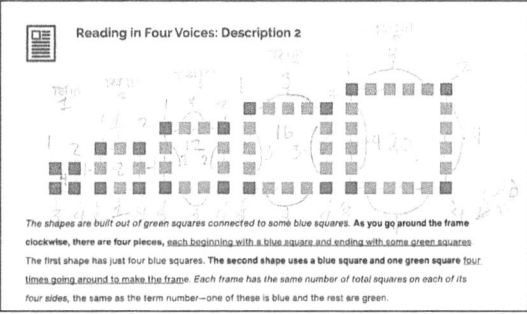

Figure 1. A student's annotations.

Note: The student has labeled the different term numbers, numbered the blue corners (1–4), counted the green squares on each side, and noted a total count of blue and green squares.

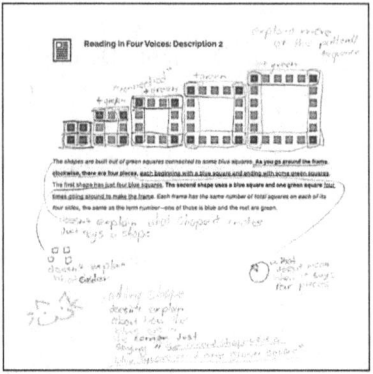

Figure 2. Another student's annotations with a sustained written critique. *Note:* The student points out the lack of specificity in the description, including the overall shapes (squares) formed and how individual elements were added.

Note: Student annotations were collected during a research study.

DISCLAIMER: The research reported here was supported by the Institute of Education Sciences, U.S. Department of Education, through Grant R305C200008 to WestEd. The opinions expressed are those of the authors and do not represent views of the Institute or the U.S. Department of Education.

REFERENCES AND FURTHER READING

Chu, H., & Hamburger, L. (2022). Educative curriculum materials for English learners: Varying the intensity of scaffolding. In L. de Oliveira & R. Westerlund (Eds.), *Scaffolding for multilingual learners in elementary and secondary schools* (pp. 181–196). Routledge.

APPENDIX A: *Sequence Cards, Terms 1-5*

APPENDIX B: *Description 1*

Reading in Four Voices: Description 1

Each of the images has four blue squares in the corners. The other squares are in between on the sides and they are green. The first shape has no green squares, while each new shape has more and more green squares. The second shape has a total of four green squares, one on each of the sides. Then, the next shape has four more green squares, for a total of eight, with two on each side.

APPENDIX C: *Description 2*

Reading in Four Voices: Description 2

The shapes are built out of green squares connected to some blue squares. As you go around the frame clockwise, there are four pieces, each beginning with a blue square and ending with some green squares. The first shape has just four blue squares. The second shape uses a blue square and one green square four times going around to make the frame. Each frame has the same number of total squares on each of its four sides, the same as the term number—one of these is blue and the rest are green.

Cultivating Digital Visual Literacy Through Data Visualization: An Intercultural Focus in Language Teaching

Huixin Wang and Qianyu Yang

Levels	Intermediate
Ages Suitable for Activity	Secondary
Aims	Build social and emotional skills
	Develop digital visual literacy
	Cultivate intercultural competence
Class Time	90 minutes
Preparation Time	30 minutes
Resources	Access to the internet on laptops or tablets
	Images (Appendixes A–B)
	Essays (Appendixes C–D)

This activity aims to enhance students' digital and visual literacy, using the SAMR model (Substitution, Augmentation, Modification, Redefinition) as a framework (Puentedura, 2013). It integrates technology-enhanced language teaching to foster intercultural learning, critical and creative thinking through multimodalities and data visualization.

PROCEDURE

Part 1: Exploring Cultural Elements Through Visuals (25 minutes)

1. *(5 minutes)* Begin the activity by presenting students with images of a Christmas tree and a dragon (from Appendixes A and B).

2. *(10 minutes)* Ask students to work in groups and reflect on the cultural and social elements associated with these two images. They should

    a. discuss cultural symbols represented in the visuals (e.g., the dragon in Chinese culture or the Christmas tree in Western culture), and

    b. relate these symbols to their own social or cultural context, sharing their interpretations and reflecting on other semiotic elements.

3. *(10 minutes)* Guide students to select a symbol that represents their personal and cultural experiences (e.g., a Christmas tree, a dragon, or another cultural image from their own background). Ask them to share stories or experiences related to that symbol. Present an example (Figure 1) of how the cultural symbol of the Christmas tree influenced one student's identity development and social experience.

Figure 1. Alex's speech about cultural symbols.

Image and text credit: Huixin Wang. Used with permission.

Part 2: Analyzing Essays Related to Cultural Elements Through Data Visualization (45 Minutes)

1. *(5 minutes)* Introduce the concept of data visualization by focusing on word clouds and word frequency.

   a. Explain how visualizing word frequency can reveal key themes, tone, and cultural focus in speeches. For example, frequently used words can highlight recurring ideas, suggest the speaker's attitude, and reflect cultural values.

   b. Introduce the website Voyant Tools (voyant-tools.org) and show how it can generate word clouds and bar charts, making speech analysis easier. To generate results, copy and paste in a sample text or a website URL, then click "Reveal."

2. *(15 minutes)* Provide students with digital copies of two essays—one related to Chinese culture (Appendix C) and the other to British culture (Appendix D)—for comparative analysis.

   a. Ask students to read the texts and discuss the prompt questions in Appendix E.

   b. After the discussion, guide students in using Voyant Tools to generate word clouds and bar charts to help them understand each essay. Walk them through the process of creating visualizations for both essays.

   c. Appendixes F and G display the generated word cloud and most frequent words for the first essay, while Appendixes H and I present the generated word cloud and most frequent words for the second essay.

3. *(10 minutes)* After visualizing the data from the two essays, ask students to use the data to compare the two essays in regards to key themes and patterns.

   a. Have students work in groups and discuss the same questions as in Step 2a.

   b. During this reanalysis, lead students to notice how the word clouds and bar charts added to their understanding of the topic.

4. *(15 minutes)* Prompt students to reflect on how visualizing word frequencies helped them understand the texts better:

   a. Ask students to discuss how their identity and voice are expressed through the culturally related essay with a combination of data visualization.

VII

b. Lead a discussion on how multimodal visual literacy enables new ways of expressing oneself and communicating complex emotions and experiences.

c. Encourage students to think about how to create other visualization methods (e.g., diagrams, graphs, network graphs, word trees) using digital platforms. Provide additional tools for students to explore different visualization techniques.

Part 3: Create a Culturally Related Speech With Data Visualization (20 minutes)

1. Assign students to select their own culturally relevant image and write a short speech about that image.

2. Using Voyant Tools, have students generate word clouds and bar charts from their own texts.

3. In the next class, have students present their speeches with data visualization as a formative assessment.

CAVEATS AND OPTIONS

Be mindful of cultural differences when interpreting visual elements and symbols. Ensure a respectful and inclusive environment where all student responses are valued.

REFERENCES AND FURTHER READING

Puentedura, R. (2013). *SAMR: A contextualized introduction.* http://www.hippasus.com/rrpweblog/archives/000112.html

Romrell, D., Kidder, L., & Wood, E. (2014). The SAMR model as a framework for evaluating mLearning. *Journnal of Asynchronous Learning Network, 18*(10).

APPENDIX A: *Image of a Christmas Tree*

APPENDIX B: *Image of a Dragon*

APPENDIX C: *Essay 1*

Cultural Elements in China: What They Mean to Me and What Motivates Me to Learn More

When I reflect on Chinese culture, I am instantly drawn to the rich traditions that shape our lives. One cultural symbol that stands out is the dragon, a representation of strength and power. Since childhood, the dragon dance during Chinese New Year has fascinated me, creating a deep connection to our cultural heritage. The dragon is more than just a mythical creature—a dragon is a symbol of luck, prosperity, and protection. This strong connection to the dragon and other cultural symbols enables me to learn more about Chinese culture.

Another key element that holds deep meaning for me is the concept of family and reunion. In China, family is at the heart of everything, from New Year's reunion dinners to everyday life. The respect for elders, the importance of unity and reunion in family, and the value of togetherness are central to Chinese culture. These traditions continue to shape my identity as indispensable with family and reunion, and understanding their evolution makes me explore Chinese traditions even further.

Cultural festivals, such as the Lantern Festival, fill our streets with light and celebration. These events reflect the hope and harmony we seek as a community. The sight of lanterns drifting into the sky inspires me and reinforces my desire to study the depth of Chinese culture. It's these cultural symbols—the dragon, family, and festivals—that encourage me to delve deeper into our traditions and their modern interpretations.

Finally, I am driven by the desire to preserve history. Learning about our ancestors' history, their struggles, and their triumphs through rituals like ancestor worship let me keep these cultural traditions alive. The profound legacy of the Han Dynasty history, which significantly shaped Chinese culture and identity, inspires me to delve deeper into our historical roots. I've come to realize that Chinese culture is a dynamic blend of history, symbolism, and modern adaptation. This blend is what makes our culture so captivating, and it sparks me to continue my studies.

APPENDIX D: *Essay 2*

Cultural Traditions in the UK: The Cultural Meaning and What Inspires Me to Learn More

When I think of British culture, one of the first images that comes to mind is the Christmas tree, a symbol of celebration and tradition. The sight of a beautifully decorated Christmas tree in homes and public spaces evokes feelings of warmth, joy, and togetherness with family. Christmas is more than just a festival—it represents a long-standing tradition of bringing family and friends together during the holiday season. The Christmas holiday season is filled with festivities, from caroling and gift giving to family meals and holiday gatherings. The idea of giving, of showing appreciation to loved ones, is at the heart of this tradition. These festive moments remind me of the power of family and community, which are central British values.

The emphasis on togetherness during Christmas is what makes it such an important celebration for its culture, and it inspires me to learn more surrounding this holiday.

Also, British arts and literature have long been a defining feature of the nation's rich cultural heritage, with a legacy that spans centuries. From the timeless arts of William Shakespeare, whose plays continue to shape modern storytelling, to the romantic poetry of William Wordsworth and the literature of Jane Austen, British literature has influenced generations around the world. In the visual arts, movements like the Pre-Raphaelites and artists such as J. M. W. Turner have left a lasting impact on art history, reflecting Britain's deep connection to arts, nature and social commentary. Literature and the arts not only celebrate beauty and creativity but also often explore the complexities of human nature, society, and historical events. This enduring tradition of arts and literature achievement continues to inspire and evolve, making British culture a dynamic blend of the classical and contemporary.

In addition to the Christmas festival, arts and literature, there are other cultural symbols that reflect the nation's values. For example, the concept of royal traditions, seen in celebrations like Trooping the Color, demonstrates the country's deep respect for history and monarchy. The continuity of these customs, passed down through generations, fascinates me. I am particularly inspired by how the British people celebrate their heritage while embracing modern interpretations of these rituals.

Finally, I am motivated by the desire to understand how British culture blends tradition with modernity. Christmas, though rooted in history, has adapted to modern times, becoming a symbol of both tradition and innovation. Learning about the history of Christmas and its evolving role in British culture has deepened my appreciation for how these elements can transform over time. This dynamic blend of history, symbolism, and adaptation is what makes British culture so captivating to me.

APPENDIX E: *Prompt Questions*

1. Identify and highlight the key themes and topics in each essay. What are the most frequently mentioned cultural elements in Chinese and British traditions?

2. Compare and contrast the similarities and differences between Chinese and British culture as presented in the essays. How do the repeated words in each essay reflect the unique cultural values and practices of these two nations?

3. What do the repeatedly emphasized words tell us about the cultural significance of these traditions and events? How do these traditions serve as representations of their respective cultural identities?

4. Consider other cultural values and their embedded meanings in your life. Are there any underlying principles or values that might not be explicitly stated but are implied through the traditions mentioned (e.g., community, unity, respect for history)?

APPENDIX F: *Generated Word Cloud of Essay 1*

APPENDIX G: *Most Frequent Words in Essay 1*

		Term	Count
	1	chinese	8
	2	culture	7
	3	cultural	7
	4	dragon	6
	5	traditions	5
	6	history	5
	7	family	5
	8	tourism	4
	9	symbols	2
	10	symbol	2
	11	shape	2
	12	reflect	2
	13	new	2

Most frequent words in the corpus:
- chinese (8); culture (7); cultural (7); dragon (6); traditions (5)

APPENDIX H: *Generated Word Cloud of Essay 2*

APPENDIX I: *Most Frequent Words in Essay 2*

		Term	Count
	1	british	9
	2	christmas	8
	3	arts	8
	4	tradition	6
	5	literature	6
	6	culture	6
	7	history	5
	8	holiday	4
	9	family	4
	10	cultural	4
	11	modern	3
	12	william	2
	13	values	2

Most frequent words in the corpus:
- chinese (8); culture (7); cultural (7); dragon (6); traditions (5)

Encouraging Self-Expression: Identity Mapping Through Collage

Connie Siebold

Levels	Intermediate to advanced
Ages Suitable for Activity	Any
Aims	Develop self-expression and group cohesion
	Create and present personal narratives visually
	Practice with different art mediums
	Practice presentation, writing, and vocabulary skills
Class Time	60–90 minutes depending on chosen depth of activity and domains chosen.
Preparation Time	45 minutes
Resources	Sample identity map (as in Appendix B)
	Paper or cardboard sheets
	Art supplies (e.g., paint, crayons, colored pencils, markers, mosaic pieces, glitter)

This activity introduces the concept of identity mapping using concepts taken from community-based art education. Students represent their intersecting identities visually, orally, and in writing. They create a visually representative project based on established domains, give it an explanatory caption, and present it to the group.

PROCEDURE

1. Discuss the concept of identity. Ask students to suggest different *domains,* or categories, that their identity falls into. See Appendix A for examples of domains. List the brainstormed domains on the board.

2. Show examples of identity maps (see Appendix B). Either show an identity map that you created previously, or find examples from the internet (search *identity map*). Discuss the key components of an identity map with the class to check for comprehension.

3. Give students time to brainstorm. Encourage them to select the personality domains/categories that are most important to them, and then list their specific personality traits that fall within each category.

4. Have students think about how they can visually represent each personality trait that they have listed.

5. Distribute blank paper or cardboard sheets to students and provide a variety of craft supplies for them to utilize in their visual representation of their identity.

6. Walk around as students create their identity maps, emphasizing that there are no correct ways to visually represent the parts of their identity.

7. Have students write a brief caption explaining what they have chosen to include in their identity map, and why.

8. Allow each student time to present their identity map, encouraging other students to find similarities between their maps. This can be done through individual presentations or as a gallery walk activity.

9. Collect the maps at the end of the activity and display them in a single classroom identity mural. Leave them displayed for the duration of the term if possible.

CAVEATS AND OPTIONS

- Use discretion in Step 1 when choosing/eliciting the domains best suited for your context.
  - For adults, the domains can include additional topics, such as health, religion, career, geography, aesthetic preferences, recreational preferences, gender or sexual identity, and similar.
  - For K–12 students, adapt the domains to things they care about, such as grade level, place in family (sibling status), pet ownership, favorite activities, future aspirations, and similar.
- Provide several examples of visual formats to help students who don't see themselves as creative (e.g., the shape of a hand, interlocking circles, or a simple blank page they can fill entirely).
- Though assessing the written caption may be appropriate for this exercise, it is best to merely count participation for the visual portion of the activity.
- Encourage students who finish early to add additional domains of their choosing.
- Provide a list of guiding questions to support students struggling to express their own identity.
  - Helpful questions for older students could include: "Do you consider your religious or national identity to be more important? How do you spend your free time? What groups of people do you identify with?"
  - Helpful questions for younger students could include: "What grade level are you in? Who is in your family? What are you good at? What activities do you like?"
- Take notes on student identities to better tailor future class activities to things they have written down as a value. Refer back to the identity maps throughout the term to reinforce personal connections to the class activities and materials.

REFERENCES AND FURTHER READING

Congdon, K., Stewart, M., & White, J. H. (2002). Mapping identity for curriculum work. *Contemporary Issues in Art Education*, 108–118.

VII

APPENDIX A: *Identity Domains*

The following are identity domains drawn from Congdon et al. (2002):

- Religious identity/community
- Gender and sexual identity/community
- Geographical identity/community
- Family identity/community
- Age identity/community
- Economic identity/community
- Political identity/community
- Recreational identity/community
- Aesthetic identity/community
- Racial/ethnic identity/community
- Occupational identity/community
- Health and body identity/community

Overall Identity: Which of the previously listed identities are the most important to your identity?

APPENDIX B: *Example Identity Map*

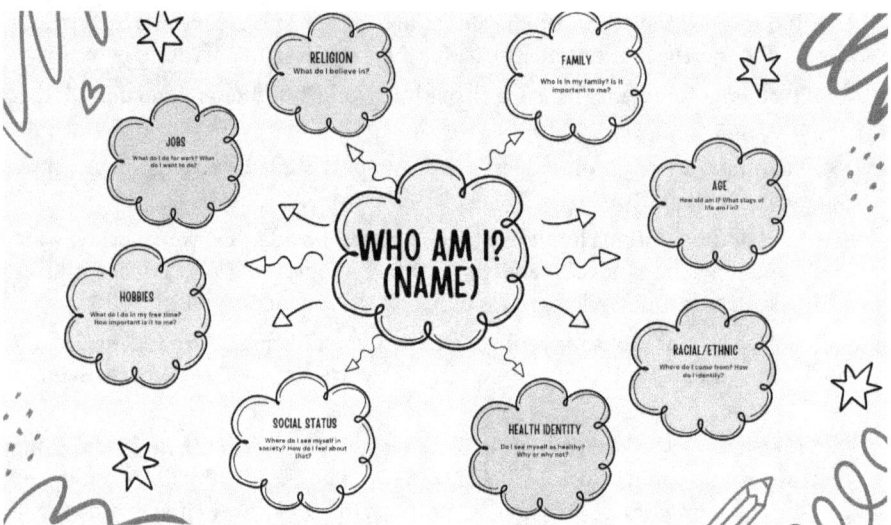

Image credit: Connie Siebold. Created on Canva.

Exploring Visual Cues From the Ocean's Deadly Creatures

Renu Milind Dhotre

Levels	Intermediate
Ages Suitable for Activity	Any
Aims	Identify and describe the characteristics and dangers posed by the most dangerous ocean creatures
	Develop visual literacy skills through the analysis of the visual cues
	Foster critical thinking and research skills
	Promote collaborative learning and effective communication
Class Time	60 minutes
Preparation Time	15 minutes
Resources	Laptop and projector
	Handout (Appendix A)
	Video: "10 minutes of fascinating deep-sea animals | Into The Deep" (MBARI, 2022; www.youtube.com/watch?v=ryRcPeOM1sY)
	Chart paper and markers
	Student notebooks or writing paper
	Pencils or pens

This activity aims to engage students in an exciting exploration of the visual cues of the world's most dangerous ocean creatures, enhancing their understanding of the diverse marine life and fostering visual literacy skills through the analysis of a captivating video.

PROCEDURE

1. *Introduction (5 minutes):* Introduce the topic of dangerous ocean creatures, discussing their significance and the fascination they evoke. Explain the objectives and relevance of the activity.

2. *Discussion Before Viewing (10 minutes):* Show images of different dangerous ocean creatures to spark curiosity and activate prior knowledge.

    a. Elicit students' ideas and perceptions about these creatures, encouraging them to share their thoughts and expectations. Draw their attention to the visual elements. Ask about specific features and what these features might communicate.

    b. Tell students they will watch a video about ocean creatures. There is no talking in this video and students should focus on the physical appearances.

3. *Viewing and Analysis (25 minutes):* Play the video from the provided link (or one similar). Instruct students to observe and analyze the visual elements, behaviors, and adaptations of each creature. Pause at intervals to facilitate discussions, asking students to share their observations, reactions, and questions.

4. *Group Research and Presentation (15 minutes):* Divide students into small groups and assign each group one dangerous ocean creature from the video. Hand out copies of the Worksheet for Group Research and Presentation (see Appendix A).

   a. Instruct groups to conduct further research on their assigned creature, focusing on its habitat, unique defense mechanisms, diet, physical characteristics, and the messages these physical characteristics communicate.

   b. Provide supplemental resources, such as books, articles, or websites, to support their research (see Appendix B for some ideas).

   c. Tell each group to prepare a short presentation highlighting their creature's key physical features and what these physical features communicate.

5. *Group Presentations (10 minutes):* Have each group present their findings. Emphasize the need for clear communication and the use of visual aids. Encourage the audience to ask questions and engage in discussions after each presentation.

6. *Reflection and Discussion (5 minutes):* Facilitate a class discussion reflecting on the activity and the students' learning experiences. Ask students to share their newfound knowledge, insights, and any surprising discoveries.

CAVEATS AND OPTIONS

- For lower level students, provide simpler research questions and tell students to focus on key visual elements and behaviors of the creatures.

- Adapt the activity based on students' proficiency level, providing more guided research for lower level students and encouraging independent research for higher level students.

- For older or more advanced learners, draw connections in Step 6 between how animals use physical features to communicate messages and how humans use our physical appearance to also communicate messages.

REFERENCES AND FURTHER READING

MBARI (Monterey Bay Aquarium Research Institute). (2022, February 10). *10 minutes of fascinating deep-sea animals | Into The Deep* [Video]. https://www.youtube.com/watch?v=ryRcPeOM1sY

APPENDIX A: *Worksheet for Group Research and Presentation*

Exploring Dangerous Ocean Creatures

Group Name: _____

Assigned Creature:_____

Instructions

1. Conduct research on your assigned dangerous ocean creature using reliable sources such as books, articles, or websites.

2. Answer the following research questions about your creature's habitat, diet, physical characteristics, and unique defense mechanisms.

3. Prepare a short presentation to share your findings with the class, following the guidelines at the end of this worksheet.

4. Collect visual aids, such as images or diagrams, to enhance your presentation.

5. Be ready to answer questions and engage in a discussion after your presentation.

Research Questions

Habitat

- Where does your creature live in the ocean?
- Does it prefer shallow or deep waters?
- Are there any specific regions or environments it is found in?

Diet

- What does your creature eat?
- How does it capture or obtain its food?
- Does it have any unique feeding behaviors or adaptations?

Physical Characteristics

- Describe the appearance of your creature (e.g., size, shape, color).
- Are there any specific features that help it survive or hunt?
- Does it have any remarkable physical adaptations?

Unique Defense Mechanisms

- How does your creature protect itself or ward off potential threats?
- Does it have any special abilities or defense mechanisms?
- Does it have any interesting strategies or adaptations for self-defense?

Presentation Guidelines

1. Prepare a 3- to 5-minute presentation.

2. Clearly introduce your creature and its name.

3. Highlight the key information in an organized and engaging manner.

4. Utilize visual aids (images, diagrams, etc.) to support your presentation.

5. Encourage participation by inviting questions and facilitating a discussion.

APPENDIX B: *Suggested Websites for Research*

Here are a few selected websites to help your students launch their research. You may also direct them to your school library or other appropriate research sources.

- "11 deadliest sea creatures: Meet the most dangerous animals in the ocean" (www.discoverwildlife.com/animal-facts/marine-animals/deadliest-sea-creatures)
- "20 of the Most Dangerous Sea Creatures in the Deep Blue" (animals.howstuffworks.com/marine-life/most-dangerous-sea-creatures.htm)
- "Ranked: The most dangerous sea creatures in the world" (www.loveexploring.com/gallerylist/326468/ranked-the-most-dangerous-sea-creatures-in-the-world)
- "13 of the most venomous sea creatures lurking in the water" (www.livescience.com/animals/13-of-the-most-venomous-sea-creatures-on-earth)
- "The Most Dangerous Sea Animals: Nature's Deadliest Underwater Threats" (www.wildlifenomads.com/blog/the-most-dangerous-sea-animal)
- "Five Sea Creatures to Avoid at the Shore" (oceanservice.noaa.gov/hazards/beach-dangers/sea-creatures-to-avoid.html)

Gaining Meaningful Insights Through Data Visualization

Florence Elizabeth Bacabac

Levels	Low advanced to high advanced
Ages Suitable for Activity	Adult
Aims	Analyze and interpret data graphics effectively
	Use data graphics to communicate information clearly
Class Time	120 minutes
Preparation Time	60 to 90 minutes
Resources	Laptop and projector
	Sample data graphics (Appendixes A–D)
	Access to the internet in a computer lab or on laptops

In this activity, students explore how to interpret data effectively through graphics. By engaging with various types of charts and graphs, students not only learn to analyze data critically but also develop the skills to communicate information clearly and persuasively.

PROCEDURE

1. Display a few different types of data graphics (see Appendix A). Discuss what data graphics can show:

    a. trends and patterns, such as increases, decreases, upward or downward movements, stability, rises, falls, or fluctuations

    b. comparisons and relationships between elements, such as *more than, less than,* or *equal to*

2. Display a data graphic that students haven't seen before (see Appendix B). Ask students to examine the data graphic and, with a partner, discuss key insights they can gather from the data. They should focus on patterns, trends, or interesting details that stand out. After 5–8 minutes, have students share their thoughts with the rest of the class.

3. Show some examples of data graphics with captions (see Appendix C). Explain that the purpose of captions is to introduce or summarize the graphic and its context for the viewers.

    a. Specify that captions are used to help viewers quickly grasp the meaning of the graphic, highlight key points, and clarify any ambiguity or complex details in the graphic.

    b. Explain that captions can influence perception because they are not always neutral. They can shape how we interpret data graphics by either emphasizing certain aspects of the graphic while omitting others or framing the data in a positive, negative, or neutral light.

c. Discuss how the example captions could make viewers feel differently about the same data.

4. Assign a group activity on caption writing for a graphic. Have students work in small groups and write two or three captions for the last data graphic in Appendix C. Then, discuss in class how the various captions can manipulate perception.

5. Provide students with a simple dataset sourced from a website, such as Data.gov, Kaggle, Google Trends, or Tableau (see Appendix D), and ask them to do the following:

   a. Create a visual representation of the dataset using Canva (canva.com).

   b. If the dataset is already represented graphically, redesign it in a different format—for example, transform a pie chart into a line chart.

   c. If importing an existing data graphic from another website into Canva, modify elements such as colors, wording, scope, or layout to ensure originality and avoid copyright infringement.

   > **How to Use Canva**
   >
   > - Open a web browser and type "canva.com/templates" in the address bar.
   > - Create a free account or log in to an existing account.
   > - Enter "charts" or "graphs" in the search box.
   > - Select a template to edit, and use the editing tools creatively.
   > - Write a one-sentence caption that introduces or summarizes the graphic.

   d. Compose a one-paragraph description of the visual. Explain the graphic's insights to someone unfamiliar with the data. Describe what the graphic conveys.

6. Hold a peer-review workshop in class where students exchange rough drafts with one another to provide feedback and suggest areas for improvement. Where applicable, teachers should offer individual support to those who might struggle or need help in class.

7. Collect the compositions and do a quick show and tell of the graphics, captions, and descriptions.

8. Ask students to reflect on the following questions and discuss their reflections as a class:

   a. What did you learn about the importance of using visuals to communicate information?

   b. Why did you visualize the data in the way you did?

   c. What difficulties did you experience while creating the graphic and/or writing the caption and its one-paragraph description?

   d. What other feedback do you have on the overall process?

VII

CAVEATS AND OPTIONS

- This activity can be spread across two 60-minute sessions. For example, the first session could cover Steps 1 (introduction to data graphics) through 5 (composition assignment), while the second session could focus on Steps 6 (workshop) through 8 (reflections).

- For Step 1, the teacher may consult an introductory textbook on data analysis, business communication, or technical writing and include information on graphic data representation. Look for chapters that cover visuals, charts, and graphs.

- Before Step 5, you may need to introduce the digital tool Canva and guide students in setting up a free account.

- Adapt the activity for advanced learners by asking them to analyze how data can be manipulated or represented differently, using the following steps:
  - Look at an existing data graphic, and describe how the data is currently represented.
  - Identify any biases in the graphic's design, such as emphasis on certain data points or omission of context.
  - Suggest a different way the same data could be visualized.
  - Reflect on how this change might influence viewers' interpretations.

- To extend this activity, ask students to write a critical analysis of a data graphic from Google Trends or Tableau, evaluating its effectiveness in presenting data. Tell students to consider the graphic's clarity, design (e.g., colors, layout, scale), accuracy, and potential bias. Discuss how the graphic influences viewers' perceptions and suggest improvements if necessary.

REFERENCES AND FURTHER READING

Bider, L., Callejón, M., & Tselova, S. (2024). *How data visualization can empower students in a data-driven world.* Canva. https://www.canva.com/learn/data-visualisation-for-students/

Google. (2025). *Google trends.* https://trends.google.com

Kaggle. (2025). *Kaggle: Your machine learning and data science community.* https://www.kaggle.com

Tableau. (2025). *Free public data sets for analysis.* https://www.tableau.com/learn/articles/free-public-data-sets

U.S. General Services Administration. (2025). *Data.gov.* https://data.gov

APPENDIX A: *Sample Data Graphics*

Graphics created in Canva.

BUDGET PIE CHART — Monthly Budget

Donut Chart

CLASS SCHEDULE

Time	Period
7:55am	First Bell
8:00 – 8:40am	1st Period
8:40 – 9:20am	2nd Period
9:20 – 10:00am	3rd Period
10:00 – 10:30am	First Break
10:30 – 11:10am	4th Period
11:10 – 11:50am	5th Period
11:50 – 12:30pm	Second Break
1:10 – 1:50pm	6th Period
1:50 – 2:30pm	7th Period
2:30 – 3:10pm	8th Period

Table

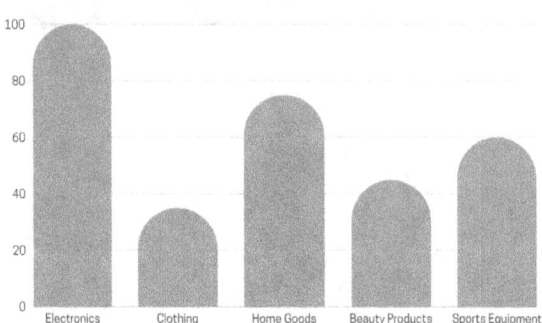

Bar chart

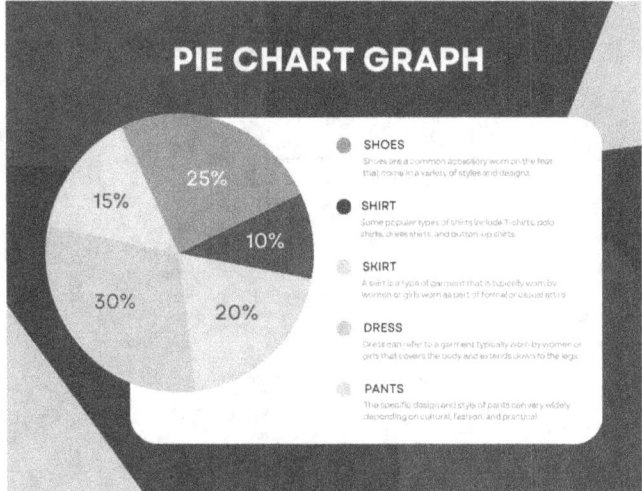

Pie chart

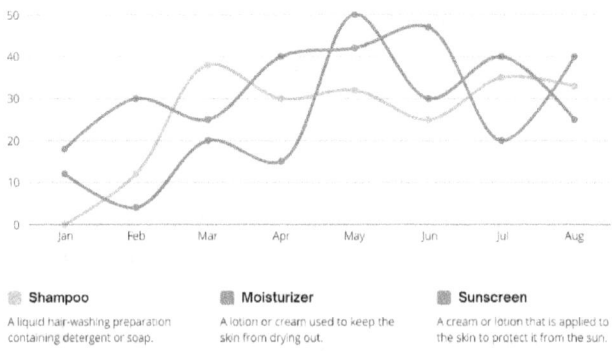

Line graph

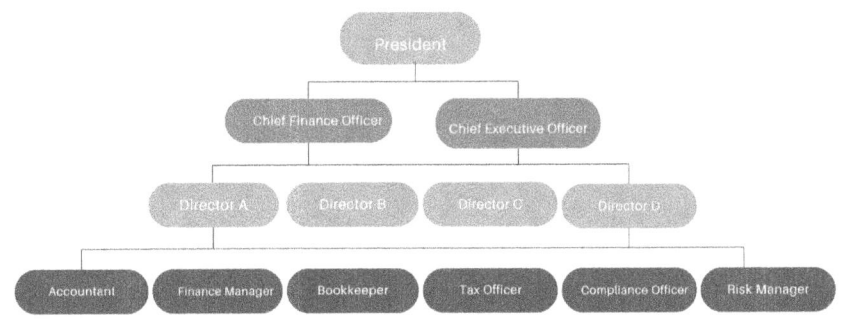

Organizational chart

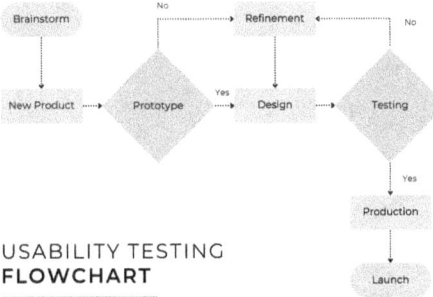

Flow chart

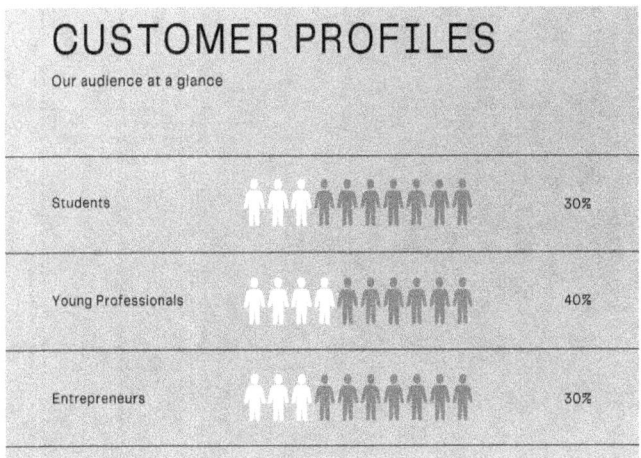

Pictograph

VII

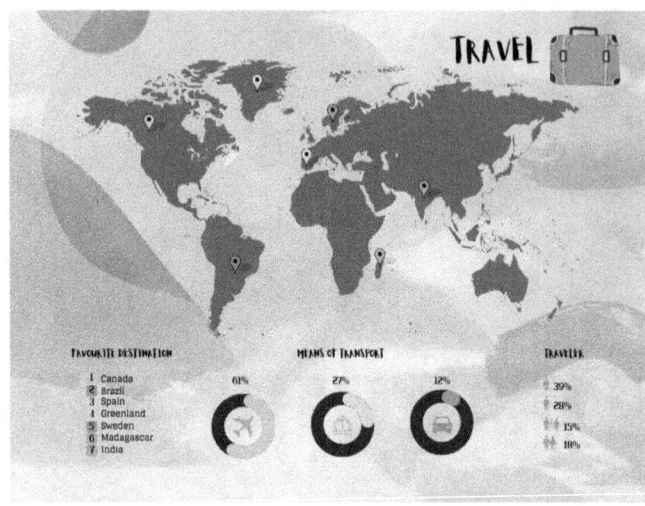

Map

APPENDIX B: *Sample Bar Chart*

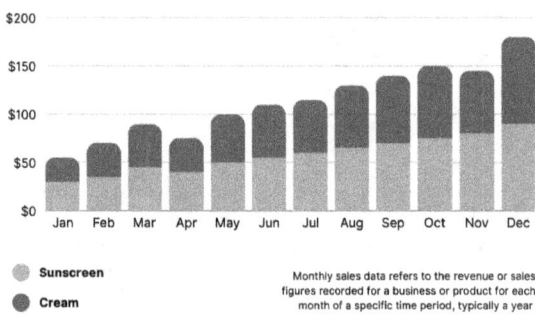

Bar chart showing monthly sales data.

Note: Created in Canva.

APPENDIX C: *Data Graphics With Captions*

Bar chart showing an increase in awarded scholarships with a caption under the visual

BAR CHART

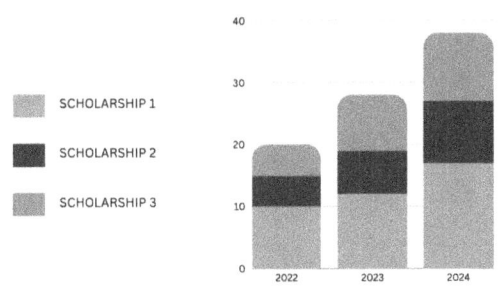

www.reallygreatsite.com

Figure 1. The increase in scholarships awarded from 2022 to 2024.

Line graph showing an increase in website traffic with a caption under the visual

Our Company's Website Traffic

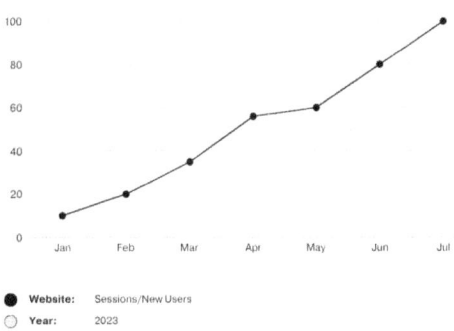

Figure 2. Website traffic increased from January to July 2023.

Line graph showing a decrease in monthly product sales with three caption options that can influence perception under the visual

VII

Figure 3. Sales have decreased over the past year. (Neutral)

OR

Figure 3. Sales stabilized after an earlier decline. (Positive Spin)

OR

Figure 3. Sales continue to plummet, showing poor market performance. (Negative Spin)

Line graph showing a decrease in sales rate for Group Activity on caption writing

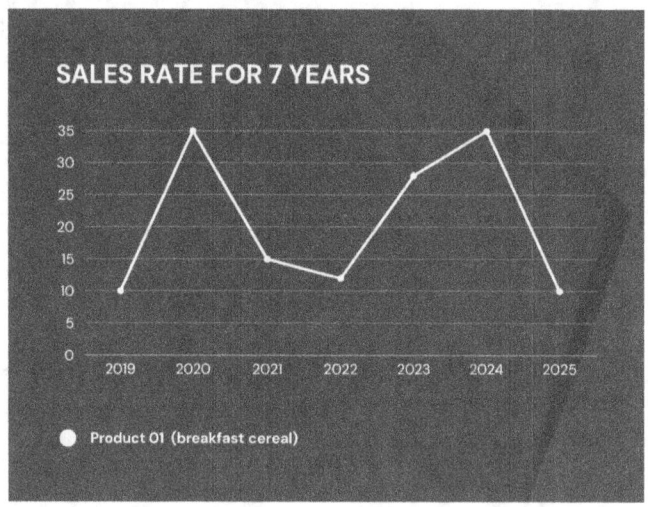

Figure A. _____

APPENDIX D: *Sample Data Sets*

- Electric vehicle population data (U.S. General Services Administration, 2025; catalog.data.gov/dataset/electric-vehicle-population-data)
- Anemia detection dataset (Kaggle, 2025; www.kaggle.com/datasets/shahriar26s/anemia-detection-dataset)
- 2025 NBA Playoffs (Google, 2025; trends.withgoogle.com/trends/us/nba-finals/)

Helping Hens: Grapheme Awareness with H

Monica Girard Farris

Levels	Low beginner to beginner
Ages Suitable for Activity	Any
Aims	Develop grapheme awareness of the letter *h*.
	Practice listening as they follow one-step directions to draw a hen.
Class Time	30–40 minutes
Preparation Time	10–15 minutes
Resources	Writing surface (paper, digital tool)
	Writing utensils (pencils, markers, digital tool)

This activity integrates letters and sounds to actively engage beginning language learners and foster literacy development (Levesque et al., 2021). The scaffolding process allows students to engage in visual literacy and develop grapheme awareness in a fun and interactive way, suitable for English learners of all ages.

PROCEDURE

1. Distribute paper and colored pencils (or tell students to get out their notebooks or digital writing tools).

2. Write a capital *H* on the board for students to see. Have students write a capital *H* on their paper (or digital tool).

3. Ask students if they know the name of the letter: "H". Elicit the sound the letter makes: /h/.

4. Ask students if they can think of any words that start with the sound /h/.

5. Tell students you will show them a way to remember that the letter *H* says /h/.

6. Add details to the letter *H* to make it look like a hen (see Appendix). Tell students to do the same on their paper (or digital tool).

7. Direct students to draw a setting for their hen, such as a park, the playground, outer space, school, the moon, the beach, the farm, or the market. Then, invite students to orally tell where their hen is and what their hen is doing.

8. Review the letter *H*, the sound /h/, and the word *hen*.

9. Pair students and have them practice saying the /h/ sound.

10. In pairs, have students brainstorm more words starting with *h* (e.g., *hat, house, hippo*). Alternately, in groups, have students make the shape of the letter *H* with their bodies while repeating the sound /h/.

11. With remaining class time, or as a follow-up activity, have students draw another *H* and add details to turn it into a different *H*-object of their choice (e.g., *H* into a house).

12. Display students' drawings around the room or share them digitally to reinforce grapheme recognition.
13. Finish with a game: Play Letter Hunt, where students look around the classroom or their home space to identify objects that start with /h/.

CAVEATS AND OPTIONS

To deepen learning, ask students to share a memory related to hens (alternatively, adult learners can share a favorite chicken recipe).

REFERENCES AND FURTHER READING

Levesque, K. C., Breadmore, H. L., & Deacon, S. H. (2021). How morphology impacts reading and spelling: Advancing the role of morphology in models of literacy development. *Journal of Research in Reading, 44*(1), 10–26. https://doi.org/10.1111/1467-9817.12313

APPENDIX: H *Makes Hen Grapheme Illustration*

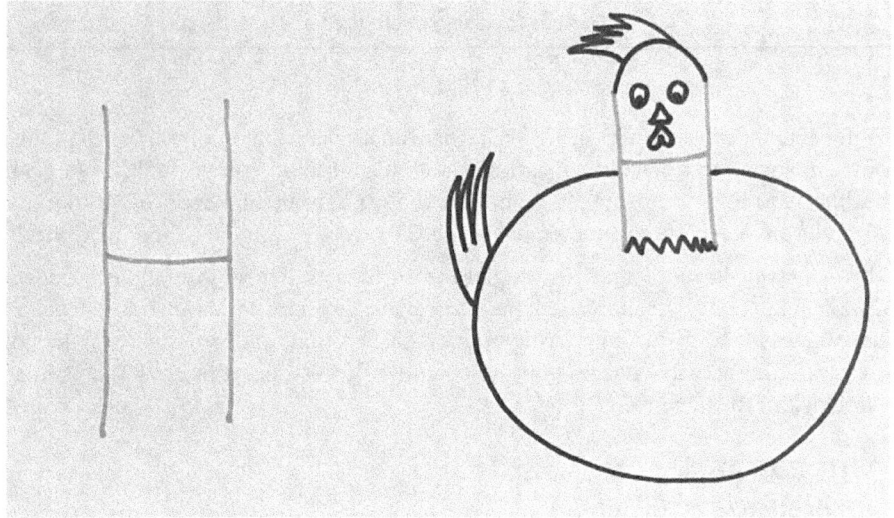

Human Machine: Visualizing and Discussing Complex Systems and Processes

Brittany Renee Gnau

Levels	Intermediate to advanced
Ages Suitable for Activity	Early secondary to adult
Aims	Develop listening and speaking skills
	Narrate the work of a machine through visual storytelling
	Describe complex processes and sequence key events
	Develop creativity and collaboration skills
Class Time	1 hour
Preparation Time	30 minutes
Resources	Pen and paper
	Devices for taking photographs (e.g., tablets or smartphones)

Students today are inheriting a world that functions through a proliferating range of technologies and machines. Machines are integral to all sorts of industries, from healthcare to manufacturing. To manage schoolwork, to handle finances, or to move around from one place to another, people need to know how to talk about machines.

This activity invites students to investigate the world around them through the perspective of an interactive machine designed to produce a specific kind of work. It involves active listening and speaking, group work, collaboration, and generous amounts of creativity. This activity engages multiple cognitive processes as it builds visual literacy through kinesthetic movement.

PROCEDURE

Introduction (5–15 minutes)

1. Begin by brainstorming: Ask students to create a list of various types of machines. Write responses on the board as they share their ideas.

2. Invite students to discuss what a machine is and what machines do. They might answer that a machine performs work for us, a machine makes noises or does motions, or a machine prepares a product by following a certain design.

3. Ask students to demonstrate an imitation of different mechanical actions. Individually, in groups, or as a whole class, have students brainstorm about how they might visually and kinesthetically represent the action of any of the following: a smoothie machine, a washing machine, an airplane, or a water sprinkler.

Brainstorming and Planning (15 minutes)

1. Put students in groups of three to eight. Ask students to plan how they can create a human machine.

    a. They must decide what kind of machine they will perform. Encourage them to come up with at least three ideas and then choose the best machine to represent.

    b. Each person must perform a different part of the machine's work, and each person should be able to explain how all parts of the machine function.

    c. As a team, they need to think critically about how to creatively represent complex processes in an understandable format. They must construct a visual narrative with a beginning and an end that tells a kind of story about how work is done.

    d. Provide the following prompts: What will each part of the machine look/sound like? How will the machine start, and how will it come to a stop? Who will play each part of the machine? Can you describe how each person does a different part of the work? How can you work as a team to tell the story of your human machine through the sequence of actions, or visual cues, that you create?

Rehearsal (10 minutes)

1. Tell learners to rehearse how their machine starts, works, and stops at least three times.

2. Encourage them to be creative and play with different ways of replicating the actions of their chosen machine. Their machine can move and make noise as appropriate. Give them time to choose how they feel comfortable connecting the shapes together to make their machine. Make any revisions as necessary.

3. Remind students that every member of the group must do some work/action that somehow connects to the greater machine's shape and processes. For example, they might need to put all their feet together to create a certain visual effect, or fist bump to represent a transfer of energy, or link arms to represent some movement between all of the members combined. Encourage critical thinking, problem solving, and playful creativity.

4. Ask a few members to step outside of their role and look at the group machine from an outside view. Give groups a chance to edit and consider how their representation looks from the audience's perspective. Guide students to make adjustments to help the action translate visually to the audience.

5. Encourage groups to incorporate variations (e.g., sounds, vibrations, shudders, glitches, jitters, jerky movements, delays) to make the fascinating functions and challenges of real machines more authentic in their performance.

Performance and Audience Reflection (20 minutes)

1. Have teams take turns performing their machine for the class in a designated performance area.

VII

Reflection (10 minutes)

1. Ask students to discuss key takeaways from their human machine activity. (See examples of technical vocabulary in the Appendix.)

2. Lead a comparison of the differences between human and mechanical machines. Encourage students to consider how machines simplify tasks and improve efficiency.

3. Finally, ask students to elaborate on the challenges and rewards involved in creating their visual performance of a machine.

CAVEATS AND OPTIONS

- If you have video capabilities, consider showing students examples of various machines in motion. Excellent examples can be found in clips from television shows like "How It's Made" (www.discoveryuk.com/series/how-its-made/).

- Show examples of different Rube Goldberg machines that break down a relatively simple task into a series of specialized and overly complicated motions, from Rube Goldberg's official YouTube channel (www.youtube.com/@RubeGoldbergOfficial).

APPENDIX: *Examples of Technical Language*

Following are some samples of appropriate technical vocabulary by level.

Beginner

"I had to stir the food very fast."

"I was the part that moves the clothes to make them clean in the laundry."

"She was making coffee. She used a machine to turn beans into espresso."

"He could stop all the machines quickly. He was like a special button."

Intermediate to Advanced

"I was the whisker in our human machine. My job was to rapidly mix the food in our breakfast machine."

"I was the drum of our human machine. My job was to shake, rotate, and rinse clothes to get them clean in the laundry."

"She was grinding the fresh coffee beans in our espresso machine."

"He was the emergency shut down button that halted all the production on our assembly line."

Image Interpretation Scavenger Hunt

Elena Taylor

Levels	Intermediate to advanced
Ages Suitable for Activity	Any
Aims	Develop interpretive skills
	Promote diverse perspectives through peer-to-peer interaction
	Practice target vocabulary and grammatical structures
Class Time	60 minutes
Preparation Time	10 minutes
Resources	List of prompts (see Appendix)
	Devices for taking photographs (e.g., tablets or smartphones)
	Optional: A shared online platform for displaying images

In this activity, students identify and capture images that represent descriptive prompts. They then interpret the images collected by their classmates. The activity develops students' visual literacy by encouraging them to explore and analyze different visual elements.

PROCEDURE

1. Introduce the activity by telling students they will use their smartphones (or tablets) to take photos that represent textual prompts describing objects, such as "something that seems welcoming" or "something that requires a lot of attention."

2. Give each student a list of prompts, such as the one found in the Appendix. Ensure the prompts are open-ended and allow for individual interpretation.

3. Illustrate the activity by explaining that, for example, if they are working on the prompt "something that seems welcoming," the students could take a photo of a smiling friend or a cozy chair. Encourage students to be creative and use their imagination when looking for items.

4. Give students about 10–15 minutes (or longer if needed) to walk around the designated space (e.g., classroom, hallway, library, an outside area) and capture images.

5. Bring students together and divide them into small groups (or remain as a whole class).

6. Ask students to share their images with their group members/classmates by displaying them on their smartphones. (If technology allows, the students can upload their images to a shared online platform, such as Padlet [padlet.com].)

7. Tell the rest of the group to interpret the images and guess which prompt from the list each image represents. Have the students explain their guesses. During this stage, the photographer should not reveal the intended meaning behind their images.

VII

8. After each student shares their images and everyone explains their interpretations, allow the photographers to describe the intended meaning behind each of their photos. Encourage students to discuss their diverse perspectives and individual interpretations.

CAVEATS AND OPTIONS

- Choose open-ended prompts that stimulate students' imaginations. Avoid prompts that encourage simple, literal answers. For example, instead of "something yellow," use prompts like "something that represents comfort."
- Adapt the activity for higher or lower levels by varying the difficulty of the language in the prompts.
- If students do not have access to cameras, bring several magazines/newspapers and have students find printed images that represent the prompts.
- Use this activity to practice adjective (relative) clauses: Create prompts that include both subject–adjective clauses (e.g., "an object that seems old") and object–adjective clauses (e.g., "something that many people enjoy looking at"). You can also design prompts to target specific vocabulary items.

APPENDIX: *Examples of Prompts*

- An object that represents strength
- Something that seems mysterious
- Something that requires a lot of attention
- An item that reminds you of home
- Something that seems welcoming
- An object that symbolizes wisdom
- Something that encourages adventure
- An item that exemplifies change
- A color that conveys happiness
- Something that feels calming

In the Eye of the Beholder

Claudia Rosenhan

Levels	Intermediate
Ages Suitable for Activity	Secondary
Aims	Use descriptive and sensory language
	Interrogate images for both literal and inferred meaning
	Distinguish between different perceptions
	Narrate a multimodal story
Class Time	2 (50-minute) sessions
Preparation Time	30 minutes
Resources	Papers with colored blotches
	Access to the internet on tablets or smartphones
	Images (see Appendix A)
	Video 1: "Why Do We See Faces in Objects?" (Science Channel, 2016; www.youtube.com/watch?v=LzdjRah9fwA)
	Video 2: "What It Means If You Can See Faces in Objects - Susan G. Wardle" (TED-Ed, 2023; www.youtube.com/watch?v=zpOoBtFNYuw)

This activity challenges learners to consider whether we perceive reality as given, or whether our brain creates a reality (Zhou & Meng, 2020). Through completing the activity, learners explore how we make sense of the world by interpreting our sensory perceptions—and how a similar meaning-making process is going on when we use language. In this activity, students explore the concept of pareidolia (i.e., seeing faces in everyday objects) and create a multimodal narrative with self-created images.

PROCEDURE

Activity 1: Introducing Pareidolia

1. *(10 minutes)* Ask learners to discuss in pairs whether they see faces in everyday objects (e.g., in the clouds). They can do this in a shared home language or in English. After the discussion, explain that this human tendency has a special name: *pareidolia.*

2. *(20 minutes)* Hand out sheets of paper with randomly shaped color blotches (or ask learners to create color blotches on a blank sheet of paper). Ask learners to give these blotches a face, as in the book *Hirameki* (Peng + Hu, 2016). Then, ask learners to share their drawings and explain their ideas. Support students by scaffolding vocabulary if necessary.

3. *(10 minutes)* Show examples of pareidolia; play Videos 1 and 2 (first 30 seconds only) and display the images in Appendix A. Alternatively, ask learners to conduct an internet search for the term *pareidolia* themselves. Invite learners to share the images they find.

4. *(10 minutes)* Lead a discussion about the concept of pareidolia, using the following guiding questions:

   a. Why do you think we see faces in everyday objects?

   b. Does everyone always see the same image?

   c. Ask them whether the faces they see are "male" or "female."

   This can be done as a whole class or in small groups. If groups, circulate to support comprehension and scaffold language use.

5. *Homework*: Ask learners to observe their environments, take pareidolic images with their smartphones or cameras, and bring them to the next class. Students can print images or upload them to a shared platform (e.g., your learning management system, Google Slides).

Activity 2: Extension

1. *(30 mins)* Ask learners to write a narrative story that presents the character in their pareidolic image as the hero. They can work on paper or digitally.

2. *(20 mins)* Create an exhibition of the students' photographs and invite learners to present their narrative and photo in front of the class. Then, have all students add their stories to the exhibition (whether on paper or digitally).

CAVEATS AND OPTIONS

- This class depends, to a large extent, on access to the internet and digital resources. In contexts where such resources are limited or nonexistent, use the *Hirameki* exercise (Step 2) as the material for Activity 1. This can be further extended for Activity 2, for example, by having students create inkblots for homework.

- Learners are expected to engage with the homework. If learners are not able to do so (for instance, if cameras are not available), provide a number of sample images for learners as the basis for their stories (see Appendix A).

- If older learners find the activity too childlike, choose specific reference images that tap into the preferences of older teens and adults (e.g., creating memes from pareidolic images).

- As images may be culture specific, take the opportunity to invite a larger discussion about diversity of perspectives.

- Images may be manipulated via generative artificial intelligence. If learners encounter such images, spark a discussion on what is "real."

REFERENCES AND FURTHER READING

Kalaja, P., Dufva, H., Alanen, R., & Barkhuizen, G. (2013). Experimenting with visual narratives. In G. Barkhuizen (Ed.), *Narrative research in applied linguistics* (pp. 105-131). Cambridge University Press.

Peng + Hu. (2016). *Hirameki: Draw what you see*. Thames and Hudson.

Science Channel. (2016, April 18). *Why do we see faces in objects?* [Video]. http://www.youtube.com/watch?v=LzdjRah9fwA

TED-Ed. (2023, June 13). *What it means if you can see faces in objects - Susan G. Wardle* [Video]. http://www.youtube.com/watch?v=zpOoBtFNYuw

Zhou, L. F., & Meng, M. (2020). Do you see the "face"? Individual differences in face pareidolia. *Journal of Pacific Rim Psychology, 14*, e2. https://doi.org/10.1017/prp.2019.27

APPENDIX: *Sample Images*

View the front cover of Peng + Hu's *Hirameki Draw What You See,* which shows how simple ink blots can be turned into imaginative doodles:

cdn.waterstones.com/bookjackets/large/9780/5002/9780500292488.jpg

Image credit: Brett Jackson on Wikimedia Commons (upload.wikimedia.org/wikipedia/commons/8/81/Pareidolia_3.jpg)

Image credit: Danamania on Wikimedia Commons (upload.wikimedia.org/wikipedia/commons/3/3a/Pareidolia_clouds.jpg)

Image credit: Procsilas Moscas on Wikimedia Commons (upload.wikimedia.org/wikipedia/commons/3/36/ Pareidolia_%2815468122%29.jpg)

Image credit: Thom Quine on Wikimedia Commons (upload.wikimedia.org/wikipedia/commons/e/e5/Pareidolia.jpg)

Mapping Identity: Visualizing Self Through Graphic Organizers

Hayriye Ulaş Taraf

Levels	High beginner
Ages Suitable for Activity	Early secondary
Aims	Understand the importance and functionality of graphic organizers
	Identify different types of graphic organizers and their specific purposes
	Reflect on personal traits such as likes and dislikes, strengths and weaknesses, and hobbies
	Enhance self-awareness through the creative use of graphic organizers
	Practise higher order thinking skills, such as brainstorming, comparing, reflecting, and questioning
Class Time	80 minutes
Preparation Time	15–20 minutes
Resources	Graphic organizers (Appendixes A–F)
	Copies of survey (Appendix H)
	Colored pencils or pens
	Blank paper
	Access to the internet on laptops or tablets

This activity engages students in reflecting on the self, combining visual literacy and higher order thinking skills. Students visually organize ideas about their identities by incorporating graphic organizers, fostering self-reflection, and connecting with their peers. This approach promotes 21st-century learning by encouraging the exploration of personal and shared experiences in a creative, visually engaging way.

PROCEDURE

1. Greet the students and introduce the activity by displaying several examples of graphic organizers (Appendixes A–F).

2. Explain what a graphic organizer is and ask students to discuss how we can use it in both life and school.

3. Introduce the different graphic organizers in the appendixes and describe their purposes and functions, as follows:

   - Story map (Appendix A): Summarizes a story's plot, characters, setting, and sometimes a moral or lesson taught

   - Venn diagram (Appendix B): Compares and contrasts ideas

   - Fish bone diagram (Appendix C): Explores cause–effect and problem–solution relationships

VII

- Concept map (Appendix D): Useful for categorizing and brainstorming ideas
- Timeline (Appendix E): Visualizes events chronologically
- K-W-L chart (Appendix F): Organizes what we know, wonder, and learn about a topic

4. Create a quick class discussion with the following question prompts: "Which of these do you think is the most useful for your school life? How about for personal tasks?"

5. Shift focus to how concept maps can help students reflect on themselves. Say, "Let's try using one of these tools to explore who we are!"

6. On the board, start creating a concept map about personal traits. Guide students to brainstorm categories for such a visual.

7. Encourage active participation by asking for examples in each category. List students' suggested answers, such as *personality, likes, dislikes, strengths, weaknesses, hobbies,* and *goals.* Possible answers are shown in the concept map in Figure 1.

Figure 1. Sample concept map for personal traits and identity.

8. Ask students to brainstorm words or phrases to describe themselves (e.g., personality, hobbies, likes). Have them draw a large letter *I* on paper (as in Appendix G).

9. Ask students to write their brainstormed phrases and sentences about themselves around the letter *I*. Optionally, ask them to take it a step further with a free-writing activity: Give students 5–7 minutes to write freely about themselves—who they are, what they like, how they feel—without worrying about grammar or structure. The idea is to let their thoughts flow naturally.

10. Now, introduce a digital word cloud tool, such as WordArt (wordart.com). Have students open the website on their mobile devices and type in phrases, sentences, or incomplete sentences. Students can watch as the tool turns their submissions into a visual word cloud. Encourage students to play around with different colours, fonts, and shapes to make the results personal and unique.

11. Once their word clouds are ready, have students share them with the class. Do a gallery walk where they print and display their word clouds around the room, or have students present their work digitally.

12. Wrap up the activity with a short class discussion and reflection.

13. Hand out the "Who Are You?" survey (Appendix H). Tell students to fill it out based on their own answers and then ask a partner the same questions, recording their responses.

14. Have students draw an outline of their hand on a piece of paper, followed by their partner's hand overlapping it. This will form a Venn diagram for comparing similarities and differences in their answers (see example in Appendix I). Explain that they should write their similarities in the overlapping section and their differences on the fingers, to symbolize their unique identities.

15. Discuss the concepts of uniqueness and individuality as a class using handprints (or fingerprints) as a visual metaphor.

CAVEATS AND OPTIONS

- Adapt the activity for higher levels by asking students to create acrostic poems or song lyrics to express who they are.

- For younger students, simplify the brainstorming by focusing on fewer categories (e.g., only personality and hobbies).

APPENDIX A: *Story Map*

Topic: Summarizing the Fable "The Town Mouse And The Country Mouse"

APPENDIX B: *Venn Diagram*

Topic: Comparing the Book and Movie "Harry Potter And The Sorcerer's Stone"

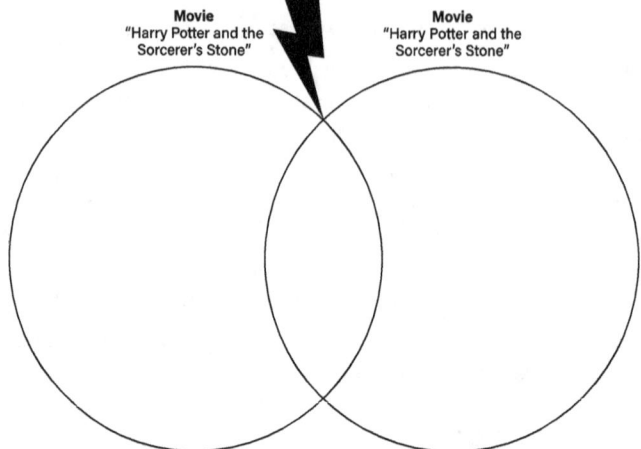

APPENDIX C: *Fish Bone*

Topic: Identifying Causes and Effects

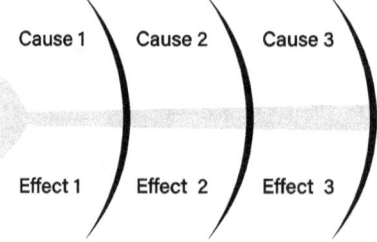

APPENDIX D: *Concept Map*

Topic: Brainstorming About Personal Traits

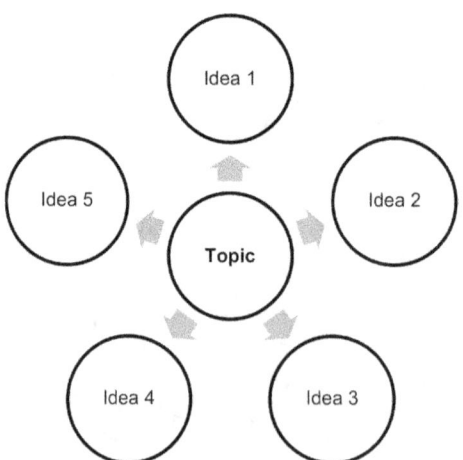

APPENDIX E: *Timeline*

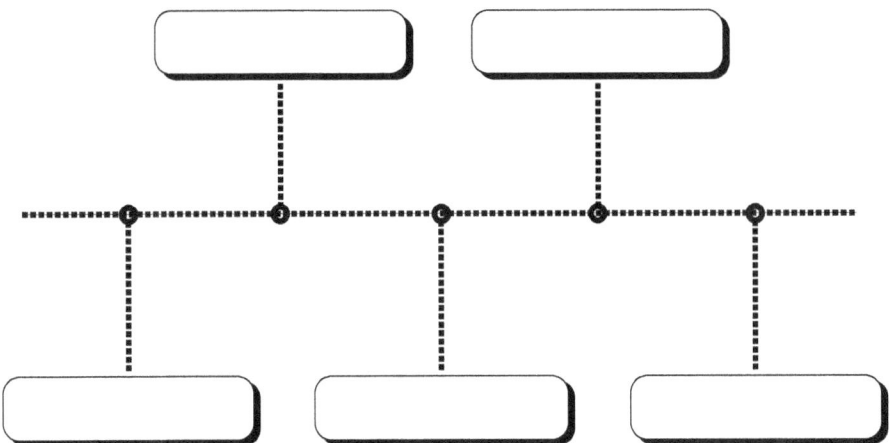

APPENDIX F: *K-W-L Chart*

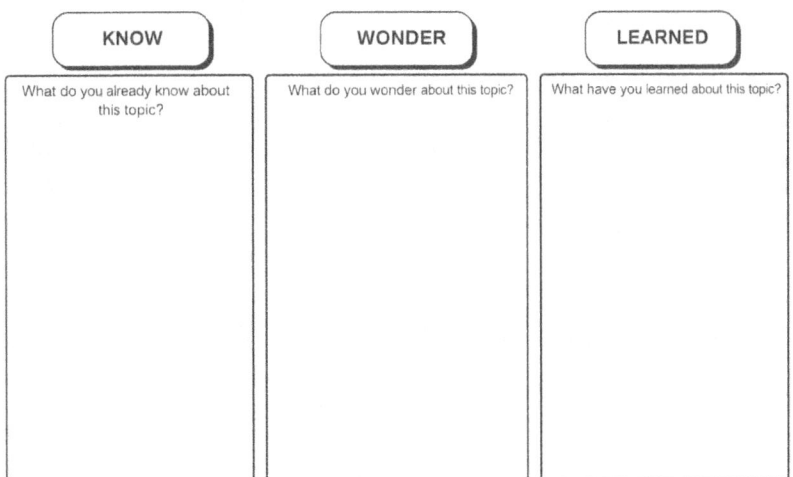

KNOW	WONDER	LEARNED
What do you already know about this topic?	What do you wonder about this topic?	What have you learned about this topic?

VII

APPENDIX G: *Letter Visual*

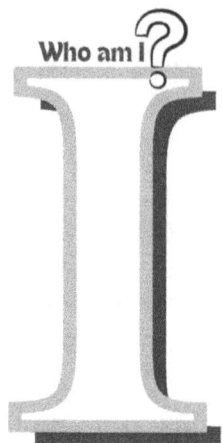

APPENDIX H: *"Who Are You?" Survey*

How are you the same as and different from your partner? Complete the survey with your answers. Then, ask a partner the questions. Write your partner's answers in the chart.

	You	Your Partner
What three words best describe you?		
What three words best describe you in the morning?		
What three words best describe you at school?		
What three words best describe you at home?		
How would your family describe you?		
How would your friends describe you?		
What are your goals or dreams?		
What is something you are proud of?		
What makes you feel happy?		
What are your greatest strengths?		
What are your weaknesses?		
Where do you like to spend your free time?		
What place are you most comfortable in?		

APPENDIX I: *Hand-Shaped Venn Diagram*

Nature's Alphabet

Heidi Haavan Grosch

Levels	All
Ages Suitable for Activity	Any
Aims	Heighten visual awareness through practicing the skill of noticing
	Build visual literacy
	Develop creative writing skills
Class Time	15–60 minutes
Preparation Time	None
Resources	Model alphabet photos (Appendix)
	Devices for taking photographs (e.g., tablets or smartphones)
	Access to a shared online platform

To become agents of change, we need to become more aware of the world around us. Honing our awareness also helps us become better at noticing language and how it is used in its different forms. This activity is designed to enhance the skill of paying attention to hidden details and seeing things that may not be obvious at first glance, leading to interactive discussions and increased vocabulary.

PROCEDURE

1. Divide the class into pairs. Provide each pair one digital device to take photographs.

2. Share a couple of model photos so students know what you are looking for (see Appendix). Practice finding alphabet letters in the sample photos as a whole class.

3. Give the students 10–15 minutes to take pictures of as many letters of the alphabet as they can find in their environment, either outside or inside the school building.

4. Return to the classroom and have each pair upload their images to your online platform.

   a. Show students how to upload photos to a school site that you use to share digital resources or to a free online platform, such as Padlet (padlet.com) or Google Docs.

   b. Have learners upload photos to your platform in a random order, or create columns/sections with letter groups (e.g., A–E, F–I, J–M, N–R, S–V, W–Z).

   c. Alternatively, have the learners send all the images to you digitally. Then, you can print them out in a physical format.

5. Review the photos together as a whole class and talk about the letters found and/or do one of the writing activities given in the Caveats and Options.

CAVEATS AND OPTIONS

- If working with younger learners, try the following adaptations:
  - Limit the number of available digital devices to take photos. Have children look for letters in the environment around them, then call out, "I found an *A!*" and ask the designated photographer to take that picture. This makes the activity feel a bit like a letter scavenger hunt.
  - As the teacher, work together with the students to discover things that make the shape of the different letters and then brainstorm words that begin with each found letter. This would be a way to work on expanding vocabulary.

- For older or more advanced learners, you can do a variety of writing activities:
  - Practice alliteration (i.e., a sentence or phrase where all the words begin with the same letter) using one of the found letters as a starting point. Here are examples of alliteration with the letter *T*: "Tom Turtle tripped two times on Tuesday" or "Tongue-tied teenagers talk together on Twitter."
  - Have students present an oral report, in the style of a news reporter, on their unique find and how it got there or what makes it special. Tell them to start with a phrase like "You'll never guess what I discovered..." or "Guess what I found..."
  - Have a class competition to see how many images of a certain letter you can find in a week. Make a letter board with those images.
  - Print the alphabet photographs and combine them to create words. Take a picture of the new words you create with the alphabet pictures!
  - Have students write a simple text in which one of the letters is the main character. Here is an example introduction: "*T* was just hanging around the garden when he met a bird..."

- You can find additional inspiration if you investigate land art, also known as earth art. This is a genre of art that is created directly in the landscape using natural materials.

APPENDIX: *Example Photos of Nature's Alphabet*

Image 1. Can you find the letter *T* and the letter *H*?

Image credit: Heidi Haavan Grosch. Used with permission.

Image 2. Can you find the letter *C* and the letter *O*?

Image credit: Heidi Haavan Grosch. Used with permission.

Image 3. Can you find the letter *L* and the letter *V*?

Image credit: Heidi Haavan Grosch. Used with permission.

Photovoice: Mediated Reflective Practice for Preservice Teachers

Sandi Ferdiansyah

Levels	Advanced and high advanced
Ages Suitable for Activity	Preservice teachers
Aims	Mediate preservice teachers' reflective practice
	Build identity as a reflective practitioner
	Build critical thinking and creativity through visually mediated reflection
Class Time	90 minutes
Preparation Time	None
Resources	Video recordings of students' teaching practice
	Devices for taking photographs (e.g., tablets or smartphones)

Photovoice (Wang & Burris, 1997) is a photo-mediated reflection that can be used to engage preservice teachers in reflecting on their teaching practice (past), reflecting in their teaching (present), and reflecting for their future teaching (Farrel, 2007). In this activity, preservice teachers learn how to assess their own teaching, evaluate their practice while teaching, and plan for better future teaching. In addition, they write a reflective journal and enhance it with digital photography to express their thoughts.

PROCEDURE

Before-Reflection Activities (30 minutes)

1. Ask the preservice teachers to watch a video recording of their past teaching practice and reflect on it in writing:

   a. As they observe their teaching, have them make note of critical incidents which occurred in their teaching. A *critical incident* refers to a specific moment that has a significant impact on either students or preservice teachers.

   b. Ask them to reflect on why they selected those critical incidents, how the incidents may impact their future practice, and what other preservice teachers can learn from them. These questions promote preservice teachers' critical thinking and creativity in evaluating their teaching practices.

   c. For example, have them write about how students' collaboration worked, how their pedagogical approach impacted students' learning, or how they provided one-on-one feedback on the student's work.

While-Reflection Activities (45 minutes)

1. Ask the preservice teachers to take one or more photographs inside or outside the classroom which best represent their reflective voice on the critical incident.

a. Explain that their photographs must have either an original or metaphoric meaning:

   i. The *original* category includes images that depict real objects or scenes related to the critical incident. These objects could include anything inside or outside the classroom, such as students, tables, or teachers.

   ii. In contrast, the *metaphoric* category consists of images of real objects that carry a metaphorical or symbolic meaning. For instance, a photograph of a yellow flower might symbolize the fresh and beautiful smile of a teacher.

b. Tell teachers that all photographs must be taken by the teachers themselves, not downloaded from the internet.

2. Ask the preservice teachers to write a photovoice (a visually mediated reflective writing) of 100–150 words below each selected photograph (see Appendix for an example):

   a. Each photovoice should include the following rhetorical moves: explain the context or situation, describe the critical incident, and reflect on what they learned.

   b. In the context and situation part, have teachers describe the photograph they have selected, where it was taken, and reason why it was taken.

   c. In the critical incident part, have teachers write the important moments of their teaching practice that they believe are worth sharing from their observation.

   d. In the reflection part, have teachers write about activities learned from the critical incident.

After-Reflection Activities (15 minutes)

1. Create groups of three or four. Have preservice teachers exchange and discuss their photovoices. They should share how their photographs symbolize the critical incidents and how the critical incidents impact their decision-making for their future teaching practice. Tell teachers to write down interesting points from the discussion.

2. Have the preservice teachers present their reflections—and activities learned from each other—to the whole class. Finally, ask participants to share their learning experience after writing their first photovoice.

CAVEATS AND OPTIONS

- To engage preservice teachers in reflection for action, have them write potential strategies that they believe effective to improve their previous teaching practice. To help them support their selected strategies, require them to provide reasons and references for the potential instructional design.

- Have students create an e-portfolio on a new social media account, using Instagram, Facebook, or a similar platform. Have them post their photovoice reflections and ask other teachers to provide feedback via comments.

VII

REFERENCES AND FURTHER READING

Farrell, T. S. C. (2007). *Reflective language teaching: From research to practice.* Continuum.

Wang, C., & Burris, M. A. (1997). Photovoice: Concept, methodology, and use for participatory needs assessment. *Health Education & Behavior, 24*(3), 369–387. https://doi.org/10.1177/109019819702400309

APPENDIX: *Student Photovoice Example*

Image credit: Riskiyah's photovoice. Used with permission.

Using Graphs to Promote Critical Thinking

Shelley A. Saltzman

Level	High advanced
Ages Suitable for Activity	Adults
Aims	Describe and interpret information presented in graph form
	Develop critical thinking skills
	Evaluate and recognize misleading graphs
Class Time	40 minutes
Preparation Time	None
Resources	Example graphs and tables (Appendix)
	Laptop and projector

Visual literacy demands that students are capable of not only describing and interpreting the graphs they encounter, but also critically examining them. Through a sequence of group activities, students discover that graphs can be created with the intent to deceive. In this activity, students develop the critical thinking habit needed to avoid being manipulated by such misleading graphs.

PROCEDURE

1. Divide the class into two groups (Group A and Group B).
2. Show Graph 1 to Group A and Graph 2 to Group B (see Appendix for all sample graphs and tables). Provide printed copies, or have students view the graphs digitally where possible.
3. In each group, ask students to discuss the following questions about their bar graph:
   a. What do you notice?
   b. Is this change slight or dramatic?
   c. Where in the graph is the evidence to support that claim?
   d. What is the overall message of the graph?
   e. Create a title that captures the graph's main idea.
4. Ask each group to present their bar graph and title to the other group.
5. Ask both groups to add the data from their graph into Table 1. (Collect the data digitally on a projected slide of Table 1 or, if technology is not available, recreate Table 1 on the board.)
6. Guide students to notice that the data is the same, but the graphs give different impressions. Lead a discussion about how the scale of a graph affects the viewers' impression of the data presented in the graph. (You may want to point out that

when the y-axis does not start at zero, the difference is made to appear more significant than it really is.)

7. Next, show Graph 3 to Group A and Graph 4 to Group B.

8. In each group, ask students to discuss the following questions about their line graph.

    a. What do you notice?

    b. Is this change slight or dramatic?

    c. Where in the graph is the evidence to support that claim?

    d. What is the overall message of the graph?

    e. Create a title that captures the graph's main idea.

9. Ask each group to present their line graph and title to the other group.

10. Ask both groups to fill in Table 2 with data from their graph.

11. Guide students to notice again that the data is the same, but the graphs give different impressions. Lead a discussion about how the scale range of a graph affects the viewers' impression of the data presented in the graph. (You may want to point out that when the top range is much higher than any of the data points, the change over time appears less significant than it really is.)

12. To close the activity, encourage students to use what they have learned from this activity to read charts carefully so that they will not be misled by them.

CAVEATS AND OPTIONS

- If time is limited, teach half the activity, focusing on only bar graphs (Graphs 1–6) or line graphs (Graphs 7–12).

- Make your own graph (e.g., using Microsoft Excel) on any topic the students are interested in. In fact, you might start by surveying your students on a topic of interest and then create a graph using Excel.

- Choose graphs from popular websites or news sites. If you do so, you may want to vary the sources so as not to imply that misleading graphs occur on one news site more frequently than another.

- To add a vocabulary component, preteach verbs and adverbs commonly used to describe change and then ask students to use those words to describe the graphs. Here are some examples of relevant vocabulary:

    — Verbs for positive change: *increase, rise, jump, soar, skyrocket, double*

    — Verbs for negative change: *decrease, decline, dip, shrink, drop, fall, plummet*

    — Adverbs: *slightly, marginally, moderately, sharply, considerably, dramatically, rapidly*

- Ask students to finish sentence frames by supplying a verb in present perfect tense and an adverb from the pretaught list. This helps students learn to express a graph's main message (e.g., "This graph shows that in the last five years, the number of her students who use grammar checkers has increased dramatically.").

REFERENCES AND FURTHER READING

ACRL Task Force on Information Literacy Competency Standards. (2000). ACRL standards: Information literacy competency standards for higher education. *College & Research Libraries News, 61*(3), 207–215. https://doi.org/10.5860/crln.61.3.207

Glen, S. (n.d.). *Misleading graphs: Real-life examples.* Statistics How To. https://www.statisticshowto.com/probability-and-statistics/descriptive-statistics/misleading-graphs/

Huff, D. (1954). *How to lie with statistics.* W. W. Norton & Company.

The Learning Network. (2021, July 28). Introduction to 'What's going on in this graph?' *The New York Times.* https://www.nytimes.com/2021/07/28/learning/introduction-to-whats-going-on-in this-graph.html

Sanches, T., Lopes, C., & Antunes, M. L. (2022). *Critical thinking in information literacy pedagogical strategies: New dynamics for higher education throughout librarians' vision* [Conference session]. 8th International Conference on Higher Education Advances, Polytechnic University of Valencia. http://dx.doi.org/10.4995/HEAd22.2022.14476

APPENDIX: *Example Graphs and Tables*

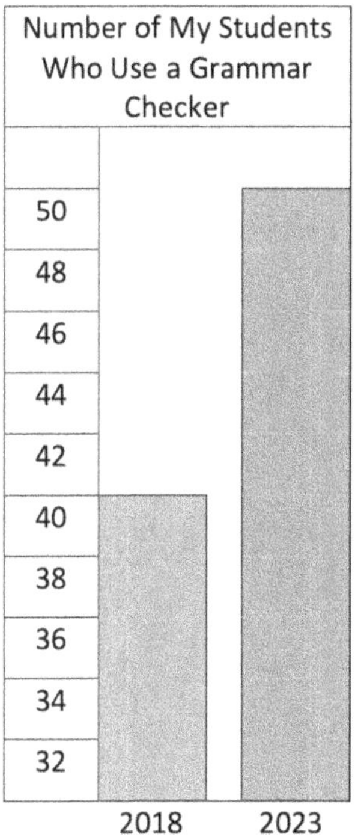

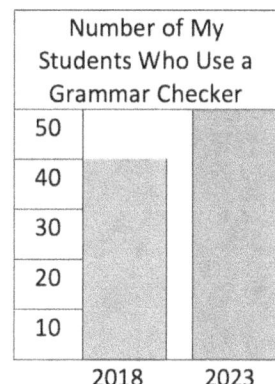

Graph 1. Grammar checker usage

Graph 2. Grammar checker usage

VII

Table 1. Number of Students Who Use a Grammar Checker

	Chart 1	Chart 2
2018		
2023		

Table 1b. Answer Key

	Chart 1	Chart 2
2018	40	40
2023	50	50

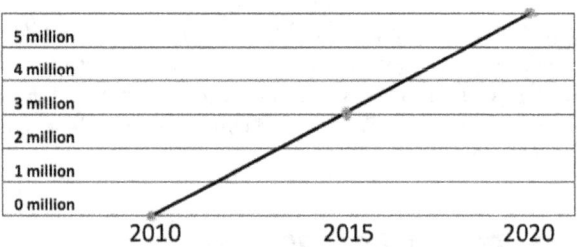

Graph 3. The number of U.S. citizens aged 95 and older.

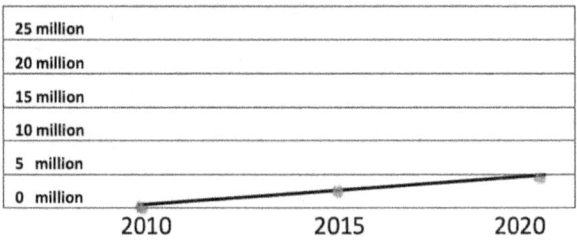

Graph 4. The number of U.S. citizens aged 95 and older.

Table 2. The Number of US Citizens Aged 95 and Older

	Chart 1	Chart 2
2010		
2015		
2020		

Table 2b. Answer Key

	Chart 1	Chart 2
2010	0	0
2015	3	3
2020	5	5

A Visual Template for Narrative Tenses

Emily Bryson

Levels	Low intermediate to advanced
Ages Suitable for Activity	Primary to adult
Aims	Develop skills for language analysis and critical thinking
	Practice reading, writing, listening, and speaking
	Review and consolidate understanding of narrative tenses
	Use visualization strategies to understand grammar
Class Time	5–45 minutes
Preparation Time	10 minutes
Resources	Example prompt text (Appendix A)
	Blank visual template (Appendix C)

Learning to use English grammar correctly, especially making distinctions between tenses, can be challenging for learners. Expressing time and tense through a visual metaphor can support learners to interpret, understand, and remember these distinctions. In this activity, learners use a visual template to analyze examples of narrative tenses. This activity promotes critical thinking, language analysis, and the development of visual thinking skills. It is intended as a review and consolidation activity after teaching the forms of past simple, past progressive, and past perfect.

PROCEDURE

1. Give students a short text using narrative tenses. A sample is provided with this activity (see Appendix A), or you may want to find or create your own. Ask students to read it and identify examples of past simple, past perfect, and past continuous tenses.

2. Ask students to work in pairs to check their answers and describe the usage of each tense. For extra support, optionally ask learners to match each tense to the following categories:

   a. finished actions in the past and the main events in a story [past simple]

   b. background information or events [past progressive]

   c. an action that happened before another action [past perfect]

3. Check answers and analyze the text as a whole class. Explain the form and meaning of each tense (see Appendix B).

4. Distribute, display, or draw the visual template on the board (see Appendix C, Image 1). Tell students that each part of the template represents one of the tenses. Ask students what they think each section may refer to and help them to find the appropriate solution. For example:

   a. Which tense refers to background information? [past progressive] What is in the background of this image? [a mountain]

b. Which tense do we use to show one action happening before another? [past perfect] Which image here has two actions? [the two arrows]

c. Which tense is for the main actions in a story, often short and complete? [past simple] What tense could all these short arrows refer to? [past simple]

5. Instruct students to write sentences about the sample narrrative on each part of the visual template. They may use their own ideas or copy structures from the text, depending on their ability.

6. Ask students to work in pairs to write their own very short stories using past continuous, past simple, and past continuous tenses. Then, ask them to draw the visual template and add their story to the template (see Appendix C, Image 2).

7. Invite a few students to the front of the class to tell their stories using the template.

CAVEATS AND OPTIONS

- This teaching technique is best used as a review and consolidation. Consider providing more detailed practice with contextualized grammar examples prior to this activity.

- Read the first paragraph of the example story aloud. Ask students to guess what the bird had in its mouth and to give an alternate ending to the story.

- Extend the learning by having learners draw their own visual templates to interpret other tenses.

- Discuss with learners other ways they like to remember, interpret, and visualize grammar. Encourage them to share any innovative ideas with the rest of the class.

- Extend the activity by encouraging further discussion and research on the ethics, challenges, and benefits of feeding animals in their natural habits.

FURTHER READING

Bryson, E. (2025). *Emily Bryson ELT.* https://www.emilybrysonelt.com/

APPENDIX A: *Example Narrative Tenses Short Story*

This morning, I saw something that surprised me. I was looking out the window on the bus when I saw a huge bird! It was white with gray stripes and a yellow beak. It had something in its mouth. I didn't know what it was, but it looked strange. It was much bigger than anything a bird that size should eat!

As I got off the bus, I noticed that the bird had dropped a pizza! Other birds were flying toward it. There were so many birds. I couldn't believe that a seagull had had a whole pizza in its mouth!

APPENDIX B: *Meaning and Form*

Past Simple

- Shows finished actions in the past
- Use the past form of the verb
- Example: *go > went*

Past Perfect

- Shows that one action in the past happened before another
- Use *had* + past participle
- Example: *had gone*

Past Continuous

- Shows a longer action that happens at a certain time in the past, often interrupted by another action or used for background information
- Use *was/were* + verb + *-ing*
- Example: *was going*

APPENDIX C: *Visual Template*

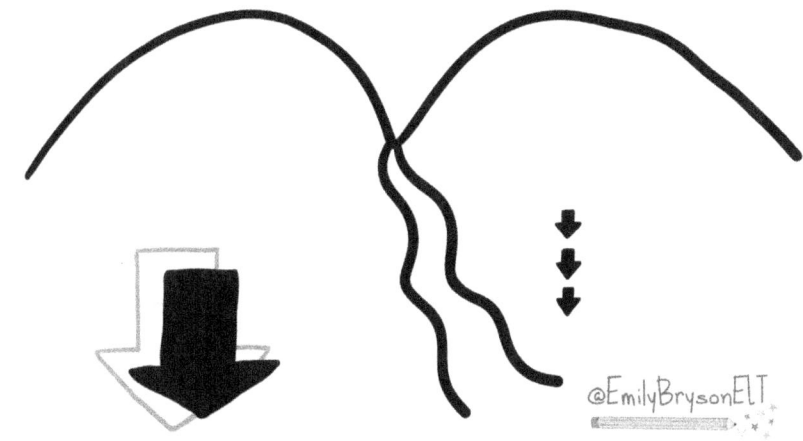

Image 1. Visual story template.

Image credit: Emily Bryson. Used with permission.

Image 2. Visual story template with added text.

Image credit: Emily Bryson. Used with permission.

VII

Visual Verbiage: Enhancing Reading Comprehension With Image-Based Annotation

Sara Zohoor, Hoda Parvaneh, Zohreh Eslami

Levels	High intermediate to advanced
Ages Suitable for Activity	Secondary to adult
Aims	Develop visual literacy skills
	Integrate visual cues with textual information
	Enhance reading comprehension and facilitate deeper understanding of a text
	Encourage critical thinking and creative responses
	Reduce reading time by increasing the efficiency of the reading process
Class Time	1 hour–90 minutes
Preparation Time	30 minutes–1 hour
Resources	Access to digital reading materials (articles, journals, etc.)
	Access to the internet on laptops or tablets
	Laptop and projector

In today's fast-paced academic environment, university-level and advanced students are expected to process a large volume of reading material in a timely and thorough manner. However, for multilingual learners of English, reading comprehension can often be hindered by the lack of contextual and visual cues that support understanding. This activity aims to enhance visual literacy and reading comprehension skills by introducing the concept of image-based annotation, which uses personalized visual cues to aid recall and facilitate deeper understanding of reading materials.

PROCEDURE

1. Introduce the concept of visual literacy and explain its relevance to reading comprehension. Point out how images are easy to remember and, when we add images to our annotations, they help us better remember the information.

2. Provide students with an interesting article to read on their laptops or tablets in .PDF format. Alternatively, allow them time to select their own articles. Instruct students to read through the text once without annotating.

3. Provide a brief demonstration of how to add annotation to a .PDF document using a digital annotation tool (see Caveats and Options for suggested tools). Explain and model how to create personalized visual cues that will help students remember key points from the text.

4. Instruct students to reread their texts and, while reading, create visual annotations that highlight key information, concepts, or themes. They can use images,

symbols, colors, or any other visual elements that help them recall and understand the information.

5. Have students share their visual annotations with their peers, either in small groups or in a whole class discussion. As students share their annotations, encourage them to point out how specific visual elements help them remember key information.

6. Discuss the effectiveness of the students' visual annotations in facilitating understanding and recall of the reading materials.

7. Assign a follow-up task that requires students to integrate their annotations into a summary or analysis of the reading materials.

CAVEATS AND OPTIONS

- Make sure students have access to the necessary digital tools and are familiar with their use before starting the activity. A few tools that work well for this activity include Adobe Acrobat, Foxit PDF Reader, and Kami for Google Chrome.

- Encourage students to be creative and experiment with different visual cues but also remind them to keep their annotations relevant and informative.

- Allow students to choose the level of detail and complexity of their annotations, depending on their individual reading and comprehension abilities.

- Consider using this strategy in combination with other reading comprehension techniques, such as active reading or summarization.

- Do an experiment:
  — Give students a text to read. Ask comprehension questions.
  — Then, give them a different text to read at the same level of difficulty.
  — This time, allow them time to annotate the reading before asking comprehension questions.
  — Ask students if they noticed a difference in their ability to recall information after annotating the second reading.

REFERENCES AND FURTHER READING

Ghavifekr, S., & Rosdy, W. A. W. (2015). Teaching and learning with technology: Effectiveness of ICT integration in schools. *International Journal of Research in Education and Science, 1*(2), 175–191.

Hobbs, R. (2010). *Digital and media literacy: A plan of action.* The Aspen Institute.

VII

Visualization of Synonyms

Qianhui Sun

Levels	Intermediate to advanced
Ages Suitable for Activity	Adult
Aims	Raise awareness of English varieties
	Improve data visualization skills with the GloWbE corpus
	Develop understanding of cultural differences reflected in synonym usage
Class Time	40 minutes
Preparation Time	10–15 minutes
Resources	Access to the internet on laptops or tablets
	Images (Appendix)
	Laptop and projector

By exploring the Corpus of Global Web-based English (GloWbE; Davies, 2013), students can visualize how synonyms for a word or phrase are used across different national English varieties. The visualization enables them to notice that certain synonyms are more commonly used in some varieties of English than in others, fostering their awareness of the characteristic lexical features of different English varieties.

In this activity, students focus on visualizing synonyms for *wife* in Great Britain and the United States, improving their data visualization skills, enhancing their understanding of synonyms, and fostering their intercultural understanding. The activity is adaptable to explore any English variety available in GloWbE.

PROCEDURE

Warm-up Discussion (5 minutes)

1. Begin by asking the whole class, "Do you think language use changes based on cultural context? If so, can you think of examples of different words used for the same idea in different varieties of English, like *plaster* in British English versus *Band-Aid* in American English?" Elicit examples.

2. Inform students that today they will explore global English variations by visualizing synonyms for *wife* in British and American English using GloWbE (Davies, 2013).

Corpus Exploration (30 minutes)

3. Introduce students to the GloWbE website (www.english-corpora.org/glowbe/) by projecting it on a screen for the whole class. Ask students to open the website on their own laptops or tablets and follow your exploration in the next steps of the activity.

4. Explain that GloWbE contains approximately 1.9 billion words of text available on the internet across various national English varieties, enabling students to compare differences between these varieties of English.

5. Ask students to choose "List" (see Item 3 in Figure 1 of the Appendix).

6. Instruct students to type "=wife" in the search box (see Item 4 in Figure 1). Explain that placing the equals sign before the word *wife* allows students to explore the synonyms of *wife* across different English varieties available in GloWbE.

7. Ask students to click on "Sections" (see Item 6 in Figure 1), allowing them to select the subcorpora they want to compare.

   a. In the first column, they should select "Great Britain" (see Item 7 in Figure 1).

   b. In the second column, they should select "United States" (see Item 8 in Figure 1).

   c. Explain that this selection will allow them to compare how synonyms for *wife* are used in these two countries (i.e., Great Britain and the United States) side by side.

8. Have students click on "Find matching strings" (see Item 10 in Figure 1).

9. Explain that the search results will show the synonyms for *wife* in both countries, such as *mate* and *consort* in Great Britain, versus *spouse* and *helpmeet* in the United States.

10. Explain that "TOKENS 1" and "TOKENS 2" (see Item 12 in Figure 2) represent the number of times synonyms for *wife* appear in the selected subcorpora (Column 1 for Great Britain, Column 2 for the United States).

11. Explain that "PM1" and "PM2" (see Item 13 in Figure 2) represent the normalized frequency of occurrences (tokens per million words), which allows a comparison between subcorpora of different sizes.

12. Explain that the "RATIO" (see Item 14 in Figure 2) represents the relative percentage in the two subcorpora. For example, if a word has a ratio of 2.0, it means the word is used twice as often in one subcorpus compared to the other.

13. Show students the bar chart (Chart 1 in the Appendix) and ask them to discuss the following question with a partner or as a whole class: "Which country has a higher usage of the word *mate*?" Encourage them to explain their reasoning based on the visual data in the chart.

Group Discussion (5 minutes)

14. Once students have finished exploring the corpora, have them discuss what they have learned in small groups. Provide the following questions for reflection:

   a. What do the differences in synonym usage tell us about cultural norms or attitudes in each country?

   b. Why might certain synonyms be more prevalent in one country than another?

CAVEATS AND OPTIONS

- Ask students to register (for free) to use the GloWbE corpus prior to the activity to avoid delays during class.

- Depending on the class's familiarity with the GloWbE corpus, allocate more time for exploration.

VII

- Extend the activity, if students are interested, by showing them how to compare other synonyms or related words across various national English varieties.
  — To do this, type the search word or phrase (see 1 in Figure 3 of Appendix), click the check box next to "Sections" (see 2 in Figure 3 of Appendix), and then click "Find matching strings" (see 3 in Figure 3 of Appendix). The result is shown in Figure 4.
  — Codes in GloWbE for each national variety are shown in parentheses: Australia (AU), Bangladesh (BD), Canada (CA), Ghana (GH), Great Britain (GB), Hong Kong (HK), India (IN), Ireland (IE), Jamaica (JM), Kenya (KE), Malaysia (MY), New Zealand (NZ), Nigeria (NG), Pakistan (PK), Philippines (PH), Singapore (SG), South Africa (ZA), Sri Lanka (LK), Tanzania (TZ), United States (US).
- Create a bar chart (Chart 2 of Appendix) displaying the frequency of the word *wife* across various national English varieties (or for advanced students, ask them to make one). Each bar represents the number of occurrences of the word *wife* in a specific English variety.
- Create a pie chart (Chart 3 of Appendix) showing the proportional frequency of the word *wife* across various national English varieties (or for advanced students, ask them to create one). Each slice represents the contribution of a specific English variety to the total occurrences of the word *wife* in GloWbE, providing a clear and visual representation of its global distribution.

APPENDIX: *Instructional Visuals for Synonyms in GloWbE*

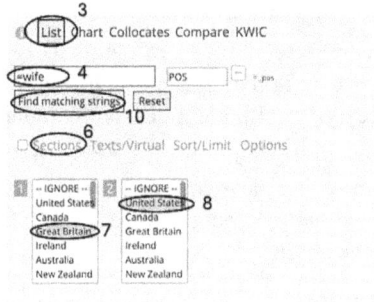

Figure 1. How to search for the synonyms of *wife* in GloWbE (Great Britain vs. United States subcorpora).

	WORD/PHRASE	TOKENS 1	TOKENS	PM 1	PM 2	RATIO		WORD/PHRASE	TOKENS 2	TOKENS 1	PM 2	PM 1	RATIO
1	MATE	11310	4766	29.2	12.3	2.4	1	SPOUSE	7225	2880	18.7	7.4	2.5
2	CONSORT	456	264	1.2	0.7	1.7	2	HELPMEET	19	9	0.0	0.0	2.1
3	PARTNER	30534	20694	78.8	53.5	1.5	3	WIFE	50185	45318	129.7	116.9	1.1
4	COMPANION	4642	4495	12.0	11.6	1.0	4	COMPANION	4495	4642	11.6	12.0	1.0
5	WIFE	45318	50185	116.9	129.7	0.9	5	PARTNER	20694	30534	53.5	78.8	0.7
6	SPOUSE	2880	7225	7.4	18.7	0.4	6	CONSORT	264	456	0.7	1.2	0.6
							7	MATE	4766	11310	12.3	29.2	0.4

Figure 2. List of the synonyms of *wife* in GloWbE (Great Britain vs. United States subcorpora).

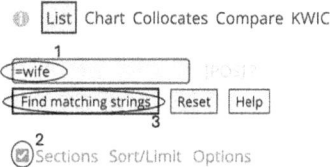

Figure 3. How to search for the synonyms of *wife* in GloWbE (globally).

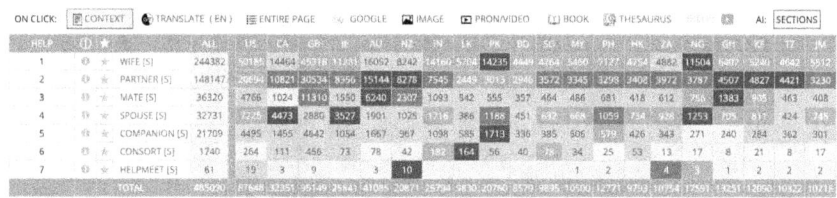

Figure 4. Frequency of the synonyms of *wife* in GloWbE (globally).

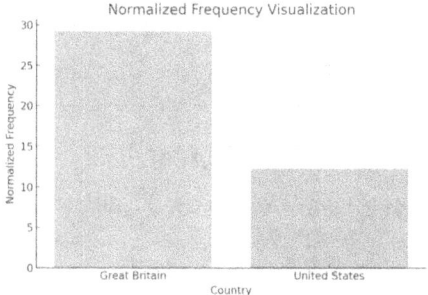

Chart 1. Normalized frequency of *mate* (Great Britain vs. United States subcorpora)

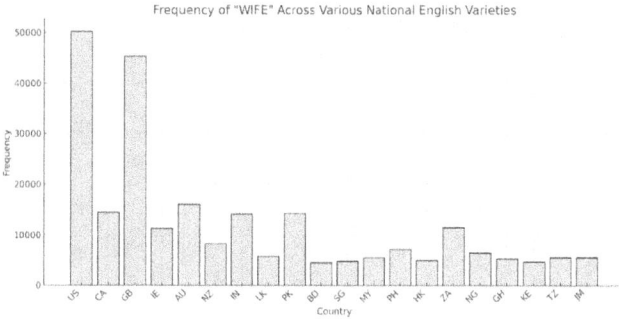

Chart 2. Frequency of *wife* across various national English varieties.

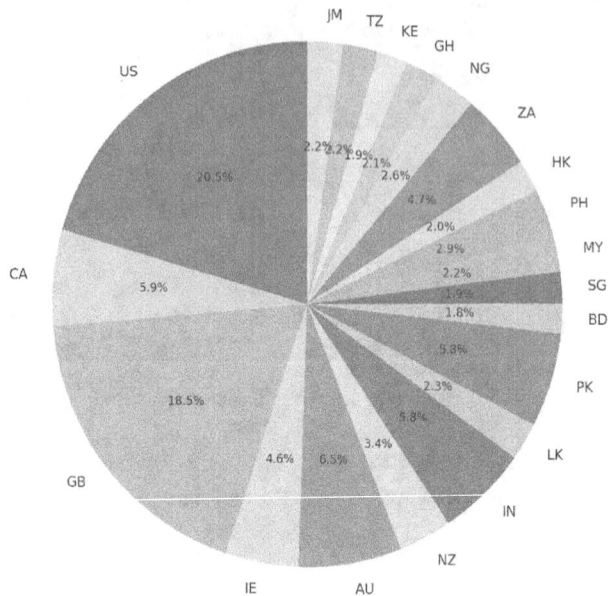

Chart 3. Proportional frequency of *wife* across various national English varieties.

REFERENCES AND FURTHER READING

Davies, M. (2013). Corpus of Global Web-based English (GloWbE). https://www.
english-corpora.org/glowbe/

Visualize Your Dreams: Crafting an Inspiring Vision Board

Ana Ibis Rojas Herrera

Level	Intermediate
Ages Suitable for Activity	Secondary
Aims	Recognize the importance of setting goals for personal growth and success
	Identify and define short- and long-term goals in various areas (e.g., academic, personal, social, extracurricular)
	Design a vision board that represents their goals
	Apply a growth mindset to the goal-setting process
Class Time	90 minutes
Preparation Time	1 hour
Resources	*For physical vision boards:* magazines, newspapers, scissors, glue, markers, crayons, colored pencils, and poster board or large paper
	For digital vision boards: access to the internet on laptops or tablets

n this activity, students explore the power of visualization by creating their own vision boards. Participants will learn how to identify their goals and aspirations, gather meaningful images and quotes, and design a board that reflects their personal vision for the future.

PROCEDURE

Introduction to Vision Boards (10–15 minutes)

1. Ask students if they have ever heard of a vision board or visualization. Provide the following simple definition: A vision board is a collection of images, words, and symbols that represent the goals and dreams you want to achieve.

2. Display and discuss a few samples of vision boards (physical or digital) to give students a clear idea of what they will be creating.

Goal-Setting Reflection (15–20 minutes)

3. Guide students in identifying personal, academic, or career goals to include on their vision boards. You may conduct a whole-class brainstorm session, or for higher level students, ask them to reflect individually or in groups.

4. Explain the concept of SMART goals (i.e., goals that are specific, measurable, achievable, relevant, and time-bound). Give students examples of SMART goals they could set.

5. Have students write down three to five short- and long-term goals they would like to work toward. Encourage them to think about different areas of their lives (e.g., academics, health, hobbies, relationships).

VII

Gathering Materials (5–10 minutes)

6. Provide students with the materials needed to create their vision boards:

   a. If creating physical vision boards, hand out a variety of materials, such as magazines, newspapers, scissors, glue, markers, and poster boards.

   b. If creating digital vision boards, show students how to use one or more online platforms, such as Canva (canva.com) or Google Slides, to find images and design their boards.

7. Encourage students to start thinking about images or words that represent their goals, values, or dreams.

Creating the Vision Board (30–40 minutes)

8. Have students assemble their vision boards using images, words, and symbols that represent their goals and aspirations.

9. Encourage creativity! Remind students that this is their personal vision board, so there are no wrong answers. They can use any (school-appropriate) images, drawings, quotes, and symbols that inspire them.

Sharing and Reflecting (15–20 minutes)

10. Invite students to share their vision boards with their peers and reflect on the design process. Have students either present their boards in small groups or, if comfortable, share with the entire class. Encourage them to explain one or two key goals and why they chose certain images.

11. Lead a group discussion or provide journaling prompts for students to reflect on the experience (e.g., How did creating this vision board help you think about your goals? or What steps can you take to start working toward one of these goals?).

12. Optionally ask students to give feedback on each other's boards in a supportive and positive way.

Closing and Next Steps (5–10 minutes)

13. Encourage students to use their vision boards as a tool for ongoing motivation and goal setting and to place their boards somewhere visible (e.g., at home or in their notebooks) to serve as a daily reminder of their goals.

14. End the activity by sharing an inspirational phrase or quote about perseverance, self-belief, and working toward your dreams.

CAVEATS AND OPTIONS

- For a follow-up activity, revisit the vision boards after a few months and ask students to reflect on their progress.

- Consider inviting a speaker (e.g., a successful community member) to talk about the importance of setting goals and how visualization helped them achieve their dreams.

About the Editors

Lisa Horvath is a curriculum specialist and independent researcher with more than 20 years of experience in English language teaching, teacher training, and materials development. She has taught English to students of all ages, from preschool through university and beyond. For 10 years, Lisa used collaborative storytelling based on student-generated artwork to teach English to young learners in Hungary. Currently, she develops English language teaching materials for publishers and ministries of education worldwide.

Susan Iannuzzi has been a materials writer, curriculum designer, and teacher of English as an additional language for more than 25 years. With degrees in film studies, linguistics, law, instructional management, and leadership, she has explored the power of visual media throughout her academic and professional careers. She has developed a course on the intersection of documentary films and legal advocacy and another on the use of popular movies as vehicles for teaching culture and language skills.

www.ingramcontent.com/pod-product-compliance
Lightning Source LLC
Chambersburg PA
CBHW081527120626
46550CB00009B/2645